HEALING
BODY, MIND, & SPIRIT

A Guide to Energy-Based Healing

About the Author

Howard Batie was raised in Centralia, Washington, and is a graduate of the University of Washington in Seattle, the U.S. Naval Postgraduate School in Monterey, California, and he received his doctorate in metaphysics from Delphi University in McCaysville, Georgia. During and after his twenty-year navy career, he served as program coordinator of several navy satellite communications systems, and participated in the initial concept development, technical and operational design, and operational management of these vital, worldwide command and control systems for the navy.

Dr. Batie received national recognition from the Johns Hopkins Institutes for development of innovative and practical techniques for using personal computers to aid the physically handicapped. He has also designed, developed, and constructed several custom environmental telemetry systems (Volcano Monitors) for the U.S. Geological Survey. He has also authored over twenty-five general and technical articles published in the computer and electronics fields.

Dr. Batie is now in private practice as a holistic practitioner of complementary and integrative energy-based therapies, and is the director of the Evergreen Healing Arts Center in Chehalis, Washington. He is a Certified Hypnotherapist, registered with the American Board of Hypnotherapy, and a member of the Ro-Hun Professional Association.

Dr. Batie is also an Usui and Karuna Reiki® Master Teacher and Instructor, a Healing Touch Therapist, a Certified Clinical Ro-Hun Therapist, a Certified Energetic Healing Therapist, a Certified Reflective Healing Therapist, a Certified Color & Sound Therapist, a Certified Christopher Method Practitioner, a Certified Holographic Healing Therapist (the Melchizedek Method), an ordained minister, and is author of *Awakening the Healer Within*. Dr. Batie was honored as the 1998 Distinguished Alumnus at Centralia College where he is also an instructor of energy-healing techniques, and at Lower Columbia College in Longview, Washington.

To Write to the Author

If you wish to contact the author or would like more information about this book, please write to the author in care of Llewellyn Worldwide and we will forward your request. Both the author and publisher appreciate hearing from you and learning of your enjoyment of this book and how it has helped you. Llewellyn Worldwide cannot guarantee that every letter written to the author can be answered, but all will be forwarded. Please write to:

Howard F. Batie
℅ Llewellyn Worldwide
P.O. Box 64383, Dept. 0-7387-0398-2
St. Paul, MN 55164-0383, U.S.A.

Please enclose a self-addressed stamped envelope for reply,
or $1.00 to cover costs. If outside U.S.A., enclose
international postal reply coupon.

Many of Llewellyn's authors have websites with additional information and resources. For more information, please visit our website at:

www.llewellyn.com.

HEALING
BODY, MIND, & SPIRIT

A Guide to Energy-Based Healing

Howard F. Batie, Mh.D.

2004
Llewellyn Publications
St. Paul, Minnesota 55164-0383, U.S.A.

First Edition
Second Printing, 2004

Book design and project management by Michael Maupin
Cover design by Lisa Novak
Cover image ©2003 Digital Vision
Editing and typesetting by Liz Tufte & Sid Korpi
Interior illustrations by Gavin Dayton Duffy

Library of Congress Cataloging-in-Publication Data
Batie, Howard F. (Howard Franklin), 1939 –
    Healing body, mind, & spirit : a guide to energy-based healing / Howard F. Batie
        p. cm.
    Includes bibliographical references and index.
    ISBN: 07387-0398-2
        1. Vital force—Therapeutic use. 2. Healing. 3. Mental healing. I. Title: Healing body, mind and spirit. II. Title.3

    RZ999.B284 2003
    615.8'51—dc22   2003061061

Llewellyn Worldwide does not participate in, endorse, or have any authority or responsibility concerning private business transactions between our authors and the public.
    All mail addressed to the author is forwarded but the publisher cannot, unless specifically instructed by the author, give out an address or phone number.
    Any Internet references contained in this work are current at publication time, but the publisher cannot guarantee that a specific location will continue to be maintained. Please refer to the publisher's website for links to authors' websites and other sources.

Disclaimer: The practices, techniques, and meditations described in this book should *not* be used as an alternative to professional medical treatment. This book does not attempt to give any medical diagnosis, treatment, prescription, or suggestion for medication in relation to any human disease, pain, injury, deformity, or physical condition.
    The author and publisher of this book are not responsible in any manner whatsoever for any injury which may occur through following the instructions contained herein. It is recommended that before beginning any alternative healing practice you consult with your physician to determine whether you are medically, physically, and mentally fit to undertake the practice.

Llewellyn Publications
A Division of Llewellyn Worldwide, Ltd.
P.O. Box 64383, Dept. 0-7387-0398-2
St. Paul, MN 55164-0383, U.S.A.
www.llewellyn.com

Printed in the United States of America

Dedication

This book is dedicated to each reader who has been drawn to pick it up, read it, and hopefully be inspired to continue his or her own journey home. May your journey be made easier, quicker, and filled with a greater understanding and appreciation of the incredible potential within each one of us.

Acknowledgements

I'd like to recognize each person who has contributed to the material in this book, but since we all learn something from every single person we meet, that would be a bit impractical. However, there are a few very special people who have guided me to where I am now, and I would like to publicly acknowledge their patience, kindness, wisdom, special insights, and talents. They have gently pointed me toward a path I had forgotten was so special and important to me: the path of healing.

I am indeed indebted to my wonderful wife Anita for her untiring encouragement and support during the writing of this book. August Armstrong first awakened within me the faint stirrings of healing experiences from long ago, and Elaine Griffin introduced me to a very special group of loving and compassionate healers led by Dottie Graham, who opened my mind and heart to what we are capable of as spiritual human beings.

And special thanks go to Patricia Hayes, Marshall Smith, and the other wonderful teachers at Delphi University for providing the spiritual tools needed to prepare and develop myself as an instrument of healing for others.

I am also indebted to the wonderful team of editors at Llewellyn for the very professional way they have massaged my words and brought forth my thoughts with clarity onto the printed page. Nancy Mostad, Sandy Leuthner, Michael Maupin, Lisa Novak, Gavin Duffy, Nanette Peterson, Liz Tufte, and Sid Korpi have all been most helpful in bringing my manuscript into your hands in its present form.

And lastly, thanks and gratitude go to all those spiritual beings who have lovingly chosen to guide my feet along this exciting new pathway home.

Contents

Chapter 3
Healing the Emotional and
Mental Energy Bodies / 115

Chapter 4
Healing the Spiritual Energy Body / 159

Chapter 5
Growing Home / 223

Preface

It's good to be a seeker,
But sooner or later you have to be a finder.
And then it is well to give what you have found,
A gift into the world for whoever will accept it.

— Richard Bach,
Jonathan Livingston Seagull

In this high-tech age when we have split the atom, have put men on the moon, can talk to one another nearly anywhere in the world, and are inventing newer and better diagnostic machines to probe the human physiology, why are Americans returning in great numbers to a simpler form of medicine? Why have over two-thirds of the U.S. population tried one or more of the many forms of alternative treatments and healing techniques that are enjoying a recent and astounding revival?

Perhaps one reason is that we are steadily becoming aware that we are truly much more than just flesh and bones, tissue and organs, chemicals and minerals that all work together in an exquisite but delicate balance. As Eastern philosophies have taught for millennia, our multidimensional body also includes several invisible energy fields that surround the physical body. These energy fields play a very large part in our physical health; in addition, they can influence how we interact with our environment and others—emotionally, mentally, and spiritually.

However, until recently, training has not been available in our medical colleges for students, interns, and physicians to receive instruction and knowledge about the effect of these unseen human energy fields on the physical body. Instead, Western allopathic medicine has emphasized the use of drugs and surgery to treat disease. Modern surgical techniques and procedures are astounding in their ability to repair the human body, but often these techniques are not affordable or available to all who need them. Furthermore, the recent proliferation of new drugs has led to a situation wherein many physicians simply are not able to keep up with all the new drugs being produced. Side effects and unknown interactions between two or more drugs are also a real cause for concern.

In addition, most physicians no longer have time to discuss their patients' histories on anything but a clinical level. The time actually spent by the doctor discussing how patients feel and why they might feel that way is shrinking more and more, and patients resent being quickly shuffled in and out of the doctor's office. Still, most physicians agree that how patients think and feel about themselves is a major factor in influencing their overall state of health.

Another significant factor in the changing landscape of medical treatment is that many patients are no longer simply accepting what their doctor says at face value. They are getting more involved in their own health by becoming better informed on their own particular disease, condition, or symptoms, and are asking hard, detailed questions of their physicians regarding their suggested treatment plans. And they want information on disease prevention, not just disease treatment. Patients are beginning to take responsibility for their own health instead of leaving their health solely in the hands of their doctor. After all, it is their body!

And the more questions we ask, the more information we find about alternative, or nontraditional, methods of promoting health and healing the body of disease and symptoms. Books and magazine articles abound on the positive effects of diet, nutrition, acupuncture, herbs, homeopathic and naturopathic medicines, energy-based healing (laying-on of hands), megavitamins, chiropractic, meditation and prayer, and many other techniques to restore health to the complete emotional, mental, and spiritual human being we are.

So we need to become aware of emerging theories of health, disease, and treatment if we are to carry forward the best of traditional medical science and at the same time incorporate alternative metaphysical healing techniques that have consistently proven effective. This will allow us to integrate these two approaches into the most effective, affordable, and complete healing regimen, one that eliminates disease and its symptoms on all levels of the human being. This is the new movement toward what is being called "Integrative Medicine."

PURPOSE

The purposes of this book are: (1) to discuss basic principles and characteristics of the Human Energy Field that surrounds each physical body; (2) present and describe several different types of energy-based healing techniques that are now becoming available for those seeking alternatives to traditional medical treatments; and (3) describe how these techniques may be integrated into a truly holistic healing program that addresses the physical, emotional, mental, and spiritual needs of the client. If you are investigating alternative methods of healing, you have a steadily growing and often bewildering spectrum of techniques from which to choose. And the list seems to grow each time a new magazine article on the subject appears. But which healing techniques or modalities are recommended for addressing specific diseases or sets of symptoms, and do they really work?

This book discusses several energy-based healing techniques that have repeatedly demonstrated a positive effect on clients who want to accelerate their healing process in a wide range of diseases. By "energy-based" healing techniques, I mean that subset of alternative healing techniques that makes use of the Human Energy Field, sometimes called the aura, by a trained practitioner to bring about a more harmonious energy field in the client. This can result in greater overall physical health in the client, as well as a more balanced and healthy aura.

But I want the reader to be skeptical of what is presented here—keep an open mind, but do not let your brain fall out! Do not just automatically believe what you read. You need to decide if it makes sense to you. Does it fit into the information and belief systems you use in your daily life, or is it too "radical" for you to consider at this time? A wise man once said, "Don't believe anything for more than two hours." If you cannot see and feel the truth of it within that time, just put it up on the shelf until it does make sense, and only then include it as part of your own evolving Truth. But, conversely, do not prejudge anything just because you do not understand it. As we continue to experience new situations and learn from them, our own personal Truth expands to include this new knowledge.

For now, you the reader will have to *believe,* or *not believe,* in the Truth of what you read here. But if you experience a healing as either the healer or the client, then you will come to *know* the Truth of it for yourself, either positive or negative. You will not have to believe with blind faith what is written here. If you know for a fact that your healing experience is real, you can then freely take the knowledge of that experience into your own Truth, and your awareness will expand to include a new realization of that of which we are all capable.

This book also addresses several questions regarding the current state of energy healing. What kinds of alternative healing techniques are available? Can energy-based healing techniques be used to cure disease? Is healing temporary, or can energy-based healing provide a permanent cure? What does a "healer" really do? Is healing a special gift for only a few, or can anyone learn to be a healer? How can energy-based healing techniques and traditional medical treatments be integrated into an overall holistic program to provide a permanent cure for a specific disease? These and other intriguing questions are discussed in detail in the hopes that this additional information can help provide a personal roadmap for greater health that meets the specific needs of each seeker.

What kinds of alternative healing techniques are available? Chiropractic, acupuncture, massage therapy, natural remedies, flower essences, vibrational sound therapy, homeopathic medicine, Ayurvedic medicine, and energy-based techniques such as Reiki, Healing Touch, Polarity, Johrei, Bioenergy, etc., are only a small fraction of those available. Many insurance companies are now beginning to cover many of these alternative techniques simply because people get well quicker, require less medication, have fewer complications, and hospital stays are reduced when a balanced program of traditional and alternative medical therapies are used.

Of the many different categories of alternative therapies now available (e.g., natural herbs and remedies, structural integration techniques, yoga and meditation exercises, energy-based techniques, etc.), this book concentrates on several specific energy-based techniques. These techniques repeatedly have been shown to be effective and can easily be integrated into an overall holistic healing program tailored for a specific individual. These techniques address healing of not only the physical body, but also of the higher energy bodies in the Human Energy Field.

Can energy-based healing techniques be used to cure disease? Yes, but here we must understand the difference between treatment and healing. Many traditional medical procedures involve the treatment of disease symptoms, such as the pain associated with arthritis or a life-threatening cancerous growth, through drugs and/or surgery. Although these techniques can be very effective in the short term, they merely mask or temporarily control the symptoms of the disease instead of removing the original cause of the disease. For example, a cancerous organ may be simply removed from the body rather than eliminating the cause of the cancer. However, both drugs and surgery are powerful tools that can provide improved conditions for the body to heal itself. Yet in many cases, the disease may recur for reasons that may not be completely understood. We will examine in depth the reason disease occasionally recurs.

Is healing temporary, or can energy-based healing provide a permanent cure? When we remove the cause of a disease as well as its symptoms, we have gone beyond just treating the disease; we have ensured that the reason the disease exists is completely removed, and we can be confident that it will not recur. This is true healing and is accomplished through a holistic healing program that is much more comprehensive than only the traditional medical techniques in use today. If a holistic approach is adopted that addresses all levels of a person's being (physical, emotional, mental, and spiritual), the healing is usually permanent. The range of energy-based healing techniques discussed here provide a holistic approach to healing all levels of a person's being; these techniques can also be supplemented by additional lifestyle changes such as diet, exercise, and stress reduction.

What does a "healer" really do? An energy practitioner or "healer" (see Glossary) is one who has been trained to transfer or direct healing energies to a client for the purpose of healing. Energy healers have also been trained to see, sense, or feel the various layers of the client's energy field, or aura. And, depending on the specific healing technique involved, the healer has been trained in specific procedures to alter or repattern the client's energy field in a positive way such that the result is greater health.

Is healing a special gift, or can anyone learn to be a healer? Both. Some people are born with a special ability to heal, and some are given this gift later in life. Still other healers have developed the innate healing ability that is in each of us to varying degrees. One example of a person who was born with the ability to heal is Mietek Wirkus, a Polish healer who, at the age of six, was repeatedly able to stop his sister's asthma attacks merely by placing his hand on her arm. He later developed his own healing technique called "Bioenergy," which he teaches to others.[1] Another example is "Mr. A" whose story is told in Ruth Montgomery's bestseller *Born To Heal*.[2] Dr. Usui (see chapter 2, Reiki) is an example of one who was given special healing gifts later in life. On the other hand, I am an example of one who has developed my own innate healing abilities through instruction, self-development, and continuing experience in my own healing practice.

What should I expect if I go to an energy healer? This depends both on the healing technique received (Reiki, Reflective Healing, etc.) and the individual healer's style and preferences. If you came to me for any of the techniques discussed in this book, you would be asked to remove only your shoes, jewelry, and any crystals, and lie down on a comfortably padded healing table. I usually have soft, relaxing music playing in the background. Pillows are provided for your comfort and a blanket if you wish. During some techniques, such as Reiki or Healing Touch, you may choose to stay very alert or drop into a state of relaxation wherein you may or may not be aware of what I am doing. During other techniques, such as Hypnotherapy or Ro-Hun, you would be placed into a deeply relaxed state but would remain conscious of everything that goes on so you could conduct an active dialog with me during the session. Other specific details and procedures are discussed in the chapters for each healing technique.

How can energy-based healing techniques and traditional medical treatment be integrated into an overall holistic program to provide a permanent cure for a specific disease? The most important ingredient in a holistic healing program is a knowledgeable client who is well informed about both traditional medical procedures as they apply to his or her own specific disease/symptoms, and also about the available alternative therapies that may be of benefit to his or her health.

More and more, individuals are becoming responsible and proactive for their own health programs and treatment regimens. They are educating themselves in the medical options available to them and are discussing the details of their proposed treatment program with their doctors. And they are also becoming aware of the alternative medical therapies available and are asking their doctors how these therapies may be used to complement these doctors' traditional medical knowledge and surgical skills.

It is heartening to note that nearly all of the medical universities in the United States now offer courses in alternative medical therapies, although it is usually as an elective. Nevertheless, doctors are becoming aware of a wider range of therapies that can be used against specific diseases and conditions. They, like their patients, are beginning to understand the complex and intricate mechanism of the human body and the interaction of its energy field with the fields of others. Both the doctor/healer and patient/client are becoming more aware of what they are. Overall physical health can be improved and disease eliminated by using techniques that address the entire being on the physical, emotional, mental, and spiritual levels of the individual.

My Introduction to Healing

Each step we take along our own path in life awakens us to greater and grander vistas of who we are and why we are here doing the things we do. Each step we take in our unfoldment as an individual allows us greater choices in the steps we lay before ourselves. My own childhood dream to be a doctor gave way to the engineering and scientific fields. But even with a well-established career as a satellite communications systems engineer and technical program manager, one day I was led to a fork in the road that would change my career, my life, and how I perceived myself and others around me. One fork in the road read "Status Quo—Climb the Corporate Ladder" and the other fork read "Come Be a Healer and Learn About Yourself."

I chose the "Healing" fork. But I quickly found out that healing is not the ultimate goal in this process; it is only the means to an even greater end. As I use my tools of healing to help others and myself, I begin to better understand the nature of my own reality. I do not recommend healing as the only or best way to gain greater insight into your own self, but it is the way that has been right for me. Each person should find the way that resonates deep down inside and says, "This is what I am really all about; this is what I am supposed to be doing."

When I was a young child, my family would drive several hours to the home of my grandparents in Seattle for festive holidays such as Thanksgiving and Christmas. One day, I asked my grandmother about the picture of a mountain she had hanging in her kitchen. It was a great mountain that grew up out of a peaceful valley below to majestically high peaks covered with snow, and I wanted to know if it was nearby Mt. Rainier. She said, "No, that is just a picture of life. There are a thousand pathways up the mountain, but they all lead to the same place. It does not really matter which path you choose, but CHOOSE ONE and START WALKING!"

As I grew up, I began to understand her deep wisdom. We all come from different areas in the valley. Some look up and just wonder what the mountaintop might be like. Others have to start climbing from wherever they are to experience what is at the top and to see the valley below from a higher perspective.

I had been working for a large company that provides technical and engineering services in the satellite communications field to both the commercial and government sectors. I was leading a well-trained group of hardware and software engineers, and our company had just successfully negotiated an expanded contract for an additional five years. Everything was coming up roses. Then, one morning as I was waking up, I heard a very clear and distinct voice say, "Howard, it's time!" I shot up in bed to see who was there, but the room was empty. At the same time, I knew completely what it was time for: it was time to move to the Virginia Beach, Virginia, area. But I did not know why at the time.

Several times during my lifetime, I heard that very clear voice which would usually say something short like "No!" or "Don't do that!" or "Do not worry about this. It does not matter." Once, while I was test-driving cars before I bought one, "the Voice" in my mind said very clearly and distinctly, "This car will be very reliable and economical to operate." I bought the car and drove it more than 230,000 miles with no repairs needed. Over the years, I have learned to trust the advice given me by this unseen counselor. It has always been right and always in my best interests. The one time I ignored the Voice and did not take its advice, I was placed in a situation that proved to be financially disastrous. Now, when the Voice speaks, I listen!

So when I heard "Howard, it's time!" I knew I must heed the call. That day, I gave my notice at work and began preparations for moving, and within a few months, I had relocated to a comfortable house in the Chesapeake countryside with just over *three* acres. It was a welcome change from the pressure-cooker of the Washington, D.C., beltway scene. In just a few short weeks, doors began to open for me, and new opportunities to explore my own development suddenly presented themselves. First, I received a brochure in the mail for Reiki, a Japanese method of healing the physical body similar to the laying on of hands. Intrigued, I was soon initiated as a Reiki Practitioner and began my fascinating odyssey into energy healing.

About the same time, I became aware of workshops teaching other forms of physical healing, such as Healing Touch, Reflexology, Shiatsu, Acupressure, and Polarity Therapy. Of these, I was particularly drawn to Healing Touch and, within several months, had taken the first three workshops that taught all of the thirty individual Healing Touch techniques. While I was becoming familiar with the experience and practice of Healing Touch and Reiki, I attended a "getaway" weekend at Delphi University, a metaphysical institute in the Cherokee Hills of northern Georgia. There, I was introduced to an eye-opening array of advanced healing techniques that included Ro-Hun, Reflective Healing, and other energy-based assessment and healing processes. Additional courses were also available for rapid development of one's natural psychic and intuitive abilities. I was hooked!

Over the next several years, my path was guided by my desire to help others in a down-to-earth, practical way for physical and emotional healing, as well as a constant tug and pull on my inner psyche to heal and develop my own inner being. It has been said that you cannot heal others until you heal yourself. But I have also found that in learning how to bring healing to others, I have been able to bring healing to myself as well . . . not only physical healings, but also the comforting certainty and knowledge of what I am, who I am, and why I am here on this Earth doing what I am doing. Knowing one's purpose in life, and being confident and comfortable in that purpose, is a strong motivator for fulfilling those inner urgings and yearnings we often tend to shove aside or ignore. I know that at least one of my purposes is to gather together the information and knowledge about our energetic nature from many diverse sources and present it in this book for all who are ready to see, hear, and embrace the greater Truth of what we are as humans, as well as our relationship to each other and all there is.

It is my hope that with this book, I am able to inspire you to take a grand adventure up your own path on the mountainside of life. Let me point the way with illustrations from my own chosen path, healing. I hope this will give you a greater appreciation of this broader perspective of life and of ourselves as we keep climbing. I also hope you will realize that a broader perspective and clearer purpose in life is really what we are all climbing toward, not just greater abilities as a healer, as a merchant, as a tailor, or whatever path you have chosen. That broader perspective and awareness of who we are as universal citizens is available to each mountain climber, not just those on the healing path. Come climb with me!

ORGANIZATION OF THE BOOK

In order to understand energy-based healing and the principles that allow one to be a conduit or channel of healing energy for another, we must begin by understanding the energetic nature of our bodies. Therefore, chapter 1 provides the reader with a discussion of the Universal Energy Field and the Human Energy Field, along with an overview of energetic principles as they relate to human healing, as I understand them at this point in my own development. Chapters 2 through 4 provide a discussion of those significant modalities which pertain to the healing on the physical level (Reiki, Healing Touch, and Color and Sound Therapy), etheric level (Spiritual Surgery and Reflective Healing), emotional and mental levels (Hypnotherapy and Ro-Hun Transformational Therapy), and the spiritual level (an advanced meditation technique and Spiritual Regression). Lastly, chapter 5 provides a summation and overview from a broader perspective of the principles and information in the first four chapters.

This work contains much new material not found in my first book, *Awakening the Healer Within*. In chapter 2 (techniques that address the Physical and Etheric Energy Bodies), the previous treatment of Reiki has been greatly expanded, and a new technique, Color and Sound

Therapy, has been added. A large amount of information about the practice of Reiki in Japan historically on to the present time has recently been made available in English and significantly expands the original perspective of Reiki beyond what is normally taught in most Western Reiki classes. Color and Sound Therapy is an exciting technique I have been exploring recently and is the most effective technique I have yet found for balancing and harmonizing the human chakra system. The version in which I have been trained uses a combination of Tibetan singing bowls, the human voice, tuning forks, and a powerful musical mantra as background music.

In chapter 4 (techniques that address the Spiritual Energy Body), an exciting advanced meditation technique and a discussion of Spiritual Regression have been added. Since publication of *Awakening the Healer Within,* the works of the late Rev. Paul Solomon of Virginia Beach, Virginia, have been made available through the Paul Solomon Foundation, and the foundation has graciously given permission for me to present the meditation Paul developed as the Seven Terraces Meditation. I have modified it slightly yet kept Paul's original focus and process intact, calling it the Inner Light Consciousness (ILC) Meditation in honor and recognition of the greater Inner Light Consciousness works Paul has left as his enduring legacy. These may be found at the Paul Solomon Foundation website, *www.paulsolomon.com.* An audio CD that provides the guided imagery for the Inner Light Consciousness Meditation and the instructions on how to use this CD for the most effective meditation experience, is available (see Appendix C).

The remaining significant addition to chapter 4 is an overview and description of the technique known as Spiritual Regression that was developed by Dr. Michael Newton and discussed in detail in his books *Journey of Souls* and *Destiny of Souls.* After meeting Dr. Newton and discussing with him the elements of his groundbreaking work in exploring the spiritual consciousness of his clients, I knew for certain that Spiritual Regression provides one of the most significant and life-transforming experiences one can have, one that clearly brings into conscious awareness the true, spiritual nature of each client. Other hypnotherapists who are doing similar and very significant work are Shepherd Hoodwin, author of *The Journey of Your Soul,* and Dr. Shakuntala Modi, author of

Memories of God and Creation; these titles are included in the Bibliography section.

It should be noted here that the healing modalities chosen for discussion in this book are only a small fraction of the available energy-based healing techniques, and this is not to imply that the ones examined here are the best or most effective modalities. I have elected to discuss these because they are the ones to which I have been drawn, they provide a wide range of therapies that can be made available to address each level of our being (physical, etheric, emotional, mental, and spiritual), and because I have received detailed training and practical experience with each of them. They are all included in my healing practice.

Howard Batie
Chehalis, Washington
March 2003

Chapter One

Introduction to Energy-Based Healing Concepts

The human energy field responds to stimuli even before the brain does. I think we have way overrated the brain as the active ingredient in the relationship of a human to the world. The mind's not in the brain. It's in that darn field.

—Valerie Hunt, quoted by Michael Talbot
in *The Holographic Universe*

1

SINCE THE DAWN OF TIME, mankind has looked up toward the night-time sky and wondered how many stars there are, and how far away they are. Intricate designs of animals, warriors, and other symbols were seen in the heavens, and these patterns and constellations were used to interpret the cycles of life on this great planet. Then, as telescopes and other instruments came into use and these stars were closely observed, the then-prevalent geocentric concept of the universe began to crumble, and a new awareness of our place in it came into the consciousness of mankind: the Earth was no longer the center of the universe. It was now merely one of several planets that circle our sun, which is, in turn, just one of the infinite number of stars in the heavens.

As instruments began to improve in accuracy and several scientific branches of investigation came about to examine the heavens, we began to be able to estimate the size, shape and mass of the universe. However, as astronomers gaze farther and deeper into the heavens, they continue to come across processes in other galaxies and other worlds for which they have no explanation. Clearly, our present understanding of the composition of the universe is less than perfect.

In an attempt to correct this situation, astronomers and astrophysicists have begun to reexamine some of their basic theories and concepts of nature. The Newtonian concept of our physical world worked very well when we were not aware of the vast fields of energy that permeate all levels of the universe, from the largest galaxies to the smallest atom. Not only is Newtonian physics being reevaluated in the light of the more recent quantum physics, but also the limitations of Einstein's Theory of Relativity are now apparent. However, Einstein's famous equation $E = mc^2$ stated a fundamental truth that energy and matter are interchangeable. We have learned how to transform matter into energy through the atomic fission process. In addition, we have now demonstrated in the laboratory a limited capability to create matter using only focused beams of light from high-energy lasers.

The Universal Energy Field (UEF)

There appears to be a source of energy within our universe that is, as yet, unexplained by modern science. However, more than one physicist has speculated that our universe began its existence as a subtle energy field of very high vibrational frequencies, and in some places this field gradually became denser and denser over time, with subsequently lower vibrational patterns. Eventually, these areas of denser vibrational patterns coalesced into what we now perceive as our physical universe of galaxies, stars, and planets. It is also speculated that, in the immensity of space within our universe, the energy field from which all matter coalesced is still there. This original energy field is of a higher vibratory rate and is theorized to contain the holographic pattern for all of physical creation. This vast sea of vibrational energy is beyond the reach of today's instruments, and is termed the Universal Energy Field, or UEF.

In her groundbreaking book on energy-based healing, *Hands of Light,* Barbara Brennan lists several potential characteristics of the UEF.[1] According to her, the UEF is probably composed of a type of energy previously undefined by Western science, which may exist in a state between what we consider matter and energy. Furthermore, she speculates that this energy permeates all animate and inanimate objects in the universe, and connects all objects with each other. It can also be perceived or sensed by our inner senses of touch, taste, smell, sound, and luminosity (not the five normal physical senses). And last, she sugggests this energy is creative in that it is consistently building form, as opposed to degenerating form, i.e., it is synergistic instead of entropic.

If Brennan's observations are accurate, we are indeed becoming aware of our universe as much, much more than we can see and measure with today's instruments.

The Human Energy Field (HEF)

The Human Energy Field (HEF) is ". . . that part of the UEF associated with the human body"[2] and can be described in terms of three different perspectives: (1) the major and minor chakras throughout the body, (2) the subtle energy fields or energy bodies that surround the physical body, and (3) the energy meridians within the physical body that provide the means of circulating and distributing energy (prana, chi, ki, etc.) to the tissues and organs of the body. Each of these perspectives is discussed below.

THE CHAKRA SYSTEM

The Sanskrit word *chakra* means literally "spinning wheel." To those who can clairvoyantly see energy fields, a major chakra resembles a spinning wheel when looked directly into. However, when viewed from the side, it looks more like an energy vortex somewhat resembling the shape of a tornado or a funnel. This energy funnel is tight and compact near the surface of the skin, and gradually widens as it extends outside the physical body to the outer edge of the aura.

The chakra system within the human body consists of seven major chakras and many minor chakras. The location of the seven major chakras is shown in Figure 1. Each major chakra, from the Root through Brow, has four energy vortices associated with it: one spiraling upward, one downward toward the earth, one out the front of the body, and one out through the back of the body. The upward projecting vortex from one chakra and the downward projecting vortex of the chakra just above it join to form an energy column that runs vertically through the physical body from the bottom of the spine (Root Chakra) up in front of the spine and out through the top of the head (Crown Chakra).

The Crown Chakra also has vortices; however, they are spatially so close to the vortices of the Brow Chakra that they are often confused. The Brow and Crown vortices emanate from the area of the pituitary and pineal glands, respectively. These glands are physically very close to each other in the center of the brain. The result is that the vortices of the Brow Chakra overlap in much of the same space as those of the Crown Chakra. However, they can easily be distinguished since they are of different vibratory frequency.

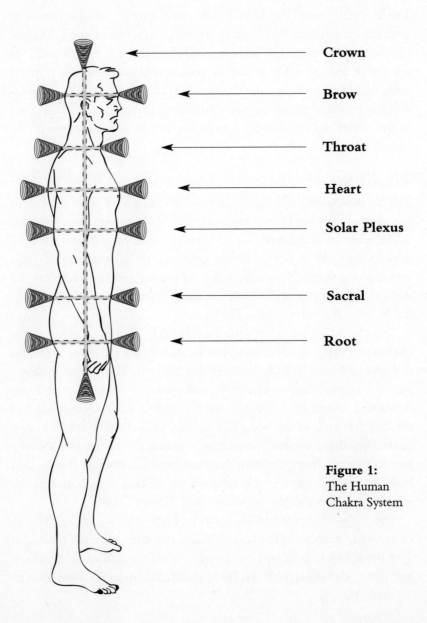

Crown

Brow

Throat

Heart

Solar Plexus

Sacral

Root

Figure 1:
The Human
Chakra System

When a chakra is healthy and balanced, its front and rear vortices spin in a circular motion. However, if there is a disturbance or blockage in the flow of energy within a chakra, the circular motion may become elliptical or, in extreme cases, severely flattened on its sides. This distortion may be sensed by those able to see or feel energy fields, or indirectly sensed by a pendulum (discussed later). Further, each chakra has its own specific "frequency," or rate of spin, with the lowest rate of spin in the Root Chakra and steadily increasing up to the highest rate of spin in the Crown Chakra.

The purpose or function of the human chakra system is to take in higher-dimensional energy from the Universal Energy Field all around us and translate or step down its frequency of vibration to that which can be used within the physical body. Each major chakra vibrates or spins at a different rate, and each chakra will absorb energy from the UEF that is harmonically related to its own frequency. Thus, energy from several frequency bands within the infinitely broad UEF spectrum is absorbed by the different chakras and is directed to those organs with which each

Chakra	Associated Organs	Endocrine Gland
Crown	Upper Brain, Right Eye	Pineal
Brow	Ears, Nose, Lower Brain, Nervous System, Left Eye	Pituitary
Throat	Lungs, Larynx, Alimentary Canal	Thyroid, Parathyroid
Heart	Heart, Blood, Vagus Nerve, Circulatory System	Thymus
Solar Plexus	Stomach, Gall Bladder, Liver	Pancreas
Sacral	Reproductive System	Testes, Ovaries
Root	Spinal Column, Kidneys	Adrenals

Table I: Major Chakras and Associated Organs and Glands

chakra is associated. (See Table I.) A good analogy of how this occurs is to visualize all the many TV signals existing around us all the time; by tuning to a specific channel (frequency), we get the specific information or programming being sent on that frequency. The human chakra system can then be said to act as a sort of multichannel receiver of vibrational frequencies from different portions of the energy spectrum all around us.

Through the internal human energy distribution system (see "Meridians" on page 15), each chakra is connected to specific organs and endocrine glands, as shown in Table I. For instance, the particular energy vibrations or frequencies absorbed by the Solar Plexus Chakra are linked energetically to the stomach, pancreas, gall bladder, and liver. Likewise, the reproductive organs receive their components of energy from the UEF through the Sacral Chakra (sometimes called the Spleen or Splenic Chakra).[3]

Many minor chakras are also located throughout the body, and are usually associated with joints such as the knee, shoulder, elbow, etc. Additional minor chakras are found in the palms of both hands and the soles of the feet, as well as at the ends of the fingers and toes. These minor chakras appear as beams of energy emanating from the body rather than as the spinning vortices of the major chakras. As will be discussed later, at least two major healing modalities, Reiki and Healing Touch, take advantage of these beams of energy coming out of the center of the palms and from the fingertips to stimulate and accelerate the body's own healing processes.

ENERGY BODIES

The Human Energy Field, or aura, is made up of a number of individual but harmonically related energetic bodies, each vibrating at its own frequency. All these subtle energy bodies are actually spatially superimposed over the physical form. Above the vibrational energy of the Physical Body are the Etheric Body, the Emotional Body, the Mental Body, and the Spiritual Body.[4] That is not to say that finer gradations do not exist; however, the groupings chosen are adequate to discuss the healing modalities presented here. Each energy body surrounds and interpenetrates all lower energy bodies, including the Physical Body. For example, the Emotional Body surrounds and penetrates the Etheric and Physical

Figure 2:
Energy Bodies of the
Human Energy System

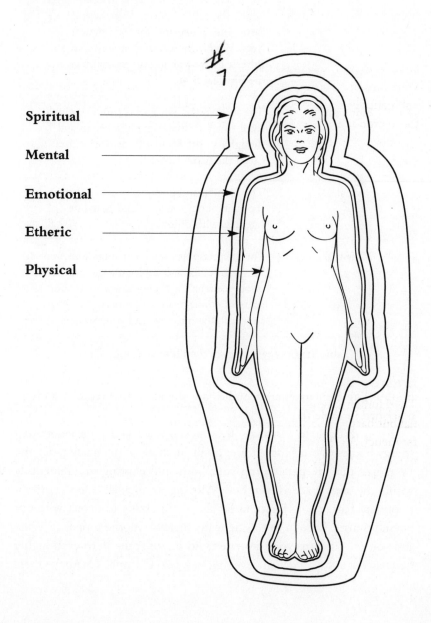

Spiritual

Mental

Emotional

Etheric

Physical

Energy Body	Contents, Characteristics
Physical	The Physical Body, organs, cells, and tissues with which we are familiar.
Etheric	An etheric matrix of energy gridlines upon which the cells of our body grow and take form. The "blueprint" for the Physical Body. Whatever pattern is present in the Etheric Body will, in time, be reflected in the Physical Body.
Emotional	The feelings and emotional patterns which are formed in response to the beliefs and thoughts in the Mental Body. Sometimes called the Astral Body.
Mental	The cultural and personal belief systems and thoughts about one's self and how one interacts with others.
Spiritual	Your higher purposes, goals, intentions, and inner senses for accomplishing the greatest good possible. Your "conscience" and your sense of connection with others, your environment, the universe, and your Source.

Table II: Energy Bodies of the Human Energy Field

Bodies. The human energy bodies are depicted in Figure 2 and are described in Table II.

If it is difficult to visualize the superimposed and interpenetrating energy bodies of our Human Energy Field, think of the many radio and TV signals that are penetrating your body and existing simultaneously within the same space as your body. Moving through all "solid" matter is a constant barrage of vibrations far above our ability to detect with our physical senses. Tune in to the right frequency with the proper receiver, and you can listen to your favorite radio station; tune in to even higher frequencies, and you get the evening news on Channel 12. Above these frequencies are heat, light, ultraviolet radiation, x-rays, and highly ener-getic particles of cosmic radiation. All these vibrations exist simultane-ously within the same three-dimensional space our bodies occupy, and the only characteristic that differentiates one from another is frequency, the rate at which that particular kind of energy vibrates.

The Physical Energy Body. At first, it may seem unusual to consider that the Physical Body is an energy body, but that is exactly what it appears to be. The Physical Body is the densest form of energy that our consciousness uses to explore and interact with its environment. Think about that for a moment. By the densest form, I mean that the vibra-tional patterns of the physical body are of a frequency low enough to be seen by our eyes (they are within the spectrum of visible light), heard by our ears (about 30 to 15,000 Hertz), and experienced with the senses of touch, taste, and smell, which are within the "frequency capability" of the Physical Body. And as we explore and become more accustomed to this new paradigm, we are able not only to see the Physical Body in a greater, more meaningful context, but also we begin to understand the role of disease and the nature of healing.

But there are many octaves, frequencies, and vibrations beyond the capability of our physical senses to detect. Beyond what we can see as vis-ible light are the higher frequencies of ultraviolet, x-ray, and cosmic radia-tion. We are beginning to understand that what we can physically sense is only a small portion of the vibrational energies around us. And if we look within our physical bodies at our atoms, molecules, and cells, again we find the patterns of vibrating energy we have traditionally called "matter."

We need to become aware that our Physical Body is really a field of vibrating energy that has coalesced from higher, less dense octaves. But we also need to remember that as vibrating fields interact with each other, one field can affect another field through the phenomenon of sympathetic vibration. If a violin player produces a note an octave above Middle G, and a second violin lying nearby on a table has a string which is tuned to Middle G, the second violin string tuned to Middle G will sympathetically begin to vibrate as well. So as we also begin to under-stand that there are several vibrational fields of energy around our phys-ical body, it becomes easier to understand how one field affects another through this principle. And this is the key to understanding how energy-based healing techniques can achieve such visible and profound results in the physical body.

The Etheric Energy Body. The Etheric Body is the first energy body in frequency above that of the Physical Body. It exists within the Physical Body, and extends outward about an inch or two outside the skin. Its purpose is to provide an energy template or matrix for the development, maintenance, and repair of the Physical Body. The Etheric Body contains a vibrational energy counterpart for each organ, blood vessel, and bone found in the Physical Body. Indeed, the Etheric Body contains the energetic blueprint for the pathways that guide the location and development of every cell of the Physical Body. "The bony structure, muscular, and vascular tissues, the nerves, the brain, and other substances are all represented in the etheric mold by currents of energy on specific frequencies."[5] "The physical tissues exist as such only because of the vital (etheric) field behind them; that it, the (etheric) field is prior to, not a result of, the physical body."[6]

Since the Etheric Body is the Physical Body's blueprint, the two are very closely related. As will be discussed later, the energetic vibrations of the Etheric Body determine the pattern for not only the physical tissues and organs, but also the state of health of those tissues and organs. If the etheric vibrations are not clear and pure, this disharmony will be reflected in the Physical Body as disharmonious function—what we call "disease." Conversely, traumas to the Physical Body (e.g., broken bones, burns, incisions, and scars) will in time be reflected into the Etheric Body unless there is some interceding process that either prevents this reflection or that restores the original vibrational pattern that existed prior to the trauma. The ability to work with a client's vibrating energy fields is precisely what forms the basis for rapid and effective energy-based physical healings.

As explained by Talbot, an illness can appear in the energy field weeks and even months before it appears in the Physical Body. He considers that the physical body ". . . is just one more level of density in the human energy field and is itself a kind of hologram that has coalesced out of the interference patterns of the aura. . . ."[7] Richard Gerber, a

Detroit physician, agrees, noting that "the etheric body is a holographic energy template that guides the growth and development of the physical body."[8]

The following description of the Etheric and higher subtle energy bodies surrounding the Physical Body are taken from Brennan's book, *Hands of Light*. To those who can directly observe energy fields, the Etheric Body appears as a grid of tiny energy lines that has the overall structure and shape of the Physical Body. This matrix extends from one-quarter to two inches beyond the Physical Body. It is upon this etheric grid or matrix that the cells and tissues of the body develop and are anchored. The etheric body appears as a light blue or gray matrix of lines of light that constantly pulsate or scintillate at a rate of from fifteen to twenty cycles per minute.

The Emotional Energy Body. The Emotional Body contains the emotional patterns, feelings, and vibrations that determine our personality and also how we feel about ourselves and interact with others. If we are constantly angry, always feel helpless, or are consistently fearful, these patterns or vibrations get locked in our emotional energy field and become a part of our personality. This determines to a very large degree how we interact with others on personal, social, and cultural levels.

The Emotional Body generally follows the shape of the Physical and Etheric Bodies but is somewhat more amorphous and fluid, and extends from one to about three inches outside the Physical Body. It contains energy "blobs" of all colors of the rainbow, depending on the specific feeling or emotion. Highly charged feelings, such as love, hate, joy, and anger are associated with energy blobs that are bright and clear, while confused feelings are darker and muddier.

The Mental Energy Body. The Mental Body contains the structure and patterns of all the thoughts and belief systems we consider true. There is a very strong connection between the Mental and Emotional Bodies. Although a thought or idea can in itself be very powerful, our reactions to those thoughts carry even more energy, and different people will react differently to the same thought. For example, consider the thought form: "If you are not a Catholic (or Protestant, or Muslim, or

Jew, or whatever), you cannot go to Heaven." One person might hear that thought or idea, think it was silly, and give it absolutely no energy. But another person might become very passionate, depending on his or her greater belief systems, and argue strongly either for or against the truth of that statement. The second person's Emotional Body would then record the intensity of the reaction to the thought stored in the Mental Body. However, the person who thought the statement was silly in the first place would not have any resonance with it, and no energetic pattern would be stored in either the Mental or Emotional Bodies.

The Mental Body usually appears as yellow light, radiating around the entire body from head to toe, and extends from three to eight inches beyond the Physical Body. Within this area, individual thought forms appear as small blobs of light of varying form and intensity.

The Spiritual Energy Body. The Spiritual Body (i.e., all vibrational patterns in octaves higher than the Mental Body) contains all the information related to our experiences, and reflects our gestalt consciousness of all that has been learned and experienced. It contains our higher intentions, our sense of what is right and wrong (conscience), and our desires to increase our awareness of our purpose, place, and mission for this lifetime.

These five energy bodies make up one's Human Energy Field, or aura. Its outer shape appears roughly egg-shaped and extends out to perhaps one to two feet beyond the Physical Body; however, this shape can be extended even further out or contracted closer to the Physical Body depending on the situation the person is experiencing. For example, when a person is feeling emotions of unconditional love, the aura may expand to several feet and radiate bright hues of gold or white; but if the same person is feeling threatened physically or emotionally, the entire aura may collapse for protection into a much denser pattern within only a few inches of the body.

Chapters 2 through 4 provide examples of different energy-based techniques that provide healing on these Physical/Etheric, Emotional/Mental, and Spiritual Energy Body levels, respectively.

ENERGY MERIDIANS

Within the body, many energetic pathways connect each organ and chakra, both major and minor. It is this internal energy distribution system that permits the flow of life-sustaining energy to the internal organs and tissues. This system of pathways has been known and used for several thousand years by oriental practitioners of acupuncture. In acupuncture or acupressure, the thought is that many diseases are caused or exacerbated by inadequate energy flow to certain areas of the body or organs. The fine needles used in acupuncture stimulate specific points along these energy meridians to release the blocked flow of life-force energy and thus restore health. More recently, acupressure, a variation of this practice, has become quite popular. With acupressure, stimulation of the energy meridians to release the blocked flow of energy is accomplished by applying physical pressure from the fingers or hands instead of acupuncture needles. Western medicine is just now beginning to recognize the effectiveness of acupuncture and acupressure and, encouragingly, some insurance companies are now allowing payments for acupuncture and acupressure treatments simply because some patients recover quicker and with fewer complications.

The chapters that follow describe several healing modalities for modulating the energy components of the physical and subtle energy bodies of the client. However, for the modalities discussed, it is not necessary to have a detailed understanding of the energy meridian system within the Physical Body. It is enough to recognize that when healing energy is transferred to the client's body through whatever means (such as the healer placing his or her hands on the client in a Reiki session), the energy meridians within the body provide a means of distributing the energy from the healer to wherever it is needed within the body.

The Nature of Healing Energy

A number of very interesting studies and carefully controlled experiments have been conducted to determine the nature of the healing energies exhibited by healers' hands. These studies have provided strong evidence to suggest that healing energy is magnetic in nature, as opposed to the electrical energy exhibited by the physical body. We are all familiar with the electroencephalograph (EEG), which measures the minute electrical currents within the brain, and the electrocardiogram (EKG), which measures the minute electrical currents within the heart and other body tissues. But since the development of the ultrasensitive magnetic field detector called a SQUID (Super-conducting QUantum Interference Device), it has been possible to measure and document the intensity of the magnetic field emitted by healers' hands.

In his book, *Vibrational Medicine,* Dr. Richard Gerber cites the interesting work of Dr. John Zimmerman and several others,[9] and states that Zimmerman, working at the University of Colorado School of Medicine, found that during a healing session, the intensity of the magnetic field of the healer's hands increased to several hundred times that of the "normal" magnetic intensity. Research chemist Robert Miller found copper sulphate solution exposed to either strong magnetic fields or the magnetic field of a healer's hands will always form coarse-grained turquoise-blue crystals, instead of the usual jade-green structures formed in the absence of a magnetic field.

Dr. Justa Smith found that ". . . healers can accelerate the kinetic activity of enzymes in a fashion similar to the effects of high-intensity magnetic fields."[10] Using several different enzymes, she also found one (NAD-ase) that exhibited increased activity when exposed to a strong magnetic field, but showed a reduction in activity when exposed to a healer's hands. However, when the cellular metabolic functions of this enzyme were examined, it turned out that a decrease in enzyme activity caused or was strongly correlated with a greater energy reserve within the cell. In another experiment, Dr. Smith purposely damaged the enzyme trypsin by exposing it to a strong ultraviolet light. The damaged enzyme was then held in the hands of a healer, and the structural integrity and organization of the enzyme was restored.

Therefore, Gerber has concluded that, "The activity of the enzymes affected by the healers always seemed to be in a direction that was toward greater overall health and balanced metabolic activity of the organism. . . . The suggestion here is that the subtle life-energies of healers seem to have primarily magnetic properties."[11] Gerber also points out that, through the instrument of their hands, the healer transfers these magnetic-like energies primarily to the Physical Body and its closely connected energetic template, the Etheric Body. A very strong and plausible case is made for the argument that while the matter of the Physical Body is primarily electrical in nature, the matter of the Etheric Body is primarily magnetic in nature.

Dr. James Oschman agrees, writing, "Of all the discoveries . . . the most exciting is the discovery of the huge biomagnetic fields emitted from the hands of therapists. . . ."[12] He notes also that these biomagnetic fields vibrate in the part of the frequency spectrum that resonate with natural cell, tissue, and organ functioning, and thus have the ability to affect matter on a molecular level in a way that promotes, through electromagnetic field resonance and entrainment, a rapid return to their original natural state of being, a condition we call "health."[13]

SENSING ENERGY FIELDS

In order to promote healing, the energy-based healing practitioner must modulate or manipulate one or more of the various energy bodies, including the Physical Body. This is normally done through a combination of hand motions and the healer's intentions. However, in order to manipulate an energy body, the healer must somehow be able to accurately locate it; if the healer intended to manipulate the Etheric Body, that result could not be achieved if the practitioner's hands were held higher, say, in the client's Mental Field.

There are several methods of sensing where each subtle energy body is located, as well as sensing the vibrational activity of the chakras. Some healers are clairvoyantly sensitive to energy and can actually see the vibrational movement within each separate energy body. However, this is not very common. Most energy practitioners can physically sense the presence of energy fields and spinning chakra energy vortices with their hands or fingers; this is a skill that can be easily learned by nearly anyone. And finally, a simple pendulum can be used to dowse the vibrational condition of energy centers such as the chakras. Each of these methods is discussed below.

Directly Viewing Energy Fields. Some people are able to visually or intuitively see the energy fields of others. One such person is Barbara Brennan, author of *Hands of Light*. In that book, she has provided several color illustrations of what each subtle energy body looks like to her. In addition, several examples of energy disturbances that result in disease or symptoms are shown, as they appear to her. For the vast majority of healers who have not yet developed what she calls their Higher Sense Perception and the ability to see energy, these illustrations are indeed most impressive. Yet she is also the first to say that the illustrations show only how energy appears to her and that it may appear differently to another person.

Dowsing with a Pendulum. A pendulum is a small object suspended on a thread or string about six to eight inches long and is used primarily to determine the state of the spinning vibrational energy of a chakra. As the pendulum is moved into the vortex of the chakra, it begins to move in response to the chakra energy. The direction of movement of the pendulum can be observed, and the energetic state of the chakra can be inferred from this movement. The pendulum is responding to the interaction of the healer's energetic field (aura) and the field of the client being dowsed or pendled.

The pendulum is also very useful for visually observing the condition of the energy in a minor chakra such as a joint. For example, in one of the Healing Touch techniques, each vertebral joint of the spine can be tested with a pendulum to determine if there is a smooth energy flow through the joint. Alternatively, there may be an energy blockage found that may be contributing to the physical back symptoms being experienced by the client.

The pendulum can make several different types of movement, and each can be related to a specific energetic condition of the chakra being monitored. Normally, a rotation of the pendulum in a circle of about an inch or two in diameter indicates a "healthy" energy condition within the chakra, whereas movement of the pendulum in a straight line might indicate that an energy block exists in the chakra being "pendled." In between the circular and straight movements is an elliptical motion, which might indicate that the chakra energy is still flowing, but it is doing so in a reduced or distorted manner.

When dowsing or pendling the major chakras, it is also important to pay attention to the size of the circle, ellipse, or line that is traced by the pendulum. In a healthy aura, all major chakras will cause the pendulum to move in about the same size diameter. Therefore, you should not be alarmed if you see a circle of only one inch in diameter for all chakras. But if the pendulum spins in a two-inch diameter circle over all chakras except one which is spinning with only a one-inch diameter, you could correctly infer that some physical or energetic condition is inhibiting that chakra's full functioning.

Each practitioner who uses a pendulum usually has a favorite material for the pendulum. Many prefer quartz crystals, some prefer certain types of wood, and others use a favorite ornament on their "special" necklace. However, the weight of the pendulum may have more to do with its response than the type of material of which it is made. I have made and successfully used pendulums of conducting metal, insulators such as plastic or glass, a paper clip, wood of all types, stone beads, brass nuts, and a chip of ceramic tile. They all worked equally well, with the main difference being that the heavier pendulums took longer to start rotating, and usually had a smaller diameter circle than the lighter pendulums. Also, the length and weight of the string or line connected to the pendulum will have an effect. The longer the length, the slower the pendulum will rotate and (eventually) the wider the circle will be. There is no way to say what the right length, weight, and material for you should be. Start with a string length of six to eight inches, and try several materials that "feel" good to you and give you a reliable response from client to client.

In order to receive consistent results from a pendulum, it must be programmed to respond to a specific set of conditions in the body in a certain way. For instance, you can specify that the pendulum's reaction to a "normal" healthy chakra be a circular motion and a blocked chakra be observed by a horizontal, back-and-forth movement across the chakra. You could just as easily program the pendulum to respond in the reverse manner. The essential component that determines how your pendulum will respond is your intention!

A good example of this power of intention can be demonstrated by programming your pendulum to respond to "Yes" or "Positive" in one direction (e.g., toward and away from your body if you are holding the pendulum in front of you) and "No" or "Negative" in a perpendicular direction (e.g., sideways across your body). To program it in this manner, simply concentrate your vision and mental focus on the pendulum, and say out loud or to yourself, "I intend that a motion of this pendulum toward and away from my body represents 'Yes' or 'Positive,' and a motion across my body represents 'No' or 'Negative.'" It is just that simple.

To test the pendulum, hold your left hand horizontally in front of you with the palm down and the fingers spread far apart. Now, holding the pendulum string in your right hand, place the body of the pendulum about an inch directly in front of the tip of your left index finger. In a moment, it will start to move in the direction that you have programmed for "Positive" or "Yes" (either parallel or perpendicular to your finger). Now move the pendulum to about an inch from the tip of your middle finger, and it will begin to move in the direction you have programmed for "Negative" or "No." This corresponds to the positive and negative polarities of the energy meridians that extend through these two fingers. This "spike" of energy extends several inches beyond the end of your fingertips.

Now for the fun part. Reprogram your pendulum in just the reverse fashion to respond to a "Positive" or "Yes" with a horizontal motion back and forth across your body, and a "Negative" or "No" with a horizontal motion toward and away from your body, and retest the same index and middle fingers. Miraculously, the newly programmed motion will now be observed in the pendulum! Truly, this is mind over matter, and there is no way to misinterpret what you have just seen. The intention you stated in the thought form (programming your pendulum) has caused the pendulum to move in a certain direction, and by changing your thought form, you are able to change how you influence a material object!

The movement of the pendulum can also be used by the energy practitioner to determine the state of a particular chakra on each energy level. A pendulum that moves in a circular motion in the Etheric Body, for example, may have a completely different motion (e.g., elliptical or straight) in the Emotional Body. Through intention and the ability to sense the separate energy bodies, the practitioner can ask the pendulum to indicate, for example, the state of the Solar Plexus Chakra on the

Mental level or on the Emotional level. This allows complete characterization of the state of the chakra on all levels within the aura.

Still another fascinating property of the pendulum is its ability to respond to "Yes/No" questions according to the way you have programmed it. When held in front of you where you can see it clearly, ask a question out loud which can be unambiguously answered by "Yes" or "No," and the pendulum will respond. However, in this case the pendulum is responding to the energetic response made by your Higher Self, your soul, or your spirit. Once you become familiar with the operation of the pendulum, you can easily use it in this way to provide infallible guidance that will always be in your best interests.

Scanning with the Hand. While the pendulum may be used to get an approximate quantitative evaluation of the state of a chakra, your own hand can provide additional qualitative information about the client's energy bodies. Once the energy healer's hands are developed to sense or feel energy, the healer can use them to directly determine the overall shape of the outer edge of the aura, the boundaries of the inner energy bodies (e.g., Etheric/Emotional or Emotional/Mental boundaries), the shape of a chakra within each energy body out to the edge of the aura, and the location and qualities of any areas of energy abnormalities within the energy bodies.

How energy feels, however, is unique to each individual, and each person may have a different sensation when scanning or running his or her hand through the energy field of the same client. For example, an area of energy congestion may feel scratchy, hot, angry, or prickly to one person; and another person may have a sense of vibration in his or her hands or fingers at the same location. The sensations felt are the result of the interaction of the healer's field with that of the client, and it may be very different reaction with a different client. Therefore, it is important not to anticipate what you think the sensation might be, but instead to recognize how the energy feels when you first sense it and to detect changes in the way it feels as the session progresses.

To scan a client's energy field with my hand, I usually start by getting an impression of the overall shape of the aura at its outer edge. Starting from several feet away from the client, I move my hands slowly over one area of the client's body (e.g., abdomen) until I sense the outer edge of the Spiritual Energy Body in that area. Then I repeat this in enough locations to get a rough idea of the overall shape of the aura. Particular attention is paid to the regions of the aura directly over the front chakras, Root through Brow. Normally, the aura will be symmetrical around the client. If there is any deviation noted from this symmetry, it is very useful to document it. This will allow comparison with later scans following the energy sessions.

After the shape of the aura is determined, the individual chakra vortices may be scanned with the hand to gain any additional information beyond that obtained from the pendulum. If abnormalities are noticed in the Etheric layer of a chakra, this may give the healer a clue as to which organs may be affected and what symptoms might be presented. Similarly, when the Emotional and Mental Bodies are scanned by a sensitive healer, different sensations such as hot, cold, scratchy, jagged, or strong vibration may indicate the presence of a block in the natural flow of energy on these levels. This could, in turn, indicate the source of symptoms that appear in the Physical Body.

For example, a mental belief that you are unworthy of success (Mental layer) may result in a feeling of anger at yourself (Emotional layer). In accordance with the principle of resonance through sympathetic vibrations, this in turn affects the Etheric layer, which is the blueprint for the Physical Body, and eventually ulcers may develop. Although you may be very aware of the ulcer in the Physical Body, you may not be aware that the ulcer is also present as an energetic pattern in the Etheric Body, that the ulcer's energetic pattern was created by the anger in the Emotional Body, and that the anger is your reaction to the thought form "I am unworthy of . . ." in the Mental Body.

Developing Sensitivity to Energy

Two easy exercises one can do to develop the ability to detect and feel energy are called "The Laser" and "The Hand Bounce." While doing these exercises, be very aware of any differences between your hands in the way they feel or react to your energy field. It may be that only one of your hands will become sensitive to energy, and there is no way to predict which hand that may be—each person is different. In my case, my left hand is currently much more sensitive to energy fields, so I use it exclusively to scan. However, your right hand may be the sensitive one, or perhaps you are able to sense equally well with either hand. Practice the exercises below and learn for yourself how your own energy field, or that of another person, "feels" to you.

EXERCISE: THE LASER

A simple exercise to develop sensitivity to energy is to curl your middle, ring, and little fingers into the palm of one hand and hold them there with the thumb and point with the extended index finger into the palm of the other hand. Move your index finger around in a circle about an inch or two away from your palm, and begin to sense the slight sense of motion across your palm. The beam of energy coming out of your moving fingertip is "slicing through" the energy field of the other hand, and you can sense this, particularly if your eyes are closed and you are concentrating on learning what that feels like. You can also move your pointing finger across the soft pad on the inside of the end joint of each finger to help develop sensitivity to energy fields in your fingertips.

EXERCISE: THE HAND BOUNCE

Place your hands in front of you like you are going to clap them, keeping the palms about a foot apart at first. Now hold your left hand still and begin to move your right hand toward your left hand until the palms are about one or two inches from each other, and then move them apart again to where they started. One hand is held still so that there is no possibility of sensation in it due just to the momentum of the blood flowing in your hand. "Bounce" your right hand about once or twice a second, in and out, smoothly and continuously. Concentrate on how the palms of your hands feel, particularly your left palm—put all your awareness and concentration into what your left hand is sensing and how it feels to you.

As you bounce your right hand in and it gets from one to three inches from your left hand, you may begin to sense a very subtle, very light sense of pressure in your left palm or fingertips. It may feel like a very gentle resistance to the movement, like trying to push soapy hands through a soap bubble, or like the gentle resistance of two magnets opposing each other while still far apart. Notice this feeling and keep moving your hands steadily so you can get a stronger sense of what this feels like. Keep practicing this until you are sure you are feeling something, even if you are not sure what it is.

What you are feeling is the Etheric Energy Body around your left hand meeting the Etheric Energy Body around your right hand. When they meet and compress each other slightly, that compression is reflected into your palms or fingertips as a slight sense of pressure. It is only at this point, where the outer boundaries of the two fields meet, that the pressure is felt. As you move your hands closer together, your right hand moves within the field of your left hand, and vice versa, and no pressure is felt when the field boundary of one hand is inside the field of the other hand.

Now reverse your hands. Hold the right hand still and move your left hand in toward your right hand, again "bouncing" in and out about once or twice each second. This time, place all your awareness into the palms and fingertips of your right hand, and notice if there is a difference in the way your two hands "feel" the energy boundaries meeting. Not all people "feel" energy equally well in both hands, and you will need to experiment to see if one hand is more sensitive than the other, and if so, which is the most sensitive hand.

Keep moving your hands so you feel that slight sense of pressure between them, and notice your breathing. It is probably pretty shallow because you are concentrating on your hands so intently. Now begin to breathe deeply and quickly, and notice that your hands will have to move an inch or two further apart to keep feeling that same sensation between them. This is a very clear demonstration that the energy we take in through our breath is quickly and continuously reflected into the energy fields around our bodies. In this case, the energy fields surrounding your hands expanded due to the additional energy received by deep breathing, and your hands had to move further apart to stay at that point where the boundary of the Etheric field around each hand meets.

Do not be discouraged if at first you do not feel the energy fields around your hands. Keep practicing and focus on how your hands feel. Do not try to anticipate that they feel anything specific, but just keep noticing what they do feel. And practice, practice, practice!

When you are able to sense the energy field around your own hands, ask a partner to join you. Each person should use one hand and do the same "bounce" described above until you can begin to feel that same slight sensation in your palm. When you are both confident that you have the sensation with your hands a certain distance apart, have one of the partners think of something very, very sad and depressing. Notice how the distance between your hands begins to shrink a bit as you still feel that bounce or pressure in your hands. And now have them think of something very happy, loving and energizing, and watch how their expanding field pushes your hands further apart in order to keep sensing the edge of their field. Here is proof positive that thoughts can also affect the energy levels in your aura. Perhaps you have been around someone who felt like they were draining your energy, or someone who was very positive and uplifting just to be around. What one thinks and feels is reflected in the energy bodies surrounding him or her, and others can sense this energy.

Disease and Healing

ORIGIN OF DISEASE

For many centuries, disease was thought to be caused by evil "vapors," or spirits visiting a person's body for one reason or another. Gradually, as superstition gave way to modern investigation using the microscope, the world of the microcosm began to show itself. Now with advanced equipment such as electron microscopes, we can see into the world of germs, viruses, microbes, protozoans, and parasites. To be sure, some diseases are caused by the body's inability to cope with certain bacteria, microbes, and viruses, but these are not the cause of all illnesses and diseases. Some diseases also are a secondary result of traumatic injury, such as gangrene after a bone fracture. Still others seem to be caused, or at least exacerbated, by one's emotional state, such as the person who runs around angry for decades and finally develops a stomach ulcer. And there is also growing support for the idea that some diseases are developed in response to a karmic reaction so we can learn a lesson. We will examine all these sources of disease below.

Bacteria and Viruses.   The ability to avoid becoming infected by unhealthy germs or viruses, and if infected, to destroy these unhealthy agents, is a measure of the health of a person's immune system. If the immune system is strong, infection is checked and the self-healing process of the body is allowed to complete its work. But if the immune system is not functioning well, infection can spread and secondary complications may occur. Properly prescribed medicines and antibiotics can kill some germs and bacteria, but viruses are much more troublesome. "Allopathy (traditional medicine) is clearly superb at dealing with trauma and bacterial infections. It is far less successful with asthma, chronic pain, and autoimmune diseases."[14] And there is still no cure for the common cold, although there are several practices that can lead to a higher resistance to catching a cold in the first place. Antioxidants such as vitamins C and E continue to be recommended for having a stimulating effect on the immune system.

Your medical doctor can prescribe an effective medication to combat, for instance, strep throat. But when it comes to the treatment of diseases and symptoms that are caused by viruses, modern medicine seems to be at a loss as to where to start. One form of arthritis, for example, is thought to be caused by a virus of some sort, and the symptoms are often treated by prescribing long-term use of steroids. However, although some symptoms may be temporarily reduced by the use of steroids, these drugs have an extremely damaging effect to a person's energy system.

I had an occasion to hand-scan the field of a person who had been using prescribed steroids for about ten years to treat arthritis. When I put my hand into her field about three or four inches from her body, my hand actually went numb from the intense vibration! Her energy system was so extremely agitated and vibrating so much and so wildly that my own field could not analyze it, and all feeling was temporarily disrupted.

When I removed my hand from her field, normal sensations quickly returned. Again, I put my hand into her field, and again it went numb; removing it again returned the feeling in my hand to normal. There is much we do not yet know about the body and its reactions to many chemicals and agents that are routinely prescribed to mask the symptoms of, but not actually cure, many diseases. As we learn more about the energy fields of which we are composed, we can bring this additional understanding into good use when knowledgeable medical doctors prescribe medicines for specific diseases or symptoms.

There is also a growing body of experiential evidence that a healer's application of energy stimulates the body's immune system and helps to create internal conditions that allow the person to self-heal much faster than normally would be expected. Two such healing techniques that produce this effect, Reiki and Healing Touch, are discussed in the next chapter. The use of energy-based healing techniques is becoming more and more widespread, and many Healing Touch procedures are being introduced into the recovery rooms of many of the more progressive and enlightened hospitals. Even insurance companies are beginning to compensate for the use of certain healing energy techniques simply because people get well quicker, heal with less pain, and have shorter hospital stays.

Trauma. Today's surgeons, in conjunction with modern technology, have developed an amazing ability to analyze the body's organs, blood, and tissues; and new surgical procedures are being introduced at a pace that would have been unbelievable only a few years ago. Replacement of organs and complete joints has returned many people to a healthy, fully functional lifestyle after years of crippling pain and inactivity. Surgical procedures to repair organs, tissues, and limbs, and to graft nerves have similarly allowed many to recover the use of damaged parts of their body. The list goes on and on, and it grows daily. The modern surgeon can truly be a miracle-worker for the victim of a traumatic injury.

Yet there is still the chance that after all the effort on the part of the surgeon, a simple infection may develop, spread, and, unless checked, could lead to a life-threatening disease such as pneumonia, septecemia, or a host of other secondary complications. A person's ability to recover from traumatic injury and surgery is also a reflection of the health of that person's immune system to ward off infections. It is also an indication of the person's own self-healing ability to reconstruct tissues, to grow together nerves, and to construct new capillaries and blood vessels to nourish injured areas.

Each of these self-healing activities requires energy. Healing involves the process of converting energy within the body into matter—new tissues, new blood cells, etc. Normally, the person's Human Energy Field is the energy source for the healing activity. However, regenerative healing can be significantly accelerated by applying additional energy from the Universal Energy Field, using the healer as a channel. For instance, when healing Reiki energy is applied, broken bones knit together in about one-half the normal time. Patients recovering from surgery require less pain relief medication after an energy-based healing technique is used. Bleeding can quickly be controlled, and surgical incisions tend to heal more quickly and with less scarring following energy healing sessions.

Beliefs and Emotions.   There is growing evidence that our emotional and mental health can and does affect our physical health, both positively and negatively. In her book, *You Can Heal Your Life,* Louise L. Hay lists many diseases for which the original cause may be faulty beliefs about one's self or negative emotional reactions to what we perceive about ourselves or others.[15] For example, a person who feels stifled and suppresses crying lives in an emotional pattern that prevents that person from breathing in the goodness of life. If this emotional pattern continues, it is eventually brought down into the Etheric Body and becomes a part of the overall pattern for the Physical Body, and the person may develop asthma.

Similarly, she says AIDS, caused by a weakening of the immune system, can result when a person has faulty mental beliefs about themselves to the extent that they feel defenseless and hopeless for an extended period of time, if they have sexual guilt issues, or if there is a strong belief in not being "good enough."

Karma. For some, the concept of past lives may be difficult to accept, and the idea that past lives could affect your current lifetime may be even harder to accept. Yet in many Eastern philosophies, the idea of incarnating in repeated lifetimes is one of the underlying foundational beliefs that permit a coherent understanding of an individual's existence and purpose. The principle of karma is simply another way of stating the Golden Rule, "Do unto others as you would have them do unto you." Or, "What goes around, comes around." Within the framework of karma is the expectation that everything you do is returned to you, both good and bad. However, it is not necessary that the results of your actions be returned to you during your current lifetime; it may be delayed until a later incarnation. Karma makes sense only if viewed in the context of several lifetimes.

Another way of looking at karma is that it is a mechanism for providing us the greatest potential for our own soul's growth. For example, through my free will choice, I may choose to injure a person emotionally by withdrawing my love from her. Under the law of karma, I must also experience the injury that I have caused. Therefore, in a later experience, either in this lifetime or another lifetime, a situation will be created wherein I will be able to experience a similar withdrawal of love. In experiencing this, I am now aware of both how it feels to withdraw love and how it feels to have love withdrawn. Knowing both sides of the coin, I am now in a better position to consciously choose my future courses of action. Further, by experiencing life from all possible vantage points, I would be better able to understand all of life's complexity and beauty. "By incarnating as male and female, white and black, as Indian, Chinese, and Chicano, by experiencing life from all possible viewpoints, the reincarnational scheme allows us to see the world from all possible perspectives."[16]

However, for our discussion here, it is not necessary to believe in reincarnation or past lives. There is another very effective way of looking at our actions in a similar manner. The famous psychiatrist Carl Jung postulated the idea that all actions taken by each person on Earth throughout time are recorded in what he called the "collective unconscious." He further proposed that there was some mechanism for attaching or connecting specific events in the collective unconscious with individual people. Therefore, as you choose to take a certain action, that choice and action is recorded in the collective unconscious. In addition, there is a resonance of some sort between that action and others that have already been stored, and through this resonance, these other actions are connected to your current life through your subconscious mind.

A growing number of cases from clinical hypnotherapists and regression therapists suggest that, occasionally, the original cause of a disease may be from actions taken by an individual in the past, and that those actions are now affecting the individual's present health situation. For example, Dr. Roger Woolger, a Jungian psychotherapist, has documented several physical issues that have their origin in an earlier experience.[17] Among these was a young woman who had suffered from ulcerative colitis. Through hypnotherapy, she relived the life of an eight-year-old Dutch girl rounded up and shot at a mass grave by Nazi soldiers. The colitis was an expression of the residual terror during the girl's last moments awaiting execution. Another was a man with chronic back pain; he relived an agonizing death pinned under a wagon with a broken back. His pain substantially lessened after the session. And still another example was of a woman whose chronic migraine headaches disappeared after reliving the agony of a young girl of seven, whose father had killed her with a blow to the head with an iron bar.

Holistic Healing of Disease Symptoms

As we become more aware of our own energetic nature and the many potential sources of diseases, it becomes more and more apparent that in order to effect a complete cure from disease, we must not only eliminate the symptoms of that disease (heal the Physical Body), but we must also eliminate the *cause* of the disease, which may lie in the higher energy bodies. Unless the cause of the disease is corrected, the predisposition to that disease is still there, and the disease may return.

Happily, some enlightened surgeons are becoming aware that in order to completely cure the disease (not just cover up or remove its symptoms), additional therapy beyond drugs and surgery may be necessary. Surgery may still be required, however, and can provide the patient with additional time. This time can then be used to investigate other techniques, such as Ro-Hun, which can help to repattern the higher energy bodies to a more healthy state. When the negative thoughts and beliefs one has about one's self are released (Mental Body), and how one reacts to and "feels" about these thoughts are brought into harmony (Emotional Body), these negative patterns no longer adversely affect the Etheric Body, the pattern for the Physical Body. Then and only then has the disease and its cause been completely eliminated.

In order to assist in the healing of a client's disease or symptoms, the healer must also be aware of and sensitive to the client's expectations and needs in a process that is much different from traditional medical treatments. Holistic healing is not just going in for a treatment and taking whatever the therapist or practitioner recommends. Instead, it involves creating a partnership for healing in which both the therapist and the client work jointly toward the goal of perfect health for the client. A strong rapport and sense of trust on the part of both is needed to prepare an effective healing program for the client. This program must address both the current physical symptoms and the cause of the symptoms, and it may extend over several sessions.

But how many times have you gone to a doctor and received a prescription for just one pill? Probably not very often. Similarly, energy-based healing techniques may require several sessions before positive results are seen. The number and length of sessions will be determined by the nature and duration of the illness, the overall state of health of the client, and the willingness of the client to participate actively in his or her own healing process.

Traumatic injuries, such as broken bones, burns, lacerations, etc., usually respond very quickly to energy-based healing techniques, particularly if energy healing can be begun immediately after the injury. Sometimes only a single Reiki or Healing Touch session may be required to sufficiently accelerate the healing process and speed the client back to an early recovery. But, in general, three or more sessions are required to begin the client's healing and recovery process.

Longer-term or chronic illnesses usually require a longer healing program before beneficial results are realized. For example, a client who has suffered with arthritis for many years may have the pattern of swollen and painful joints locked in his or her Etheric Body as well as in the Physical Body, and the person's healing program may need to extend over several months. However, each client is different in not only his or her symptoms, but also the cause of these symptoms and the client's willingness to completely heal his or her illness on all levels.

I have found that the key to establishing an effective healing program for the client is a thorough initial interview that addresses not only the physical problems and symptoms, but also his or her emotional state, thoughts, and beliefs about him- or herself, and his or her spiritual (not religious) well-being. This process of becoming acquainted with the client on all levels involves a degree of compassion, concern, and patience normally not found in a traditional doctor's interview. While the average doctor's interview lasts seven minutes, an hour or more is usually required to obtain a complete personal profile of the client.

The client's expectations of the healer are also of great importance. I have had several clients who said during the initial interview that they had heard that I had healed such-and-such a disease before, and they wanted me to heal them of the same disease. Basically, their attitude was, "I'm sick; heal me!" In these cases, it is most important that they begin learning how disease occurs, and how it is healed. In this process, they begin to understand that they alone are ultimately responsible for healing their disease.

Another key to an effective healing program is access to and knowledge of the energy-based healing techniques that can help the client return to total health. However, in this age of specialization, it is highly unusual to find a single medical doctor who is competent and qualified to repair the Physical Body, conduct hypnotherapy or regression sessions to remove emotional traumas and issues, enable a client to come to grips with his or her thoughts and beliefs, and attend to the spiritual needs of the patient. Not all medical doctors see the need or find the time to really understand all aspects of why the person has come to them. Yet it is just this holistic approach that is necessary to return the patient to total health. This is not entirely the doctor's fault; until recently, our medical schools have traditionally focused almost exclusively on either surgery or drugs to address all illnesses.

Happily, this situation is rapidly changing, and now nearly all of the one hundred twenty-five medical universities in the United States offer elective instruction in, or at least familiarization with, a wide range of Alternative Therapies, including energy-based healing methods, acupuncture, Ayurvedic medicine, herbs and natural curatives, etc. Many hospitals are beginning to incorporate Alternative Therapy techniques such as energy-based healing into their treatment regimens simply because patients get well quicker and have fewer complications.

From the client's perspective, it is preferable that he or she receives all required treatment from the practitioner initially visited, the one with whom they have built a strong sense of trust. However, a complete holistic program for healing the client on all levels may necessarily involve a team effort, wherein the assistance of other holistic practitioners is brought in to address the higher energy bodies.

THE CLIENT INTERVIEW

Before using any healing technique, several important considerations must be addressed. The initial session with the client should include a detailed interview that gives the healer as much information as possible about why the client has come to him or her in order that an individual healing program may be devised for that client. Often, the entire first session may be devoted only to this initial interview. At a minimum, the following areas should be addressed:

Medical History. A review of the client's medical history, diagnoses, and treatments (usually either drugs or surgery) is required for the healer to get to know why the client has come to him or her. The form I use is shown at Appendix A. The client's honesty and willingness to participate in his or her own healing program is essential. In particular, the healer needs to know any medications the client is currently taking, the reason or condition for which they were prescribed, and all disease symptoms the client desires to have addressed. This allows the practitioner to collect the information necessary for tailoring the most effective healing program for the client. It also alerts the practitioner to contraindications for healing sessions at that time.

If there is a history of mental illness or depression severe enough to warrant prescription of drugs or medications, the healer must be aware of this. No client with a current clinically diagnosed mental illness such as schizophrenia, or who is suffering from psychosis or experiencing severe delusions, should be given an energy-based healing session that addresses physical conditions. The reason for this is that energy work activates all energy bodies to some degree through the principle of harmonic resonance. If a disease in the Physical Body is to be addressed through Reiki, for example, energy patterns in the client's Etheric, Emotional, Mental and Spiritual Bodies will also be affected. If mental or emotional traumas are surfaced in a mentally unstable client and he or she is unable to deal with these traumatic energies, serious mental damage to the client may result. Only after such conditions have been successfully treated should the healer consider accepting the person as a client. At a minimum, the energy healer should require a statement by the attending psychiatrist or clinical psychologist that the mental condition for which treatment was sought has been satisfactorily resolved.

Some forms of physical diseases such as diabetes require the client to take specific doses of a prescribed drug. Due to the effectiveness of energy-based healing processes, the physician who prescribed the drug should be made aware of the fact that alternative, energy-based healing techniques will be used to address the client's condition as well. Such notification to the physician should be made and acknowledgement received before beginning any energy-based healing sessions. It does not matter if the physician believes in the efficacy of energy-based healing or not. However, this notification does take the first step in integrating traditional allopathic and complementary techniques for the client's overall best interests. The form letter I use for this notification is shown in Appendix B. As the client's healing process continues, it is incumbent upon the client to report all physical changes noticed to the attending physician, and for the physician to determine if any changes to the prescribed medications are warranted.

Healing or Comfort?   Does the client want comfort from the pain and other symptoms of his or her disease, or does the client want the disease eliminated from his or her entire energetic system? Does the client understand the difference between treatment of disease symptoms and holistic healing on all levels? Is this client prepared and willing to participate in a holistic healing program that may affect his or her entire lifestyle? If comfort from pain and symptoms is all that is ready to be accepted at that point, Reiki or Healing Touch (see chapter 2) may be considered and discussed with the client. These are both very effective in repatterning the Etheric and Physical Bodies, but sometimes do not address the cause of the disease and its symptoms. Nevertheless, they can always safely be used to control pain and accelerate self-healing.

Why Alternative Healing?   Discuss and explore the reasons why the client has come to an energy healer as opposed to the standard approach of seeking out a medical doctor. What have his or her experiences been with traditional medical doctors? Has the client had energy-based healing sessions before? If so, what techniques were used and what was the result? What was the client's reaction? Would the client consider an integrated approach, using alternative and traditional medical techniques? Why or why not?

Client's Lifestyle.   Review the client's lifestyle in detail. How a person feels about his or her relationships, home, children, job, childhood, hobbies, and likes and dislikes can significantly affect his or her overall health and outlook on life. What does the client have or not have, do or not do, that he or she would be willing to change for a healthier life? What would the client not be willing to change?

Why Do You Have This Disease?   Initiate a discussion on the specific disease condition for which the client has come for healing, including his or her thoughts as to why he or she has the condition. What does this individual believe to be the factors or reasons for disease in general, and for his or her own specific disease? Is the client open to uncovering reasons for disease beyond those generally recognized by traditional medical specialists?

Why Do You Want to Get Well?   This may seem obvious at first—we all want to enjoy good health. But good health should not be the client's only goal. If he or she got well, what would he or she do that cannot be done now? What specific interests or activities could be pursued that cannot be enjoyed now? How will the client enjoy his or her health? What lifestyle changes must be made if the client gets well? This area is also very good for recognizing the hypochondriac who wants personalized healing attention but who still needs to keep the real or imagined symptoms for his or her own identity.

Is Healing Probable? Is the client familiar with energy-based healing to the extent that he or she believes or knows he or she can be helped? The client may have only heard of a friend who received therapeutic relief and help at the hands of a certain practitioner; in this case, this person may only believe in the possibility that he or she can be helped as well. Or, the individual may have had a favorable previous experience with a healer; in this case, he or she might know that help is not only possible, but that it is probable. It is the responsibility of the healer to gain the confidence and trust of the client, and to provide an environment wherein positive healing results can be expected. The experienced energy practitioner who has successfully helped others with the client's condition can create a strong expectation for healing.

It is also important to note that even if healing does not occur, the client may be helped in other subtle but very important ways. For example, if a cancer patient has waited too long before coming to an energy practitioner and there is no possibility remaining for the physical system to heal, most forms of energy healing can still provide relief from pain, ease of mind, and a caring, comforting environment. These are significant factors in determining the quality of life one enjoys, especially if someone is approaching transition in a hospice setting.

Constructing a Holistic Healing Program

In addition to medical treatment, if required, a comprehensive healing program may include both energy-based healing techniques as well as wellness/prevention practices such as dietary changes, natural remedies, and exercise and relaxation techniques. Such a program could be constructed by discussing with the client what his or her personal health goals are and how much willingness is shown to integrate alternative health practices along with traditional medical treatments. Healing programs cannot be dictated by the healer, but must be examined, discussed, and accepted by the client with the guidance and knowledge of the healer and other holistic practitioners as required. Very rarely will one person be sufficiently versed in all alternative medical therapies that he or she can provide complete guidance for the client.

However, the healer should be knowledgeable in a variety of energy-based healing techniques to formulate an appropriate healing program based on the physical, emotional, mental, and spiritual needs of the client. If the client wants only comfort from pain, a series of Reiki and/or Healing Touch sessions may be warranted. If a truly holistic healing program is desired, and the client is mentally and emotionally ready for it, Reiki or Healing Touch may be indicated initially to alleviate the immediate symptoms of pain. This could then be followed by a series of, for example, Spiritual Surgery sessions to ensure that the energetic pattern of the diseased organ or tissue is replaced with that of a healthy organ. This new, healthy energy pattern will soon be reflected from the Etheric Body into the Physical Body for a temporary "cure."

For the greatest assurance that the disease or symptoms will not recur, a series of Ro-Hun sessions may additionally be required to remove the cause of the disease in the Emotional/Mental Bodies (see chapter 3). Finally, and only if the client is sufficiently prepared, the Spiritual Body may be awakened so that the client begins to remember who he or she really is, why he or she is here experiencing these situations, and what the true purpose of the situations are.

The true purpose of all energy-based healing is spiritual awakening. Many clients will not be ready for such a comprehensive and life-changing program, and will elect to address only those parts of it that they are comfortable with incorporating into their daily life at that time. Nevertheless, the seeds will have been planted in the client's awareness, and they will flourish and bloom in their own time. The truly holistic energy healer must be prepared to either offer techniques that address each of the five energy layers of the Human Energy Field (Physical, Etheric, Emotional, Mental and Spiritual) or must know other healers who can participate in the client's overall program.

To form a complete holistic energy-based healing program, the therapist and client need to agree on what needs to be done and what the client is willing to do. Depending on the disease, the program may, for example, start with a series of three Spiritual Surgery sessions on Monday, Wednesday, and Friday to repattern the Etheric template, and be immediately followed by a Reiki session to accelerate healing and stimulate the auto-immune system. Additional Healing Touch sessions may be scheduled until positive physical changes are seen. With satisfactory healing of the Physical and Etheric Energy Bodies, attention can then be turned to the Emotional and Mental Energy Bodies to discover and eliminate the cause of the disease. A Ro-Hun Cleanse Purification series may be agreed upon to begin this process, with additional Ro-Hun sessions as desired. If the client desires and is properly prepared, the energy-healing program may conclude with one or more Spiritual Regression sessions. Additional lifestyle changes such as meditation, diet, and exercise may also be warranted. Depending on the client's desires and prior experiences, naturopathic or homeopathic therapies may also be appropriate.

Obviously, the above sample healing program may need modification, depending on the client's needs. However, it illustrates that all energy bodies of the Human Energy Field must be addressed to ensure that both the disease symptoms and the cause of the disease have been eliminated forever. In addition to this energy-based healing approach, the client may also be referred to the proper specialists for follow-up lifestyle improvements (e.g., diet, exercise, meditation, yoga, etc.) that the client desires. It is unlikely that any single alternative healer will be able to provide all the services required in a thorough and comprehensive healing program. Therefore, each holistic healer should maintain a network of contacts to which the client may be referred for those modalities not practiced by him- or herself. Once the client is returned to a state of health on all energy levels, the new healing program and lifestyle changes will allow the client to live in a disease-prevention consciousness, rather than in a disease-correction mode.

HEALING PREPARATIONS

As one continues to experience the healing energies transferred during a session, the healer cannot help but become very aware that there is a great amount of unseen help and assistance available to call upon. The initial hope and faith that this spiritual assistance might be there is soon replaced with a firm belief that the healer is not working alone. And then at some point, the healer may actually feel or see his or her spirit doctors or angels. It is at that point that the practitioner's beliefs turn into a knowing, a personal experience that cannot be ignored or denied, that help is always available from another unseen dimension. When this knowing comes into your consciousness, there will be an automatic change in your attitudes and respect for this sacred activity of bringing healing energy to another person. You will quite naturally begin to take steps to ensure the sacredness of your healing sessions. You will also want to ensure that the healing area has been properly prepared, that you (the healer) are properly prepared, and that you have set a clear intent for what you want to happen during the healing session.

Preparing the Area. In keeping with the spirit of healing, the healing area should be quiet, except perhaps for some pleasant music playing softly in the background. The area should be dimly lit, but not so dark that the client feels uncomfortable. Fluorescent lights should not be used in the healing area; the electric discharge within them produces a disruptive electric field that is not conducive to healing. The floor should be comfortably carpeted since the healer will probably remove his or her shoes during healing, and healer comfort is quite important. A massage table is ideal as a healing table for the client to lie on; alternatively, a comfortable, straight-backed chair with no arms should also be available if the healing modality does not require a table or one is not available.

When the healing area is prepared physically, it should then be prepared energetically. This is a matter left to the preferences of each healer. But some prayer or invocation may be offered to ensure that the healing space remains sacred and that only those spirit healers who have the highest and best interests of the client at heart may enter the healing space to work with and through you. Each healer will develop his or her own prayer of purification which conforms to his or her own beliefs and practices. A typical invocation I use is: "Father/Mother/Creator, I ask that you bless this healing area as a place of holy and sacred connection between us. I ask that you surround this healing area with your white light protection so that only those who are in Service to the Light and are from the Throne of Grace may approach this healing table. So be it! Amen."

Preparing the Healer. The healer should approach the healing table and the client only after thoroughly centering and preparing him- or herself energetically for the healing session. This preparation often includes a meditation to bring up and align the healing energies within the healer's own energy system. There are many excellent meditations or guided visualizations to do this. One of my favorites is the Hara Meditation, which is described by Barbara Brennan in her second book, *Light Emerging*.[18] This particular meditation connects your internal energy centers with the energies of Mother Earth below and the Universal Heavens above. When the energies from above and below are allowed to come into your body, blend in your heart, and flow down into your arms and hands, you become a channel through which these energies can freely flow into the client to stimulate and accelerate the healing process.

Setting Your Intent.   After the area has been energetically prepared and the healer has been centered, only then should the client be approached and the healing session begun. The healer should begin the healing session by consciously stating (preferably out loud) his or her intent for the session. It is very important that both the healer and the client understand and agree that the healer's intent should not be to heal the client, and the client's intent should not be that the healer heal him or her (see "Taking Responsibility for Healing" below). The healer's intent should always be the same for each healing session: to be a clear and open channel for the healing energies, so they may be given for the client's highest and best good at that time. The client's intent should be to graciously accept the gift of these healing energies, and to use them for his or her own highest and best good at that time.

An opening prayer stating the healer's intent is always a good way to begin a healing session if the client does not object. One I use regularly is: "Mother/Father/Creator, I ask to be used as a channel of love, light, and healing for (client's name) as we begin a (Healing Touch, Reiki, Ro-Hun, etc.) session. Father, use me, use me, use me. I call on my own spirit doctors, guides, and angels, and (client's) spirit doctors, guides, and angels to be present and assist in this healing. I call now on all healing energies that may be of benefit to (client's name) and ask that they be provided to him/her for his/her highest and best good at this time. So be it!"

HEALER–CLIENT RELATIONSHIP

Developing Trust.   The relationship between the healer and the client must be based on mutual respect and trust. It must become a partnership for the purpose of healing. If clients are not convinced that the healer has only their best interests at heart, they will put up energetic blocks and resistance to the healing energies. The old adage "You can lead a horse to water, but you cannot make him drink" is still true. The healer can go through all sorts of ritual preparations and invocations, but if the client is not comfortable with the healer, the healing session probably will not be as effective as it could otherwise be.

For this reason, it is very important that when the client meets the healer for the first time, the healer should take whatever time is required to answer any questions the client may have. This includes questions about what healing techniques are available for the client's symptoms, about why one technique is recommended over the others, and what that technique entails. When the client feels confident that the healer knows what he or she is talking about, a strong basis for trust in the healer can be developed on the part of the client.

The client must also trust in the healing process itself. If the healer can provide clear information regarding the use of the recommended technique in prior similar cases, strong confidence in that healing technique can also be developed. However, if the client does not believe the healing session will be effective, it probably will not be. This negative belief or block on the part of the client may prevent the offered healing energies from being accepted by the client. The subconscious mind of the client must believe the energies will help the client's overall condition before it will agree to accept them into the client's energy system.

The client's subconscious mind is always in charge of accepting or rejecting healing energies based on its perceived answer to the question: "Are these energies in my overall best interests at this time?" One who believes in the effectiveness of the healing process, whatever it is (energy work, pills, physical therapy, etc.), and who wants to release the disease or its symptoms, may readily accept the healing energies offered by the practitioner. However, hypochondriacs whose identities require a certain set of symptoms will nearly always reject the healing energies. To accept them and lose the symptoms may cause them to lose their identities, and this would not be "allowed" by their subconscious minds.

Taking Responsibility for Healing.   The person who says "I'm a healer; I can heal you" is only fooling him- or herself and is trying to fool you as well. One of the more difficult concepts for some to accept is that each person is ultimately responsible for healing him- or herself. Occasionally, I will get a client who says, "You're a healer—heal me of my disease!" The first thing that has to happen in a case like this is a little reeducation on the part of the client. Because the client's Higher Self is always in charge of accepting or rejecting healing energies, the client is always ultimately responsible for his or her own healing. The healer can make the healing energy available, but it is the client who accepts or rejects it, and makes use of this energy to heal a disease or alleviate symptoms within his or her own body.

Similarly, medical doctors do not heal patients when they prescribe a certain drug; the drug can only create more favorable conditions in the patients so they can heal themselves. Nor do surgeons heal patients when they remove diseased organs. But by the surgery, the patients may be able to self-heal more quickly than with diseased organs. If healing energy is accepted consciously by the client (I want to be healed) and subconsciously (Healing is in my best interests at this time), it will always be directed through his or her internal energy distribution system, the meridians, to where it is most needed. This healing energy can significantly accelerate the client's own healing process, whether or not surgery or drugs were involved.

So who is the real "healer"? Our language has taught us to expect that a "healer" is a person who heals someone else. But the true healer is the one who does the healing—the client on the healing table, who accepts the healing energies from the practitioner for his or her own self-healing processes. With this in mind, I will continue to refer to "healer" as the one who transfers the healing energies required to the client—i.e., the practitioner who is trained in the techniques of delivering energy for the client's use.

Because it is the client who is responsible for his or her own healing, the energy practitioner should never have any preconceived expectations or anticipated outcomes for the healing session. In the great majority of cases wherein the client consciously wants to accept the healing energies and the practioner is properly prepared, an effective healing session will be held. However, there may be cases when a physical healing is not in the highest and best interests of the client at that time. The client's subconscious mind may have agreed to experience a certain disease in order to learn a lesson. If that lesson has not yet been learned, the disease and its symptoms are still required until the client "gets it" on a conscious level. The high-powered Type-A executive who lives in a mental pressure cooker may develop ulcers unless he or she learns to balance his or her time, activities, and emotions.

As energy therapists and practitioners become more intuitive, they begin to ask, "Why does the client have this disease? What is the underlying cause of these symptoms?" And as we begin to examine more and more cases using hypnotherapy, regression therapy, or Ro-Hun, we begin to uncover a recurring pattern. The client's soul may have agreed to experience a certain disease or set of symptoms because in the past, the client's soul was responsible for causing the same or a similar set of symptoms in someone else. The client must always follow the Universal Law of Cause and Effect.

Protecting Your Own Energy Field.   The energy coming from a healer's hands originates in one of two places: the healer's own Human Energy Field (HEF) or the Universal Energy Field (UEF). The ideal situation is to be an open channel for energy from the UEF, so your own HEF is not drawn upon or depleted. This is why it is important for the healer to properly prepare and open him- or herself as a channel for that energy. The healer may also be energetically opened as a channel of universal energy through an initiation process into the energy of certain symbols (see "Reiki" in chapter 2).

However, if the healer is not so opened and is not properly centered and prepared, his or her own HEF will be used as the source of healing energy. This is acceptable as long as the healer's HEF is constantly replenished so it does not become depleted. The easiest way to maintain an energetically full HEF is simply to breathe deeply.[19] The breath and our chakra system are our normal ways of taking in energy from the UEF. As we breathe more deeply, we take in more energy and our own HEF becomes stronger, as shown in the exercise above for breathing deeply while doing the Hand Bounce exercise to develop sensitivity to energy fields.

If the healer relies on his or her own HEF for healing energy and does not breathe deeply while transferring energy to a client, the healer's own HEF will become depleted after awhile. This will make the healer more tired physically, less alert mentally, and more reactive emotionally. In this situation, it is also entirely possible for the healer to begin feeling some of the client's symptoms, aches, and pains! And exactly this situation has been the source of much concern and discussion, particularly by many nurses, in several Healing Touch workshops I have attended.

To understand clearly what's going on in this situation, consider the energy fields of a healer and a client when the healer has not yet moved into the client's energy field (is still several feet away). Referring to Figure 3A, the glasses on the left and right represent the energy systems of the client and healer, respectively. The healer's energy level is very high, and is represented by the high level of clear water in the glass on the right. However, the client's energy level is lower and is cloudy, due to the effects of the disease and symptoms experienced. Now in Figure 3B, when the healer intentionally enters the field of the client, healing energy can flow from his or her high-level energy system to the low-energy system of the client. If the client accepts the healing energy, physical healing can occur.

But what happens if the healer is having a bad day or if the healer is a nurse who is physically exhausted at the end of a twelve-hour shift? As shown in Figure 3C, the healer's energy level may be lower than that of the client, and energy will flow, just like water, to its own level, from a point of higher energy (the client) to a point of lower energy (the healer). The pain felt by sick or injured patients has often been transferred to attending nurses in this situation, and this pain is often reflected into the same area of the nurse's body. For instance, a patient recovering from hip replacement surgery may inadvertently transfer his or her trauma and pain into the same hip area of the attending nurse. If the nurse is not aware of the energetic balancing act in this situation, he or she may be very surprised or shocked, and wonder, "What is going on here? Why does *my* hip hurt?" But if he or she understands what is causing these sensations, the nurse can quickly and easily replenish his or her own energy field with some deep yogic breathing.

Client's and Healer's Energy Fields Are Separate.

Figure 3a:
Separate Energy Fields

Healer Enters Client's Energy Field.

Figure 3b:
Healer (right) Moves into
Client's Energy Field

Client's Negative Energy Enters Exhausted Healer's Energy Field.

Figure 3c:
Exhausted Healer (right)

Chapter Two

Healing the Physical and Etheric Energy Bodies

Treatment is directed at the reduction and elimination of symptoms, and infrequently at actual cure; healing is directed at mobilizing the mind and body to enhance the natural defenses, accelerate recovery from illness, and promote full health.

— Elliott S. Dacher, M.D.
Psychoneuroimmunology:
The New Mind/Body Healing Program

The potential for a truly preventive medicine lies within a scanner that could detect illness at the etheric level prior to it becoming manifest in the physical body. By studying the etheric images representing pre-illness stages, it might be possible to utilize various types of subtle energetic therapies to correct the tendencies toward dysfunction in the system.

— Richard Gerber, M.D.
Vibrational Medicine

THERE ARE MANY TECHNIQUES THAT fall under the umbrella of energy-based healing and that have physical healing as one of their primary goals. We cannot look at all of them in depth in one chapter, but I have selected five for a closer look. The first, Reiki, uses physical touch similar to laying-on of hands to transfer healing energy through the healer directly to the client's physical body. The second, Healing Touch, uses a combination of procedures that involve physical touch or manipulation of the subtle energy bodies surrounding the physical body. Both Reiki and Healing Touch provide very impressive physical healings. The third, Color and Sound Therapy, or Healing with Color and Sound, is a very effective technique for opening and balancing the major chakras, thereby allowing all major organs to receive the proper amount of life-giving energy they need to maintain healthy functioning of the physical body. This chapter also discusses two energy healing techniques (Spiritual Surgery and Reflective Healing) that specifically address the energetic template for the physical body: the etheric energy body. Recall that the etheric energy body is the blueprint for what happens in the physical energy body, and that changes in the etheric body are soon manifested in the physical body. Therefore, it is reasonable to discuss these two energy bodies together.

Reiki

OVERVIEW

Reiki is a Japanese word that means "Divine Light" (*rei*) and "Universal Life Force Energy" (*ki*). In other cultures this life force energy is called *chi* (China), *mana* (Hawaii), or *prana* (India). The Reiki healing energy is transferred to the client through the healer's hands, which are usually placed directly on the body or clothing of the client. A typical Reiki healing session is normally conducted with the client lying down on a healing table; however, Reiki can also be administered with the client sitting in a chair. The healer's hands are placed in a series of static positions on the client's body. The healer keeps them there motionless for a few minutes, and then moves to another position on the client's body. A full Reiki healing session usually lasts between forty-five minutes and one hour.

Reiki energy is always safe for the client, and will only accelerate the return of damaged cells or weakened systems to a state of natural health. Furthermore, this energy cannot be "overdosed." If a healer continues to make Reiki energy available after the body no longer needs it, the client's Higher Self will automatically stop accepting the energy. The healing energy also flows easily through blankets, clothing, and even casts.

Reiki is an excellent healing technique to use in the case of traumatic injuries such as lacerations, bruises, broken bones, healing of operative incisions, etc. Reiki energy can significantly accelerate the body's own healing processes and strengthen the immune system to further protect against secondary infection and disease. Broken bones heal significantly faster when Reiki is applied. However, be sure that the broken bone is correctly set and immobilized before applying Reiki; otherwise, the bone cells will quickly begin to regenerate in the wrong position.

The number of Reiki sessions that would be required would depend on the nature of the client's symptoms and how long they have persisted. Traumatic injuries respond quite effectively with just one session, or one session on each of two successive days. However, chronic conditions or symptoms may require many sessions over an extended period. In this case, a good rule of thumb is to provide a Reiki session every two to three days for four or five sessions, and then once a week until the symptoms abate.

Long-term use of Reiki for a specific individual should be considered as complementary to care and treatment provided by medical doctors. The doctor should be made aware that Reiki sessions are being provided, even if he or she does not believe in their effectiveness. As mentioned earlier, this is particularly true where the client's symptoms include hormonal or chemical imbalances in the body (e.g., diabetes, anemia, etc.) for which they are currently taking prescribed medications. The licensed physician should closely monitor the patient's condition while Reiki sessions are being provided so that any required changes to prescribed medications can be made by the doctor.

16

Reiki energy can also be effectively used to aid in the release of harmful toxins within the physical body. A Reiki session on each of four successive days will move the energies within the physical body to release many built-up toxins. These toxins may be caused by allergies, environmental pollutants, smoking, drugs (either prescription or recreational), postoperative anesthesia, etc. It is essential that plenty of water be drunk during this detoxification process to eliminate the toxins from the body, preferably spring water with natural minerals. Tap water and distilled water should be avoided. It is also possible that minor temporary side effects (e.g., headache, nausea, perspiring, etc.) may be experienced during this intensive Reiki detoxification regimen.

Reiki is a universal energy that promotes only healthy growth, and this energy can be transferred to and used by all living things—people, animals, plants and trees. Veterinarians are beginning to recognize that Reiki energy significantly accelerates the healing processes in both large and small animals. Horticulturists and gardeners are able to raise larger, healthier flowers, vegetables, and fruits through the use of Reiki on their plants and trees. This is clear testimony that Reiki is a very powerful universal life force energy.

Reiki is a healing energy that comes from the Source of Life itself. Since Reiki is also multidimensional in nature and operates beyond the limitations of our physical reality, it can be a catalytic factor in one's personal evolution no matter what beliefs are held. The experience of Reiki is a vehicle to becoming fully conscious and aware of your own spiritual nature regardless of faith or religious concepts. Reiki is not a system of religious beliefs—the world does not need another.

Anyone can become an effective Reiki practitioner—it's very simple, and the only thing you need is the desire to do so. Reiki is also very simple to use, and is beneficial for all, including the Reiki practitioner. Remember, while you are channeling the Reiki energy through your own Human Energy Field down your arms and hands and into your client, you are also receiving the benefits of its healing properties!

HISTORY OF REIKI

There are different histories of Reiki, depending on who is telling it at the time. The two most significant histories are what I call Western Reiki and Japanese Reiki.

Western Reiki.   Most of what we know about Reiki as it is usually practiced in the Western world has been handed down verbally from teacher to student, beginning with Mrs. Hawayo Takata (more about her later) in the late 1940s. More recently, several books have appeared that provide a written account of this history of Reiki. Although most of these books agree fairly closely on Reiki's major historical points, there are many differences in the details, as would be expected from any history that had been handed down orally several times.

When I received the history of Reiki during my Usui Reiki Level I training, I received it orally from a lady in Virginia Beach, Virginia, who had been a personal student of Mrs. Takata through the first two Reiki levels, and she later had taken her Reiki mastership from one of Mrs. Takata's original twenty-two Reiki Masters. Therefore, I am quite certain that the following history is a condensed version of what Mrs. Takata actually taught to her students.

In the late nineteenth century, a Japanese gentleman by the name of Mikao Usui was a teacher in a Christian boys' school in or near Kyoto, Japan. As they were studying the Bible one day, a young boy asked Dr. Usui ("Dr." was an honorary title not associated with any medical practice) if he believed that Jesus could heal just by using his hands. When Dr. Usui replied, "Yes, I believe that," the young boy asked him how Jesus had healed, and Dr. Usui could not answer his student. In Japan at the time, it was considered very embarrassing for the teacher not to know the answer to any question a student might ask, so he left his profession as a teacher and began researching all the Christian references he could find. He spent many months looking through several Christian archives and libraries, but he could not find any mention of how Jesus had healed. One day, a friend suggested that he also research the ancient Buddhist archives since it was believed that Buddha had also been able to heal the sick in a manner similar to what Jesus had used.

Dr. Usui contacted a friend of his who was head of a nearby Buddhist monastery, and was given permission to search the records there, but he found nothing. He then decided to visit America since at that time, it was accepted by many Japanese people that America had more world knowledge than any other country. He spent seven years researching the extensive library at a university in Chicago, but again to no avail.

When he returned to Kyoto, his Buddhist friend remembered that in his library, there were a few old Chinese manuscripts that had not been opened for centuries because no one there could read Chinese. Dr. Usui spent several years learning to read Chinese, but the old texts yielded no information about healing. The last book in the library, however, was not written in Chinese, but in Sanskrit, and looked to be much older than the rest. Again, Dr. Usui spent several years learning to read Sanskrit, and in this ancient text or *sutra,* he found some information on a method of healing that has been passed down from the time of Buddha. This healing method used laying on of hands and certain sacred symbols, but although several symbols were included in the ancient text, the method of how they were to be used was not written, and it was assumed that this information was considered too sacred to be included in the manuscript.

Ultimately, Dr. Usui came to realize that the only way he was going to be able to understand and use this method of healing was to obtain through meditation the information that was missing from the text. He informed his wife that he intended to go up to a favorite meditation place on nearby Mt. Kurama and fast and meditate for twenty-one days in order to get the answers he sought, and if he had not returned after twenty-one days she should come and retrieve his body. Near his favorite waterfall on the mountainside there was a small cave that he used for shelter. He spread his blanket on the ground and prepared a row of twenty-one rocks in front of him, and each nightfall he would roll one rock down the hill to mark the passage of the days.

After he had fasted and meditated for twenty-one days and all the rocks had been rolled down the hill, he felt that this would be his last night alive, and that his wife would soon come to claim his body. Then just as the stars were beginning to come out, he saw a particularly bright light near the horizon that he had not noticed before. It began to get larger and larger as this point of light moved very fast toward him. He nearly ducked to avoid the onrushing light, but at the last instant before it would collide with him, he thought, "No, perhaps this is the light I have been waiting for," and he let the quickly approaching light hit him full in the forehead.

As soon as the light connected with him, he was pushed backward to the ground, and remained there unconscious for a long time. During this time, he had a dream or a vision of hundreds of bubbles rising up from the earth and going toward the heavens, and inside each bubble was a sacred sign or symbol that he had read in the ancient manuscript. At the same time he saw each symbol, he received a complete understanding of its purpose and how it was to be used to bring about healing through the use of his hands.

When Dr. Usui awoke the next morning, he was very excited about his newly found knowledge, and he quickly gathered up his blanket, put on his sandals, and excitedly began to run down the hill so he could tell his friend in the Buddhist monastery about his new information. His friend was quite willing to let Dr. Usui practice his new abilities in one of the rooms in his monastery, and soon people from all over the countryside were coming to see the miracle man and receive healing, no matter what their symptoms or disease.

Eventually, the number of people coming to him for healing was so overwhelming that Dr. Usui began training others to help him perform the healings. He developed a system of training that included three different levels of healing abilities, and many hundreds became Level I Reiki healers. Of these, dozens went on to become Level II healers, and eventually Dr. Usui trained just over a dozen Level III healers, or Reiki Masters. The Level I and II healers could perform miraculous healings on people, but only the Reiki Masters could initiate others to become healers. One of the Reiki Masters initiated by Dr. Usui was a medical doctor, and a reserve officer in the Japanese Navy, by the name of Chujiro Hayashi. After the death of Dr. Usui, Dr. Hayashi became the designated leader or head of the Reiki movement in Japan.

Dr. Hayashi established a very flourishing healing center near his home in Tokyo, and his fame continued to spread as his healing abilities were recognized throughout Japan. Dr. Hayashi also had many students, including the Reiki Masters whom he had initiated into Reiki's highest level. In addition, he was very clairvoyant, and in the mid 1930s he foresaw the impending conflict between Japan and the United States, as well as its outcome. He was convinced that Japan would be utterly destroyed in the war, and that the secrets of Reiki would be lost forever. Therefore, he secretly decided to select one person from the United States and entrust the secrets of Reiki to them so that the world would not lose Reiki.

Meanwhile, on Christmas eve in 1900, a baby girl was born to Mr. and Mrs. Takata in Hawaii, where Mr. Takata was a poor worker in the pineapple fields there. The baby was given the name "Hawayo" to remind her parents of the beauty of Hawaii. Hawayo eventually grew up, married, and had a family of her own, and they all continued to work in the pineapple fields. One day, Hawayo's older sister died and it fell to Hawayo to return her sister's body to Japan for burial.

While there, Hawayo developed a very serious disease and was told that she required an operation. As she was being prepared for surgery, she heard a voice in her head say "You don't have to do this. There is another way." She shot up on the operating table and asked the surgeon if this operation was absolutely necessary, or if there was another way she could be healed. The surgeon replied that his cousin had had a similar disease, had gone to Dr. Hayashi's Reiki clinic, and had been healed completely. Hawayo immediately got off the table, got dressed, and went to find Dr. Hayashi's clinic. After several months of receiving Reiki treatments, she was completely cured, and she insisted that she be taught how to heal using Reiki.

Dr. Hayashi initially declined, but owing to the dogged insistence of this diminutive woman, he eventually initiated her into Reiki Levels I and II before she returned to Hawaii. Very soon after this, he clairvoyantly became aware that he would soon be recalled to active duty to fight for the emperor and be responsible for the deaths of many people. This put him into a moral quandary upon which he meditated for many days. Since he had dedicated his entire life to healing, he could not morally return to active duty. But if he did not go to war, he would be executed as a traitor, his entire family would be put out penniless on the streets to beg for their living, and all his estate's wealth would be confiscated by the government.

Eventually, he decided to visit Mrs. Takata and entrust the secrets of Reiki to her. During a visit to Hawaii, he visited Mrs. Takata's healing center and, initiating her as a Reiki Master, passed on the information required to "attune" or initiate others into all levels of Reiki. However, he made her promise not to initiate other Reiki Masters for several years, and she agreed. After he returned to Japan, Dr. Hayashi publicly committed hara-kiri, which was an honorable death at the time. Therefore, he had favorably solved his dilemma, and his family was spared the indignities of poverty.

During and after the Second World War, Mrs. Takata initiated several Level I and II Reiki students, but she did not initiate any Reiki Masters until 1970. Between 1970 and her death in 1980, she had initiated a total of twenty-two Reiki Masters. The history of Reiki that we know of in the West was passed on orally from her to each of her Level I students, and included statements to the effect that all Reiki practitioners and Reiki knowledge in Japan had been destroyed during the war, and that the oral history received by each of her own students should be passed on without any changes by them if they eventually became Reiki Masters. However, as we all know, the more times a single story is told, the more chances there are for minor "details" and other discrepancies to creep in, and this certainly was the case during subsequent Reiki Level I initiations. However, notwithstanding a few well-intentioned embellishments here and there, Reiki quickly spread far and wide around the world because it was easy to learn, easy to use, and remarkable in its effectiveness.

All forms of Western Reiki, however, did have one thing in common: Reiki practitioners were taught in their Level I training that the healing Reiki energy was transferred through the hands of the practitioner, which were placed gently on the physical body over specific organs such as the liver, the spleen, the intestines, and so on. Mrs. Takata called the set of hand positions that covered the head, front torso and back torso the "Foundation Series," and this set of hand positions was always to be performed in exactly the same manner for each client, no matter what symptoms or disease they came with. More recently, different forms of Reiki may have included additional or different hand positions as well, but the hand position sequence discussed below is the one I was taught by my initial Reiki Master who was trained personally by Mrs. Takata. So, again, I am quite certain that it reflects what Mrs. Takata taught her students.

Japanese Reiki. Around 1990, two German Reiki Masters, Frank Petter and Chetna Kobayashi, moved to Japan and began an intensive investigation into the historical roots of Reiki in Japan. As researched by these two Reiki Masters, the public records of Reiki available in Japan show that Mikao Usui (or "Dr. Usui" as he later became known) was born on August 15, 1865, in the village of Yago, in the Yamgata district of the Prefecture of Gifu. He grew up as a Buddhist, not a Christian, and he married Sadako Suzuki, by whom they had two children, a boy and a girl. He was never a teacher in a Christian boy's school, but at one time, he was a private secretary to the politician Shimpei Goto, who was the Secretary of the Railroad, the Postmaster General, and the Secretary of the Interior and State. In addition, it has never been verified that he attended any university in America, despite much research by others. Dr. Usui died from a stroke in Fukuyama, Japan on March 9, 1926, and is buried in the Buddhist Saihoji Cemetery in Tokyo where a large monument has been erected next to his gravestone. This monument tells of Dr. Usui's meditation experience on Mt. Kurama, and of the gifts of healing he received there.[1]

In 1920 or 1921, Dr. Usui, as he had frequently done before, went to a peaceful Buddhist monastery near a waterfall on nearby Mt. Kurama to meditate. But this time, instead of seeking financial success and security, he took with him a strong desire to put aside his need for personal wealth, and replace the quest for money with a search for wisdom and his own spiritual growth. Under the guidance of the Buddhist monks in the monastery, he decided to meditate and fast for twenty-one days to understand the meaning of his life and to grow spiritually from the experience.

On the twenty-first day, while deep in meditation, he had a *satori,* a transcendental vision that showed him the path he could take toward this greater enlightenment—the path of enlightening himself and those around him by healing their physical, emotional, mental and spiritual wounds. Indeed, Dr. Usui considered this form of healing as having the potential for bringing spiritual enlightenment for not only those to whom he administered, but for the entire planet.

Following his vision and transcendental meditation on Mt. Kurama, Dr. Usui began to use his new healing abilities on himself and on his family. Since it worked so well, he decided to share his knowledge with the public at large. In 1921, he founded the Usui Reiki Ryoho Gakkai (Usui Reiki Healing Method Society) in Tokyo, and acted as its first president or spiritual leader of Reiki. Weekly Reiki sharing sessions were held between him and his students, and the meetings also served as a discussion forum for any topic related to Reiki.

It is also recorded that immediately after the devastating Kanto earthquake that shook Tokyo in September 1923, Dr. Usui went to the area of devastation; there he treated and healed many of the survivors. At his healing clinic in Tokyo, he held healing demonstrations and brought healing to many people during the remainder of his lifetime. His Tokyo clinic soon became too small to handle the many clients who came to him after they heard of his remarkable healing abilities. So on February 14, 1925, Dr. Usui established a larger clinic near Tokyo in Nakano, and his fame soon spread to nearly every part of Japan.

In addition to healing those who came to him, he held Reiki instruction workshops as well, and ultimately initiated about 2,000 Reiki Level I practitioners. But of these, he accepted and initiated only sixteen to the level of Reiki Master. One of these sixteen was Dr. Chujiro Hayashi; however, there is no record that Dr. Hayashi was ever a member of the Usui Reiki Ryoho Gakkai, and he certainly was not the designated successor for the Reiki movement after Dr. Usui's death.

Before he died, Dr. Usui nominated as his successor a Mr. Ushida, who became the next president of the Usui Reiki Ryoho Gakkai and the spiritual leader of Reiki. In addition to Mr. Ushida, there has been an unbroken line of successors as president of the Usui Reiki Ryoho Gakkai down to the present time. The complete line is given as: Dr. Usui, Mr. Ushida,

Mr. Taketomi, Mr. Watanabe, Mr. Wanami, Ms. Kojama, and "The seventh president, who is therefore the rightful successor of Mikao Usui, Mr. Kondo, had been in office since the beginning of 1998."[2]

During the research into the Japanese roots of Reiki, an original copy of the handbook that Dr. Usui provided to each of his students was uncovered. When it had been translated into English by Chetnya Kobayashi, it was evident that the Reiki practiced by Dr. Usui was quite different than the Reiki that was taught by Mrs. Takata to her students. As practiced by Dr. Usui and his successors in Japan, Reiki was a system to bring spiritual enlightenment to the practitioner, and to the world by bringing physical, mental, emotional, and spiritual healing to one individual at a time. Further, the initial practice of Reiki involved developing a keen sense of energy awareness on the part of the practitioner so that he/she could physically sense elements of the Human Energy Field and consciously direct the healing energies to where they were most needed. Dr. Usui taught his students to use their hands and fingers to "scan" the client's chakras and energy levels above the physical body to locate areas of energetic imbalances or blockages, and to use their hands, fingers, eyes, and breath to direct healing Reiki energies to wherever they were needed.

In addition to the regular use of energetic hand scanning and awareness of the chakras and energy bodies of the Human Energy Field, Dr. Usui taught his students specific meditation techniques that would enhance their ability to connect with the Reiki energy and direct it to the client. Basic meditation was taught to his students at the beginner's level, and many additional advanced energetic and meditation techniques were taught at Levels II and III. These techniques were designed to allow the student to systematically become aware of themselves and their clients as energetic beings, to cultivate the ability to direct healing energies to their client across space and time (distant healing), and to develop within themselves a certain knowledge and experience of the spiritual dimensions of our being.

In addition to these startling differences between Japanese Reiki and Western Reiki, it was discovered that Dr. Usui did not use any symbols at all when practicing Reiki—he simply did not need to because of the special energetic information that had been given to him during his satori.

However, when he began to teach Reiki to his students who had not received such an enlightening experience, he needed to give them specific energetic tools so they could easily invoke the Reiki energies, connect with them, and channel them to the recipient on the table or, in the case of distant healing, wherever they were in space or in time. Therefore, he devised certain symbols that could be visualized and named to allow the student to connect consciously with the particular vibrational patterns of the symbols that were provided energetically to the student during the initiation process. The fact that two of the four symbols taught by Dr. Usui are simple Japanese phrases given in Kanji characters substantiates the Japanese language origin of these symbols instead of them being "discovered" in an ancient Sanskrit text. The names of the remaining two symbols are likewise simple phrases, the words of which can be easily found in any Japanese dictionary. Therefore, it appears that the Western version of Reiki that tells of a series of symbols being given directly to Dr. Usui in a dream may be somewhat inaccurate. However, there is little doubt that Dr. Usui did receive total information and knowledge of this healing method and the healing energies from a higher dimensional source in a tremendous burst of instantaneous energy.

For whatever reason, it appears that Mrs. Takata significantly restructured both the Japanese philosophy and the practice of Reiki in many ways. During her Level I training, she taught her students only the concept of placing the hands directly over specific organs of the physical body to transmit the healing energies. Dr. Usui's emphasis on spiritual development of the healer, and his methods of directing the Reiki energies using his fingers, eyes, and breath were discarded. Perhaps Mrs. Takata believed that the Western world was just not ready to hear about spiritual meditation techniques, hand scans, and chakras, or to embrace the Eastern philosophies that had been using human energy fields for healing for thousands of years. Similarly, Dr. Usui's practices of meditation as the focus for the Advanced Reiki (Level II) practitioner's own spiritual development were not carried forward and taught by Mrs. Takata. Perhaps she realized that unless she consciously modified the techniques of Reiki to what was considered rational by the Western mind at that time (1940s to 1970s), Reiki simply would not be accepted and proliferate in the Western world.

Following the practice taught to her by Dr. Hayashi, Mrs. Takata initiated her students into three levels of Reiki: a Level I initiation (Reiki Practitioner) allows the therapist to direct healing energies to others by placing his or her hands on the client. The attunements for Level II (Advanced Reiki Practitioner) provides additional symbols and energies that permit the practitioner to transfer or channel energies for mental healing and to heal people at a distance. And finally, the Level III (Reiki Master) attunement provides the knowledge and energy of the Usui Reiki Master Symbol that enables a Reiki Master to provide attunements or initiation ceremonies for all three levels to other students.

The purpose of these progressive attunements is to gradually open the upper four chakras (crown, brow, throat, and heart) of the initiate and also to open the individual's palm chakras. This allows a great amount of healing energy from the Universal Energy Field to enter the Reiki practitioner's crown chakra, pass down to and through his heart chakra, down his arms, and out through his palm chakras to the client.

LEVELS OF USUI REIKI PRACTICE

The healing energies of Reiki are conferred to an individual through an "attunement" or initiation process, which energetically "retunes" the vibrational patterns in that person's Human Energy Field (specifically, the chakra system). This allows the Reiki practitioner to subconsciously or consciously connect with and direct this universal healing energy either to oneself or to others through the use of certain symbols. These symbols represent different forms of healing energies that can be specifically invoked and transferred to another person.

In recent times as we have begun to sense a quickening in the consciousness of humankind, and much additional knowledge has been allowed to come into the open for inspection and understanding. If you go to your local bookstore, you might find several books on Reiki, some of which even include symbols. But just knowing what a symbol looks like does not give one the ability to use it for any purpose. One must be initiated into the energy of each symbol during an attunement or initiation ceremony. In other words, you can not give what you have not received. When the energy of the symbol has been placed into the energy system of an individual during an attunement, that person is then and only then able to use the energy of that symbol, and it can be used only for healing purposes. One can be initiated into the energy of the Reiki symbols only by one who has already been so initiated, i.e., a Reiki Master Teacher.

Usui Reiki is composed of three, and sometimes four, levels of proficiency and personal development that the Reiki healer must learn and demonstrate. Although Dr. Usui provided three levels of instruction, I provide four separate levels for my students. However, the fourth Level does not involve an energetic attunement; instead, it teaches the student how to perform the attunements in Levels I–III. The following discussion describes the Japanese and Western Reiki topics of instruction at each level.

Usui Level I (Reiki Practitioner). The Level I attunements open your chakra system and your palms so that your energy field can connect with and receive the Reiki healing energies from the Universe then and transmit them for healing to yourself or to another person's physical body using your hands.* Since this level allows you perform only local, "hands-on" healings, you do not need to know the symbol, the "Power Symbol," used at this level. Instead, in the Japanese version of Reiki, emphasis at Level I is placed on developing an ability to sense the client's energy bodies and centers (chakras) intuitively and also with the hands and fingers to determine areas of disease, to learn to trust the way your hands and your inner senses provide energetic information from the client's body and energy fields, and to learn how Reiki energy feels in your hands and fingers as it is channeled to the client. A series of hand positions on the client's body was developed by Dr. Usui, but they were to be used only as a last resort in the event that no intuitive information was received from the client's field regarding location of areas that needed to be addressed. In addition, several simple meditation

---

* Most Reiki Masters open the Palm Chakras at Level II so that a significant increase in healing energy flow over that of Level I results from the Level II attunements. However, I prefer to open the palms at Level I in order to let Level I students learn as much as possible about how Reiki energy feels when it is channeled very strongly through themselves to the client.

techniques were taught by Dr. Usui for the purpose of enhancing the student's psychic abilities to discern the areas of the client's body in need of treatment.

In nearly all Western Reiki initiations, the student is not instructed in the nature of the energetic changes to their chakra system, nor is the chakra system even discussed. Instead, the instruction time is devoted to receiving the oral history of Reiki and for practicing Mrs. Takata's Foundation Series of hand positions over the physical organs. The student is also asked to learn how the Reiki energy feels when they are channeling it so they can receive some indication when to move to the next position; however, very little energy sensitivity training, if any at all, is usually provided. Usually a minimum practice period of about three months is needed to develop proficiency in either the Japanese or Western Reiki skills and prepare the student for Level II.

It is recognized that many money-hungry Reiki Masters offer weekend "intensives" where the student is given the energetic attunements for Levels I and II, and sometimes even Level III within just a few days. I consider this practice decidedly counterproductive to the energetic development of a new Reiki healer, since the student is given no time to integrate the energies of each level into his or her field (twenty-one days are required for each level) before receiving additional energies of the next level. For most students relatively new to energy healing, this creates "energetic overload" and results in incomplete or incorrect integration of the new energies. Further, a period of time is required by the initiate to learn how these new energies feel and how his or her hands sense the flow of these new energies. Different people require different lengths of time to become accustomed to these cues, and they should become quite familiar with the way they feel these energies working before moving on to new energies provided by the next level attunements.

Usui Level II (Advanced Reiki Practitioner). The Japanese Level II attunements provide additional symbols and specific detailed instruction for use of the Mental/Emotional Healing symbol and for directing healing Reiki energies remotely to a person regardless of where they are. The Japanese name of the Mental Healing Symbol can be easily translated as "to create a new habit." The specific energetic healing technique used by Dr. Usui focuses the palm chakra energies on certain areas of the brain and also includes the use of visualizations and affirmations by both the practitioner and the client.

Several different methods of using the distant healing symbol are normally taught. These include several techniques for delivering the healing energy no matter where they are in space, "distant healing," or in time, "healing the past" and "healing the future." In addition, the foot chakras are opened to allow a freer and much more effective connection to the energies of the earth. Following Dr. Usui's instructions, I teach my students how to direct the healing Reiki energies to the client with their hands, their fingertips, their eyes, and their breath. Level II initiates are also instructed in how they may, if they have not already done so, establish a regular meditation practice that includes energetic and spiritual healing techniques.

In a Western Reiki Level II workshop, the student will be introduced to the Mental Healing symbol; however, very little understanding or practice of how it is to be used was provided to me. Instruction in the use of the Distant Healing symbol usually does not include healing the past or future, but concentrates primarily on providing different ways of sending healing energy only to someone who is not physically present. For both the Japanese and Western versions of Reiki, normally about six months of regular practice in the Reiki Level II techniques is required before the student will be prepared for Level III. However, readiness for Level III may be reached much sooner by some students; others may never be ready or desire to go to the next level.

Usui Level III (Reiki Master). The Level III attunements provide one additional Master symbol that is used in Japanese Reiki specifically for heightening the practitioner's spiritual awareness of and connection with his or her own higher aspects and the spiritual dimensions. In addition, the Reiki Master symbol gives the initiate the energetic ability to attune the Human Energy Field of others into any Reiki level, including Level III. However, in my program of four levels, the specific procedures for conducting these attunements are not provided until Level IV. Dr. Usui taught his Level III students advanced energy manipulation techniques and meditation practices for the purpose of expanding the student's spiritual awareness of himself. By regular use of the Level III Master symbol not for healing, but to connect with your spiritual self during the advanced meditation practices taught at Level III, the Reiki Master becomes very aware of his or her true spiritual nature. As this awareness during meditation is brought back into your consciousness and into your daily life, the "big picture" of life and your own role or life purpose within that picture becomes clearer. This is, in itself, very healing on the spiritual level of your being. The Level III Reiki Master is expected to have established a regular meditation practice, and also is expected to provide regular Reiki healing services in a professional setting for the general public.

In the Western version of Reiki, knowledge of the Reiki Master symbol is given to the student, and they are usually told that a slight increase in healing abilities results. However, no new Reiki healing techniques specifically for the Master symbol are taught. Similarly, no specific meditation techniques using the Master symbol are taught. For both the Japanese and Western versions, when the Reiki Master is prepared to accept, instruct, and support the development of his/her own students, he/she is then ready and qualified for Level IV.

Usui Reiki Level IV (Master Teacher). No additional symbols or energies of symbols are conferred at this level; however, Level IV provides instruction and practice in the procedures for conducting attunements and the initiation ceremonies so that the initiate can gain confidence in their ability to initiate others.

KARUNA REIKI®

It has been said that our understanding of any subject grows and evolves by gradually becoming ready to receive additional information. "When the student is ready, the teacher will appear." Similarly, our knowledge of the healing power of Reiki continues to evolve as we master what we have been given and become ready to receive additional wisdom.

Karuna Reiki represents just such an example, and was developed and named in 1995 at the International Center for Reiki Training (ICRT) in Southfield, Michigan. It evolved out of Usui and Tibetan Reiki from a desire and a knowingness that there is always something greater waiting to be uncovered, and that there is no limit to the good that can come to those who seek.

But it was found that in order for one to gain the full benefit of Karuna Reiki, one must be ready. This can happen only if one's energy system has first been conditioned through the use of the Reiki Master energies. Once this conditioning has taken place, one's energy system can more easily adjust to the higher potentials available. In addition, the experience one gains as a Reiki Master allows them to make better use of the new healing tools that Karuna Reiki provides. Because the energies are stronger and the potential for healing greater, Karuna Reiki is considered as the next step after Reiki Master, and is taught only to those who are already Reiki Masters. In the same way that a student can not take Reiki II without first having taken Reiki I, Karuna Reiki is not taught to students unless they already have taken and practiced the Reiki Master level. In this way, the student gains the greatest benefit from the training and also does not miss the benefit of the Usui Reiki Master level.

Karuna Reiki brings in healing energies that are noticeably stronger and able to more quickly heal a wider range of difficulties. Many experience the energy flowing not just through the body and arms, but all around their body as well, so that it completely surrounds the practitioner on its way to the client. *Karuna* is a Sanskrit word that means "compassionate action," and this is not an ordinary kind of compassion, but one that comes from an unbounded sea of love. This is the kind of compassion that, when combined with wisdom, can take one to enlightenment.

When taking the Karuna Reiki training, one becomes both a practitioner, able to use the energies for healing and a Master who is able to teach others. Karuna Reiki has two levels and eight symbols that are in addition to the four symbols of Usui Reiki. Each of the eight symbols brings with it a different frequency and a different way of helping the healing process. There is a symbol to reduce pain, one to prepare for deep healing, one to heal deeply, one to work with karmic issues, one to ground, one to bring harmony and balance, and so on. Having more specific healing symbols can be likened to a repair person. At first, he may have only three or four tools to work with; but once he has mastered those through practice, he learns to work with a much larger number of tools, and is therefore able to repair a wider range of problems, and do it more quickly.

Karuna Reiki opens you to work more closely with all enlightened beings. This includes those enlightened ones who are physically present, as well as those in spirit. Karuna is the motivating quality of all enlightened beings who are working to end suffering on Earth, and they continually send an unlimited amount of healing energy and guidance to us. As you develop Karuna in yourself, not only are you helping others, but you also become more receptive to the Karuna that is being sent by all enlightened beings. Thus your own healing is quickened.

The Karuna Reiki Practitioner and Master workshops conducted by the International Center for Reiki Training provide standardized instruction and attunements into the energies of the eight symbols, as well as instruction in how to activate and direct the healing energy. I refer the reader to *The Book on Karuna Reiki* by Shanti Gaia for an excellent discussion of the Karuna Reiki system, its symbols, and the specific uses for which the healing energies can be directed.

HAND POSITIONS

Many different individual Reiki styles or techniques are practiced, depending on the background and training of the initiating Reiki Master. Although Mrs. Takata taught a specific series of hand positions to be used in a very quiet environment with no talking, some Reiki Practitioners have elected to include other non-Reiki formats in their healing sessions. For instance, one Reiki Practitioner I know uses a combination of traditional Reiki hand positions and other hand motions in a Native American environment with chanting and smudging. Another uses crystals and flower essences in conjunction with their own version of "Reiki."

Many of these alternative Reiki practitioners may also use additional symbols that are not part of the traditional Reiki teachings. Therefore, the person seeking a Reiki Master would do well to investigate not only the version of Reiki that he or she uses, but also inquire about the effectiveness of that Reiki Master's attunements. Most reputable Reiki Master Teachers are willing to arrange for a testimonial from their students and selected previous clients.

A typical healing session in the Western Reiki style would begin by having the client remove their shoes and lie down on a healing table. It is not necessary to remove any clothing; however, large belts, buckles, necklaces, and earrings should be removed. In addition, it is a good idea to leave keys, beepers, and other metallic or electronic objects outside the healing area. After centering and attuning themselves, the Reiki practitioner begins the session by placing their hands in a series of positions over the head, torso and back of the client. Soft music in the background helps to relax the client. Practitioner comfort is quite important while practicing Reiki. A full Reiki session can easily last for forty-five minutes to an hour, and if the client is lying on the floor, the practitioner will soon have a sore back from leaning over. It is much better for the client to be seated in a chair if a healing table is not available.

Each hand position is maintained for a few minutes, or until the Reiki practitioner feels a shift in the way the energy feels as it moves through his hands. This signifies that it is time to proceed to the next hand position. The shift in energy felt by the practitioner might feel like his hands suddenly go from warm to cool, or it may be that a constant, slight sense of vibration ceases. The key thing that the practitioner waits for is a change in the way his hands feel, whatever that change may be. The sensation of energy flowing through the hands is the result of the interaction of the practitioner's field and the client's field; therefore, the flow of energy through a practitioner's hands may feel quite different from client to client.

The hands are maintained in each position without any movement such as a rubbing, massage-like action or purposely vibrating or moving the hands. A gentle, light touch is all that is necessary. However, since the energy is being transferred through the palm chakras, full contact is desirable between the practitioner's palms and the client's body.

The traditional series of hand positions taught by Mrs. Takata, called the "Foundation Series," is described below. In my Reiki healing sessions, if I do not receive any intuitive guidance or information from hand scanning as to where to place my hands, this foundation series of hand positions is always used, regardless of the disease or symptoms exhibited by the client. However, they may be augmented as required after the Foundation Series to provide Reiki energy to specific areas for which the client has symptoms, such as bursitis in the shoulder or a stomach ulcer.

It should be noted here that different Reiki practitioners might have several hand positions that are different hand from Mrs. Takata's foundation series. This is a matter of personal choice on the part of the Reiki practitioner. Many times the practitioner will be intuitively guided to place his hands in a certain position. I always encourage my students to follow this intuitive guidance and trust their inner instincts. However, in the absence of any inner guidance, Takata's foundation series can always be used as a fallback. As mentioned before, it is the Reiki attunement process, not any specific set of hand positions, that enables the Reiki practitioner to transfer healing energies to the client. The Reiki energy will always go where it is needed.

Front of Body. The client should begin by lying faceup on a healing table with her arms at her sides. A pillow should be placed under the back of both knees to relieve any tension on the lower part of the back. An additional pillow may be placed under the client's head if comfortable (optional). Each of the positions below should be held for two to three minutes, or until you sense a "shift" in the energy under your hands. Then go to the next hand position. The following hand positions assume that the client is lying on a healing table and is being addressed by only one Reiki practitioner.

Eyes and Forehead. (*Optional:* Fold a tissue diagonally into a triangle and place the long side across cheeks and nose.) Place hands over eyes and forehead so that the fingertips of the index fingers are near but not touching the sides of the nose. Take care not to close the nostrils. Keep thumbs together at the first and second joints. Do not press down on cheekbones, but just maintain a light touch. This position covers the eyes, sinuses above the eyes, and the front part of the brain.

Sides of Head. Sit in a chair or stand at the top of the client's head. Place the little finger of each hand under the earlobe, and the tip of the fourth (ring) finger of each hand just in front of the little flap at the entrance to each ear canal. The thumb and first four fingers should be together. Place your palms gently against the side of the client's head.

This position covers the mid-brain, and balances the energies in the right and left hemispheres of the brain. The client will soon feel very calm and relaxed.

Back of Head.   Gently roll client's head to the right and place your left hand under the back of the head, then roll the client's head to the left and place your right hand under the head. Bring both of your hands together with the little fingers touching. Your fingertips should be just under the occipital ridge at the back of the skull. Pull the head toward you very gently. This position covers the back of the brain.

Throat Area.   Rest the little finger of your right hand lightly on the client's right collarbone, and overlap your right fingers with the fingers of your left hand. Place the side of the left hand lightly on the client's left collarbone. Your index fingers should be just under or in front of the chin. Do not touch the throat area itself, but cup your hands so they form an "umbrella" over the Adam's apple area. This position covers the thyroid and parathyroid glands.

Liver Area.   Stand at the right side of the client's body. Locate the point just below the sternum (breastbone) where the ribs come together. Place the tip of the fourth finger of the left hand at this point, and gently lower your left hand to the client's body. Place the right hand next to and touching the left hand. The fingers of both hands should be together, and both palms should be gently resting on the body. Pressure on the client's body is not required for the transfer of energy, and can only be uncomfortable to the client. This position covers the liver.

Spleen Area.   Move both hands directly across to the left side of the client's body. Both hands will still be kept next to each other, and the left edge of the left hand may be just on the edge of the rib cage. This position covers the spleen.

Abdominal Area.   Move both hands down the body one hand-width, and put your left hand over the right side of the client's body, and your right hand over the left side of the client's body. The fingertips of your left hand may just touch the heel of the palm of your right hand—both your hands will be lined up and gently rest on the client's abdomen. *Note:* If your hands are large and the client's waist is slender, you may need to overlap the right palm a bit on top of your left fingers; if the client is very large and you have small hands, there may be an inch or two gap between your two hands. This position covers the upper part of the small intestines.

Lower Abdominal Area/Reproductive Glands. Respecting the client's private areas, move both hands again down the body into the groin area, but remaining above the pubic bone. This position covers the lower part of the small intestines and, in women, the reproductive organs (ovaries and uterus).

Heart Area. On female clients, standing at their right side, place your left hand on the center of their sternum (breastbone) with your hand above the breasts, and your fingers pointing toward their left side. Then place the fingertips of your right hand on your left hand and form a "T" with your two hands. The first two joints of the right fingers should rest on the left hand and the right hand should be above and not touching the breasts. This position covers the Heart and High Heart (thymus gland, which regulates the immune system).

On male clients, place both hands across the chest over the heart, with the fingertips of the left hand just touching the heel of the palm of your right hand. This position covers the heart. The Heart and High Heart areas are the only places where there is a difference in hand positions between female and male clients.

High Heart Area. On male clients, place the hands above the heart with fingertips of the left hand touching the heel of the palm of the right hand, parallel to and just touching the collarbones. This position is not required for female clients since the heart position included the High Heart (left hand as the top of the "T"). This position on male clients covers the thymus gland, which regulates the immune system.

Knees (Optional). If the client has trouble with one or both knees, place the left hand under the back of the knee and the right hand on top of the kneecap. Be sure to do the knees before the client turns over on his or her stomach.

At this point, ask the client to turn over on his/her stomach. Remove the head pillow if one was used, and adjust the face cradle. Adjust the cradle so it is comfortable for the client. When the client's face is in the cradle, place a pillow under the ankles so that the toes are up off the table.

Top of Spine. Sitting in a chair at the client's head, place your right hand on the back of the neck just below the occipital ridge, and place your left hand so that the fingers overlap the right fingers. This position covers the base of the brain and its interface to the spinal column.

The remaining steps are all done with the hands across the full body—your left fingertips just touching the heel of the left palm, or with a small gap if the client is fairly large. The entire back should be covered, so each time your hands are moved, they should go down the back by the width of your hand. The following hand positions assume an average-sized client and a Reiki practitioner with average-sized hands.

Upper Lung Area. Place your hands at the top of the back near the shoulders. This position covers the upper portion of the lungs.

Main Lung Area. Move both hands down the body one hand-width to a point directly behind the heart. This position covers the main part of both lungs.

Lower Lung/Diaphragm Area. Move both hands down the body one hand-width to a point over the bottom of the rib cage. This position covers the lower lung area, the diaphragm, and the stomach.

Kidneys/Adrenal Glands. Move both hands down the body one hand-width. This position covers both kidneys and the adrenal gland, which rests on top of each kidney.

Small Intestines. Move both hands down the body one hand-width. This position again covers the small intestines.

Lower Abdominal Area/Descending Colon. Move both hands down the body one hand-width. This position covers the remaining part of the small intestines, the descending colon, the bladder, and, in men, the prostate gland.

Buttocks. Move both hands down the body one hand-width to a point just over the curvature of the buttocks. This complete the series of hand positions in the Foundation Series.

Feet (Optional). Place the center of your palms in the center of the bottom of the client's feet using any position that is comfortable for you. One such position is to have the client spread their legs slightly, and then you would turn around with your back to the client's body, sit on the edge of the massage table and gently grasp the bottom of each foot.

Specifically Requested Areas (Optional). If the client has indicated a specific problem (e.g., bursitis in the shoulder, sprained ankle, laceration, or other injury anywhere, etc.), now is the time (after the full Reiki session) to provide additional energy to that specific area. Hold the area for a few minutes in any position that is comfortable for both you and the client.

A typical healing session in the original Japanese style, however, is quite different from the Western Style taught by Mrs. Takata and that is generally practiced outside Japan. According to Dr. Usui's handbook he gave to each of his students, the Reiki practitioner would first begin with a short meditation in the presence of the client, and then bring up and connect with the Reiki energies.[3] As soon as the hands or palms begin to feel the energy of Reiki, the practitioner would set or state his/her intent for the session—to be an open and clear channel for the Reiki energies so that they can go wherever they are needed.

Following the statement of intention, the practitioner would open himself intuitively and ask for guidance as to where he should place his hands on the client to direct the Reiki energies. If intuitive guidance was received, he would place his hands at that place until he received further guidance that it was time to move to another location or to end the session. If no intuitive guidance is initially received, he would connect with the client's energy field more directly by placing his non-dominant (receiving) hand on the crown chakra of the client and await guidance. If guidance is received, he would go to that place until further guidance is received. If no guidance is received at the crown chakra after a minute or two, he would begin a hand scan of the client's etheric body to determine the location of any areas of disease or symptomatic distress such as pain or congestion. Then he would address each area in turn until he received energetic or intuitive guidance to move to the next location or to end the session. And finally, if he received no energetic or intuitive guidance during any of the above steps, he would use a series of hand positions on the client's body that covers the head and all major organs in much the same way as Mrs. Takata's Foundation Series. However, Dr. Usui taught his students to look first for and rely on the intuitively received information; the standard pattern of hand positions was to be used only as a reliable but last resort if no information was received energetically or intuitively.

Following a Reiki session in either the Japanese or Western style, the client is often in an altered state and needs to be returned slowly to full mental clarity. Have the client gently turn over again and sit on the edge of the table for a few minutes. A glass of water will help ground the client. Always discuss with your client any sensations or reactions he or she experienced while on the table. Make sure that the client is completely clear mentally before allowing him or her to drive.

Case Study #1

The following example illustrates the effectiveness of Reiki on the functions of the physical body. Jane (not her real name), a forty-nine-year-old female, came to me one day to receive Reiki for her diabetes and also hypnotherapy sessions for weight release. At age twenty she had been diagnosed with Type I diabetes and was placed on self-administered insulin injections at that time. Five years before her visit to me, a small external pump that provided a steady rate of insulin through a needle was prescribed for her and was attached subcutaneously on her abdomen. During the initial interview she reported that her blood glucose (BG) levels were ranging from well below to significantly above the normal limits set by her physician (80–120 milligrams of glucose per deciliter of blood). She was also required to monitor her BG levels every two hours while awake and supplement the dosage provided by the insulin pump as required. In addition, she stated that she had been having very erratic sleep patterns, was nearly always tired, and experienced large mood swings ranging from a feeling of depression to anger and aggressiveness. And lastly, she wanted to reduce her weight by fifty pounds to bring her weight to within the "normal" range for her height and build.

After the client interview information was taken, I suggested that hypnotherapy for weight release should wait until her BG levels had stabilized into a more normal pattern for several months; she agreed. I also advised her that, since she was currently on medication prescribed for her diabetes, I would accept her as a client only on the condition that her physician was made aware of her desire to address the diabetes with Reiki and to release her unnecessary weight through hypnotherapy. Additionally, she was to regularly check with her physician to determine if any changes were needed to her prescribed medicines. I also asked Jane to keep a written record of her BG levels each time they were checked.

Upon receipt of acknowledgement of the above by Jane's physician, I began a program of weekly Reiki sessions with her, giving particular emphasis to her abdomen and pancreas area. At the time of her first Reiki session, her BG levels had been very erratic the past two weeks with swings over just a few hours from as low as 20 to well over 400. When she came for her second weekly session, her BG levels the past week had not shown any significant improvement, and were still ranging from 25 to 400. But by the third session, the BG levels over the previous week were now ranging from 25 to 265. At the time of the fourth session, which was held two weeks after her third session, her BG levels had further reduced and were ranging from 30 to 200. Over the next several days, but before a fifth session, her BG levels were ranging from 60 to 140, a significant improvement in both the low end and high end readings. In addition, Jane reported that she now felt full of energy, could sleep soundly the whole night through, and could focus and concentrate on tasks quite easily for an extended period of time, something she could not do before. She had also released ten pounds of excess weight on her own without the aid of diets or hypnotherapy.

At this point, Jane and her husband moved to the Alaskan wilderness, and I was unable to continue monitoring her progress. However, during the period of the Reiki sessions, I did initiate her as an Advanced Reiki Practitioner (Level II) so she could continue giving herself the healing Reiki energies.

CASE STUDY #2

One evening while I was reading the paper, I suddenly heard the dog from across the street begin to yelp and howl loudly. I looked up and saw Toots, the neighbor's five-month old black Lab puppy (who was well-known for having more energy than sense), lying under their car in the driveway. As I ran over to see what the trouble was, the woman shrieked that she had run over the dog. As she ran in the house to get her husband, Toots was lying on the ground and was unable to move anything below her midsection. She was still howling loudly, and was clearly in a lot of pain.

As I placed my hands gently on Toots' hip and abdomen, I connected with the Reiki energy to provide emergency Reiki energy to Toots and said a little prayer for her recovery. I immediately felt a sort of twist in my solar plexus (my way of knowing that my prayer has been heard), followed by a tremendous surge of energy flowing through my forearms and hands. Within a few seconds, Toots stopped howling and began to lick my arms. I took this to mean that she was no longer in pain.

As soon as the husband came out, he and their twelve-year-old son gently lifted Toots onto a blanket and put her in the back of their station wagon for a quick ride to the vet. About two hours later, the boy came over to say that Toots had been x-rayed and that her hips were crushed, she had many internal injuries, and that she would be kept overnight for observation, but she wasn't expected to live through the night. As I went to bed, I invoked the Reiki Distant Healing Symbol, created a cocoon of golden energy around Toots, and placed all the Reiki symbols in the cocoon to continue working for as long as she required them. When I awoke the next morning, I again invoked the Reiki Distant Healing Symbol and sent healing energy to her once more.

That afternoon, the boy came over to tell me that Toots had somehow lived through the night, and was now able to wag her tail a bit. Toots came home three days later and was walking again, and without any cast or bandages! She had a pretty bad limp, but she was walking! Two weeks later, she was running and jumping like a normal puppy, and you couldn't tell a bit that she had miraculously healed herself of a broken hip and multiple internal injuries, thanks to the help of Reiki and the intervention of the higher dimensions.

Summary

There are two features of Reiki that tend to set this form of energy-based healing apart from many others. First, the ability to transfer Reiki energy is given to a student only through an attunement or initiation process during which the energy of specific universal healing symbols is transferred into the Human Energy Field of the initiate. Secondly (as currently practiced in the West), the Reiki energy is transferred through a series of hand positions that concentrate on specific physical organs; the Reiki Practitioner requires no knowledge of energy bodies or the chakra system.

The first Reiki feature may at first seem a bit abstract, yet powerful physical healings have been consistently documented after a student has been "opened" or "attuned" to the energy of the Reiki symbols. No specific training or spiritual development is required of the student wishing to become a Reiki Practitioner in either the Western or Japanese style. One does not have to be "born a healer" for the attunements to be effective. Quite the contrary; many of my own Reiki students had no background or experience in healing at all. But once they found within themselves the desire to help and heal others and were led to Reiki, the Reiki attunements opened their upper chakras and palm chakras so they could effectively receive Reiki energy from the universe and transmit it to their own clients.

The second Reiki feature, that of focusing only on physical organs instead of energy bodies and chakras, is a characteristic only of the Western form of Reiki. As originally taught by Dr. Usui, Reiki included techniques and exercises to develop the practitioner's sensitivity to energy so that chakras and the energy bodies of the Human Energy Field could be located, assessed, and specifically addressed by the trained practitioner. The series of twelve hand positions initially taught by Dr. Usui to his Level 1 students was to be used only when the practitioner did not receive any information, either intuitively or from hand scanning, as to where to focus his healing efforts on the client's body.

With a more modern and broader perspective of energy healing and a clearer understanding of our human energetic nature, it is believed that Reiki energy is effective because the physical energy body and its energy blueprint, the etheric body, are the direct recipients of the Reiki energy. Physical traumatic effects due to injuries or surgical procedures are quickly reduced and healing can be dramatically accelerated during and after a Reiki session.

However, Reiki and other forms of healing that concentrate primarily on the physical or etheric bodies (sometimes called "Magnetic Healing") still may not provide a permanent cure in all cases for some diseases or symptoms. Other forms of healing that are performed on the higher subtle bodies (sometimes called "Spiritual Healing") are then required to address the original cause of the disease so that a permanent cure may be provided. "Although disease may be healed at a physical/etheric level, magnetic healing may be ineffective in the long run if the ultimate cause of illness is from a higher energy level. . . . In contradistinction to magnetic healing, spiritual healing attempts to work at the level of the higher subtle bodies and chakras to effect a healing from the most primary level of disease origins. The spiritual healer works as a power source of multiple-frequency outputs to allow energy shifts at several levels simultaneously."[4]

Although Reiki is a powerful and effective healing technique, we are now learning more about the strengths and limitations of all healing modalities, and we need to keep both sides of the coin in mind when selecting a particular technique to address a particular set of symptoms. Reiki is an excellent tool to have available in your "healing toolbox" since it is easy to administer, takes little training to become an effective Reiki practitioner, and can be used very effectively in a wide range of healing situations, particularly in traumatic injury or postoperative recovery situations. However, if the cause of the disease originates in the emotional or mental energy bodies, the relief provided by Reiki, or other healing modalities that concentrate only on the physical body, may be temporary unless the Reiki energies also successfully resolve the disease origins in the higher energy bodies.

Reiki training and attunements can be provided by a Reiki Master Teacher in your area. However, you may not find "Reiki" listed in your phone book. One way of locating a reputable Reiki Master Teacher is to inquire at a local holistic bookstore or health center. Usually, local practitioners leave their flyers and brochures for prospective customers. Local "New Age" magazines or newsletters also may contain advertisements by Reiki Master Teachers. However, care should be exercised when selecting a teacher to study under, since there may be many different versions of Reiki practiced in your area. It is best to ask a prospective

Reiki Master for testimonials from their students and clients. If they are unwilling to provide success stories from their students (with the student's permission, of course), they are probably not very successful themselves—so ask someone else. Websites and other resources can be found in Appendix C.

Healing Touch

OVERVIEW

Healing Touch (HT) is a nonintrusive, complementary energy-based program developed through the nursing profession to clear, align and balance the human energy system through touch. Through this realignment, the client's energy system is restored to higher levels of functioning, and healing of the physical body is promoted and accelerated. The goal of HT is to restore harmony and balance in the energy system to help the person self-heal. This is done either by a light touch to the body or by repatterning the energy field a few inches above the physical body.

Since Healing Touch is gentle and it influences the whole person on all levels, it can be used on everyone, infants and elderly alike, and can take place in any setting: the home, hospitals, healing centers, accident scenes, schools, hospices, or a doctor's office.

Healing Touch is a collection of about thirty individual healing techniques that have been incorporated into a structured program of instruction and practice for physicians, nurses, health care professionals, and lay healing practitioners. In addition, the number of healing techniques taught within Healing Touch keeps steadily increasing as the effectiveness of new techniques is proven and they are incorporated within the HT instructional program.

HT includes specific healing interventions that address general health and well-being, stress and tension, disease prevention, grief management, pain control, neck and back problems, anxiety, wound and fracture healing, HIV and AIDS, hypertension, pre- or postsurgery, headaches, migraines, cancer, arthritis, and many other diseases and symptoms.

HT is also an ideal introductory energy-based healing modality for several reasons. First, there is usually at least one HT intervention that specifically addresses most diseases or symptoms. For example, if a client comes to a HT Practitioner with a migraine headache, there is a specific intervention technique, "Pain Ridge," which has been shown to be very effective in lessening the severity of migraines.

Second, there is a comprehensive, standardized training and certification program available from the beginner level to advanced levels. This program allows the student of energy-based healing to develop his knowledge of the human energy system; to be able to sense and correctly manipulate the higher energy bodies; and to develop himself mentally, emotionally, spiritually, and energetically with increasing knowledge of the more advanced healing techniques. The thirty or so individual techniques include several that involve physical contact with the client's body. Others involve manipulation of only the client's higher energy bodies, and some techniques include both physical contact and energy body manipulation.

Third, HT can be performed nearly anywhere, anytime. Most HT techniques are performed with the client resting on a healing table; however, several techniques can also be performed with the client sitting in a chair. HT can also be performed very effectively on bedridden clients.

HISTORY

The Healing Touch program grew out of the nursing practice of Janet Mentgen, RN, BSN, who was invited by her nursing colleagues to develop the program. Janet had been noticing for some time the beneficial effects many clients exhibited after having their energy field "manipulated" in various intuitively guided fashions. She began correlating certain hand movements within the patient's energy field and the results that energy manipulation produced. Since these positive effects were discernable and repeatable, she began to promote their use within her private practice, and also began to collect several individual techniques into a more formal, structured program of instruction for others.

In 1989, Healing Touch was offered as a pilot program at the University of Tennessee and in Gainesville, Florida. Because of the remarkably effective results obtained through HT, in 1990 it became a certificate program of the American Holistic Nurses' Association (AHNA)—primarily for nurses. The techniques of Healing Touch are also supported by the American Holistic Medical Association (AHMA)—primarily for holistically oriented medical doctors. The AHNA had the educational resources to develop Ms. Mentgen's material into sequenced, multilevel workshops that could be taught on weekends or in comprehensive training sessions.

Due to its tremendous growth, the Healing Touch program soon outgrew AHNA as the certification authority for HT practitioners for several reasons. First, the tremendously widespread popularity of HT was beginning to tax the ability of AHNA to effectively administer the program and accredit qualified HT practitioners. Second, the HT movement had very rapidly spread worldwide, and it soon became obvious that HT now clearly extended beyond the jurisdiction of the American Holistic Nurses' Association to certify HT Practitioners in other countries. Third, the movement had also spread far beyond the bounds of only the nursing profession with many ministers and lay healing practitioners actively providing HT services. Therefore, a separate credentialing authority was required, and Healing Touch International, Inc. was formed in 1996.

The primary reason for formally structuring the HT program and providing a formal credentialing process was to ensure high standards and uniformity in the training of HT practitioners. Another motive was to achieve recognition and acceptance by the professional medical and insurance communities that HT is a legitimate healing modality for which insurance payments can be authorized. When the insurance companies recognize that energy healing using HT is an effective therapeutic technique, and medical doctors are willing to prescribe such treatments where indicated, the use of energy-based healing techniques, and HT in particular, will become more widely accepted. And in many cases energy-based healing sessions can be included in a lower-cost healing regimen than traditional allopathic therapies (drugs and surgery).

In 2001 Healing Touch International applied for and received a Complementary and Alternative Medicine (CAM) billing code. This billing code, CBCAE, is used by providers for third-party reimbursement from insurance companies. The billing code resides under the category of Energy Work: Practice Specialties, Somatic Education & Massage, Energy Work, Healing Touch. In addition, this billing code affords a mechanism to systematically track services and providers, and to explore the clinical and economic efficacy of Healing Touch services.

There are growing indications that many insurance companies and the medical profession are recognizing the efficacy and positive benefits of energy treatments. As of 1996, for example, Kaiser Permanente covered acupressure, acupuncture, nutrition counseling, relaxation techniques, and self-massage.[5] Prudential Insurance covered acupuncture, biofeedback, chiropractic, massage, midwifery and naturopathy. Many others, including Aetna U.S. Health, American National, Tri-Care (military), CIGNA HealthCare, Guardian Life, and New England Mutual Life, are now recognizing insurance claims for the growing number of alternative healing and health care modalities that are being practiced openly now in the U.S.

Energy techniques are also being practiced as a complementary healing technique in many major hospitals. On page 35 of the September 1996 issue of *Life Magazine*, an energy practitioner is shown performing Therapeutic Touch in the operating room of New York's Columbia-Presbyterian hospital during an open-heart surgery. And HT continues to be taught in many major hospitals to the nursing and medical staff. For example, in January 1998, I had the opportunity to attend a class in Advanced Energy Healing Techniques held at Norfolk (Virginia) General Hospital. In addition, by 1996, many of this country's 125 medical schools, including Harvard, Yale, and Johns Hopkins, offered courses in alternative medicine.[6]

HEALING TOUCH TECHNIQUES

The thirty or so core techniques taught in the Healing Touch program include several that are very animated in terms of healer movements, many that are very static and slow-moving (similar to the laying-on-of-hands in Reiki), and others that are in between these two extremes. Some involve fairly complex hand movements and well-developed energetic sensitivity on the part of the healer; others are so simple that first or second graders can use them very effectively to help heal their own bumps, scrapes, and cuts. In addition to the healing received, another benefit of the use of the simple techniques by youngsters is to help them become aware of their own energetic makeup.

Table III describes a portion of the core HT techniques taught in Levels 1, 2 and 3.

HT Technique	Hand Placement		
Name	Level	Body	Field	Indications (Partial)
Ultrasound	1		X	Relieve pain, reduce bleeding, accelerate healing
Magnetic Clearing	1		X	Systemic relief, post-anesthesia, environmental sensitivities, release toxins/drugs
Scudder Technique	1	X		Arthritis, broken bones, joint problems
The Hopi Technique	2	X		Release energy blocks in neck and back
Pain Drain	2	X		Release severe/chronic pain
Pain Ridge	2	X	X	Migraine headache, TMJ syndrome, broken bones
Sealing a Wound	2	X	X	Repair energy field after trauma, operation, or childbirth
Etheric Unruffle	3		X	Clears and vitalizes fifth layer of auric field
Lymphatic Drain	3		X	Cleanse/stimulate lymphatic and autoimmune systems
Spiritual Surgery	3	X		Repairs Etheric Template (fifth level) and Etheric Body

Table III: Typical Healing Touch Techniques

The indications for selecting a particular technique vary from simple stress relief through release of acute pain, and from relief of specific disease-related symptoms to cleansing and repairing damage to the higher energy bodies.

Much of the mystery of energy healing, even in the simplest of techniques, results simply from not knowing what to do and from not understanding what is happening energetically. For example, the simple HT Level 1 technique called "Ultrasound" (no connection with the procedure for scanning inside the body with sound waves) is excellent for pain management (e.g., arthritic joints), for reducing bleeding, for accelerating the healing of cut or lacerated tissues, and for accelerating the healing of broken bones. Ultrasound can be administered anywhere, anytime, with no additional equipment or paraphernalia required. All you need is your hand and the knowledge of how to use it properly.

Simple Technique. The Ultrasound procedure consists of placing the tips of the thumb, forefinger, and middle finger of one hand together and imagining or visualizing the unseen energy spike that projects out the end of each digit for six-to-eight inches, being focused into a single, strong beam of energy for several inches. Now, without bending the wrist, move your whole forearm back and forth in a random motion so that your fingertips are about an inch or two above the injured area. The beam of energy projects down into the body through the injured area. If you move this beam of energy over the back of your other hand, soon you might begin to feel a faint but discernible tickling sensation as the beam of energy moves across the fine hairs.

The focused beam of energy from your fingertips is moving through the energy pattern that makes up your etheric body, and this energy interaction is felt as the light tickle. However, what happens energetically at a deeper level is that the energy beam from your moving hand is penetrating deeply within the etheric body and completely through your physical hand. This focused energy beam breaks up disturbed or blocked vibrational patterns caused by the injury. If this technique is begun immediately after a traumatic injury and continued for several minutes, the trauma to the energy pattern of the physical body will not be reflected upward into the energy pattern of the etheric body. Pain soon subsides and a quick return to the previous healthy pattern in the physical body (accelerated healing of tissue) is promoted. Animals respond especially well to Ultrasound with immediate wound repair. Large gaping wounds woven together with Ultrasound will often shrink to a small scab by the next morning.[7]

Complex Technique. On the other end of the spectrum, the sequence for addressing back and neck pain involves several separate processes that use both physical touch and energetic manipulation. After the client's energy system has been assessed with a pendulum and scanned using the healer's sensitized hand, the major and minor chakras are connected and balanced using a touch sequence where the healer's hands remain static in one position for about a minute before moving to the next position. Then the client is turned over on his stomach and the minor chakras in the legs and hips are energetically connected.

This is followed by pendling each vertebra to determine if there is an energy blockage associated with that vertebra. If a blockage is found, a completely energetic technique is used next, "Open Spinal Flow," and then followed by a physical touch technique, "Vertebral Spiral Technique," that energetically connects and balances the energy flow between the autonomic and central nervous systems. If an energy blockage persists after this balancing, a technique used by the Hopi Indians for centuries, "The Hopi Back Technique," is nearly always effective in removing the energy block from the spine. Additional techniques such as "Repair Nerve Damage," "Pain Drain," "Ultrasound," "Laser," etc., may also be drawn upon as required.

Obviously, the Back and Neck procedures are complex, and the practitioner must be able to correctly assess the client's energy states and properly apply the correct HT techniques as required. This goes also for all other HT techniques, both simple and complex. In many areas of the country, there are local HT practice groups which meet weekly or biweekly to practice on each other using, over time, each HT core technique. This maintains a high state of proficiency for the HT practitioners and also is quite beneficial in serving as a forum to keep abreast of developments in the Healing Touch program, as well as announcing events of general interest to energy healers.

HT EDUCATIONAL PROGRAM

The Healing Touch program is a multilevel educational program in energy-based therapy that ranges from beginning to advanced practice.

Core HT Techniques. The thirty or so core HT techniques are taught in a series of three workshops with fifteen or more clock hours of experiential instruction in each workshop. As currently structured, workshops typically begin with three hours instruction on Friday evening and continue with at least six hours instruction on Saturday and Sunday. Alternatively, longer sessions on Friday and Saturday can be held, with none required Friday evening. In each of the first three workshops, the student can earn fifteen-to-twenty Continuing Education credits.

Level 1 is the introductory level workshop, and is open to all persons, regardless of their background and training. The only prerequisites are a desire to help others and a strong commitment to further develop concepts and skills in energy-based therapy. In Level 1 the concept of the Human Energy Field is described as it relates to modern scientific principles. The student will apply these principles as he or she learns the basic concepts and demonstrates the sequence of steps in Magnetic Passes, an energy-based healing technique that requires sensitive hands and fingers to properly manipulate the client's energy field. The Level 1 student is also taught when and how to apply eight specific intervention techniques used in HT. Each technique is taught to the students, and then the students demonstrate the technique on each other under the supervision of a trained instructor.

Level 2 workshops are provided for those who have completed Level 1 and now wish to increase their depth and breadth in the study of HT. This level incorporates several additional healing techniques necessary to become an advanced practitioner. Emphasis is on developing healing sequences for specific client needs. Neck and back techniques are introduced, and therapeutic interventions for specific emotional and physiological problems are discussed and practiced. Objectives at this level are to review all Level 1 techniques, introduce additional healing techniques, further develop the healer's assessment abilities with both the pendulum and hand scan, and to develop client interviewing techniques. In addition, the student is introduced to a one-hour healing sequence for spe-

cific client problems, and given an understanding of energy-healing principles by describing specific techniques of various healers and healing
modalities other that HT.

Level 3 is taught only to students who have successfully completed
Levels 1 and 2. These workshops provide the forum to further develop
the healer's Higher Sense Perception and the ability to work intuitively
in response to higher guidance. Several additional advanced healing techniques are taught for working with the client's higher energy levels. Self-
healing and the student's self-development are also discussed. The student
will learn and discuss advanced studies of the human energy system and
perceptual tools of the healer, view healing from three separate perspectives (practitioner, client, observer), demonstrate and implement a full
healing sequence, and demonstrate skill in the several advanced techniques taught.

Certification Training. Level 4 is for students who have successfully
completed Levels 1, 2 and 3, and who now desire to proceed into the
HT certification process and ultimately become Certified Healing Touch
Practitioners. This two-segment practicum (Levels 4 and 5) teaches the
student how to develop and conduct a Healing Touch practice. Thirty
continuing education credits are provided for each of the two levels. A
Certified Healing Touch Practitioner (CHTP) or Instructor (CHTI) is
assigned to each student as a mentor to oversee and guide the student in
meeting the certification requirements. Level 4 and 5 workshops are
conducted in a retreat setting to allow for greater centering and focus
on the intense learning and practice.

Level 4 focuses on the advanced practitioner level of HT, business
concepts, ethics, client/therapist relationships, and ways to integrate
activities into community health care programs. In addition, the student
is monitored by his mentor in the application of healing techniques and
healing disciplines. For certification, the student will be required, within
the next year or two, to conduct and document 100 Healing Touch sessions, to demonstrate a knowledge and understanding of energetic healing
principles and concepts, and to experience and describe several different
healing techniques. In addition the student must document his own self-
development (books read, classes attended, research, and other projects

participated in, etc.), and prepare a detailed case study that documents a client's understanding of the client management process from initial interview through therapeutic addressal of his or her condition, to discharge planning. All documentation will be assembled into a journal for review by peers, instructors, other mentors and, eventually, the certification committee.

Level 5 focuses on the completion of projects begun since the Level 4 workshop, the intervening mentorship experience, integration of HT into community activities, the establishment of a healing practice, and demonstration in the expertise required for all HT healing techniques. Students will be required to describe the professional development of their healing practice, present a professional profile notebook (including a resume), and present and discuss healing practice issues. In addition, they must present a comprehensive case study for peer review and critique, present outcomes/documentation of client sessions, discuss theories of healing, report and review the apprenticeship/mentorship process, and experience ten other alternative healing modalities. Upon satisfactory demonstration and performance of all requirements of Level 5, the student is then recommended to the HT Certification Committee that independently reviews the submitted documentation. At any stage in the Level 5 review process, if the documentation provided is not clear or sufficiently substantive, the student will be asked to correct any deficiencies. Upon acceptance of the documentation by the HT Certification Committee, the student is officially designated as a Certified Healing Touch Practitioner (CHTP).

Instructor Training.   After becoming certified, the HT Practitioner can attend a Level 6 workshop at which the student will be trained in the procedures to conduct Healing Touch workshops as the instructor. The emphasis here is on group dynamics, setting up programs, and principles and methods of teaching and learning. After the workshop, the instructor trainee is then required to assist another fully certified instructor in the conduct of three Level 1 workshops, and then be an associate or assistant instructor in another five Level 1 workshops. The instructor trainee is evaluated during each of these workshops, and upon a satisfactory recommendation from all instructors, the trainee is certified as a Certified Healing Touch Instructor (CHTI) for Level 1 workshops only. A similar process is followed to become qualified to instruct Level 2, 3, 4 and 5 workshops. All instructors of HT workshops are required to first become a Certified HT Instructor by Healing Touch International in order to teach the official program of Healing Touch.

Advanced Energetic Healing Techniques: Upon completion of Level 3, the student is eligible to attend advanced Energetic Healing workshops. This is a five-part series taught by selected senior Certified Healing Touch Instructors. Each workshop provides eight-to-sixteen contact hours and can be taken as one or two day workshops, or in a shorter one-day intensive workshop. Courses are offered by Healing Touch Partnerships, Inc., throughout the United States, Canada, Australia, and New Zealand.

In Part I, "Clearing the Internal Self," the student is taught more comprehensive energy system analysis methods and advanced techniques to facilitate physical, emotional, mental, and spiritual healing.

In Part II, "Identifying and Healing Wounds," the student learns that our lives are limited by physical, emotional, mental, or spiritual wounds that are stored energetically in the layers of our aura as a result of current, recent past, early childhood, and other lifetime experiences. The student learns how to alter the patterns so that we can be returned to who we were fully meant to be.

In Part III, the student learns how beliefs are stored energetically in one's energy field, and that they dramatically influence how we lead our lives. The student learns how to recognize limiting beliefs and how to change and/or release them.

The Part IV workshop teaches one how to change relationships by changing one's energy. It is based on assessing, diagnosing, and adjusting relationships between persons using the knowledge of the seven-chakra system.

In Part V, the student learns that family dynamics shape who we are, who we have become, and who we want to be. This course explores family energy patterns and shows ways to change them in a positive manner.

HT Spiritual Ministry (HTSM). The HT Spiritual Ministry program was established in 1997 and is a continuing multilevel education program that teaches healing from a spiritual perspective. It is designed for nurses in parish and other ministry settings, and for ministers in parish and pastoral ministries; however, it is also made available to the lay community and those who seek to explore a spiritual healing ministry involving the laying-on of hands and other energy-based healing therapies from a Judeo-Christian perspective. HTSM provides a holistic, ecumenical approach to healing on all levels by combining laying on of hands using Healing Touch techniques, prayer, and anointing rituals with essential oils as described in the Bible and other theological texts.

Healing Touch Spiritual Ministry offers an exciting program born of two powerful visions of healing. The first emerges from the ancient Christian tradition of the laying-on of hands and anointing with oils that was modeled by Jesus as a major part of his ministry. Healing continued to flourish as the early church practiced healing, prayer and anointing with oil. The second vision embodies Healing Touch, an energy-based therapeutic approach to health and healing built upon a philosophy of caring. Rooted in the ancient laying-on of hands and modern day energy-based healing, the Healing Touch Spiritual Ministry Program teaches a sacred healing art that flows from the love and compassion we have for one another. When we heal from the heart with touch, we become conduits for the healing energies of our Creator.

There are six workshops offered in HTSM. Prior to instruction in the core Healing Touch techniques described above for Levels 1, 2 and 3, an eight-hour introductory workshop is held before Level 1. This Introduction to Healing Ministry workshop details the history of healing in Christianity with the opportunity to experience the laying-on of hands, and also concentrates on reviewing related scriptures for healing work and the principles and practice of the laying-on of hands. The HT Spiritual Ministry Levels 1, 2 and 3 workshops teach the same healing techniques as taught in the Healing Touch program, but from a Christian perspective. HT Spiritual Ministry Level 1 utilizes a spiritual focus to teach basic intervention methods to help with specific needs. Emphasis is on personal development of those desiring to be ministers of healing. HT Spiritual Ministry Level 2 focuses on heart-centered healing and presents advanced intervention methods to help with specific healing needs. Emphasis is on models of healing within present-day church and models of healing within present-day church and ministry settings, and ways to integrate laying-on of hands, prayer, and anointing with oils into a church/parish healing ministry. Suggested guidelines and policies are also provided for churches wishing to create and/or integrate healing ministry services as an integral part of the overall program for their members. HTSM Level 3 emphasizes working with spiritual guidance in being an instrument of healing. Each HTSM Level 1, 2, and 3 workshop provides fifteen-to-twenty contact hours of training and instruction. There is an additional workshop that precedes HTSM Level 3 called "The Art of Listening to Spiritual Guidance." This is a four-to-six-hour course that introduces the student to awareness of spiritual guidance in healing work that flows from our Divine source. Discernment of spirits and the roles of our angelic helpers and the communion of saints are discussed in relation to spiritual guidance. Meditation exercises strengthen awareness of divine guidance that is available to everyone.

This program has wide appeal for nurses, especially for those in parish and hospice nursing. It is also for both ministers and lay healing practitioners interested in exploring a healing ministry through the laying-on of hands. Those trained in HT Spiritual Ministry principles often provide church-associated healing services and administer to those in need of healing. This includes the sick, shut-ins, to those in nursing homes, hospitals and hospices. Parish nurses, prayer teams, chaplains, ministers, and the lay community have all benefited from these workshops, and are using this work to bring healing compassion into their own work with others.

The workshop contents are tailored as much as possible for compatibility with the teachings of the church denomination to which the workshop is presented, or for the more general needs of other broader target audiences such as hospitals, clinics, nursing staffs, or the general public. Healing Touch Spiritual Ministry workshops are regularly scheduled at various locations throughout the United States. Specific locations, dates, and times are provided on the HTSM website (see Appendix C) and are also published in each edition of the Healing Touch Newsletter.

Healing Touch for Animals (HTA). Veterinarians for both large and small animals are now beginning to adopt energy-based healing techniques in growing numbers. This is due simply to the fact that not only humans, but animals as well, show marked improvement and accelerated healing of wounds with less pain when energetic healing techniques are used. Several Healing Touch techniques have been modified and adapted for use on animals, and other newly developed techniques have been devised to work with both small and large animals.

The HTA Program was developed by Carol Komitor of Highlands Ranch, Colorado. She has a thirteen-year background as a veterinary technician and is also a Certified Healing Touch Practitioner and Instructor, a Certified Massage Therapist, and a Certified Hospital Based Massage Therapist. Her deep love of animals inspired her to adapt many of the Healing Touch techniques for use on specific animals. The first formal Healing Touch For Animals workshop was held in March 1996 with a horse, a dog, a pot-bellied pig, and a small burro as the subjects. The different energy fields of the various animals were experienced and tailored techniques were devised to facilitate each animal's healing process.

Carol's passion for animals brought about development of the Komitor Healing Method (KHM), a teaching method that offers a cooperative model bridging holistic health care techniques with traditional veterinary medicine. HTA workshops including the Komitor Healing Method have been taught throughout the U.S. mainland, Hawaii, Alaska, and Canada. These workshops teach modern scientific concepts pertaining to both the Human Energy Field and the Animal Energy Field, techniques for assessing an animal's energy field, and how to use HT and KHM skills to provide holistic animal health care. The techniques taught in these workshops can bring about accelerated wound healing; rapid recovery from surgery, illness or other traumatic injury; and resolution of behavioral problems and stress-related issues.

Beginning and Advanced training is conducted in a group setting where you can experience hands-on healing work with animals. Periodic Canine and Equine workshops are regularly scheduled for small and large animals, respectively. The Canine Workshop features dogs, and you may bring your own well-behaved, leashed dog. The Equine Workshop offers hands-on experience with horses. Equine participants are taught how to approach and safely work around the large animals, so even if you've never ridden or been around horses, you can comfortably participate. Both workshops also teach techniques for applying HTA,

KHM therapy to any small or large animal, including birds, mammals, reptiles, aquatics and exotics. Several HTA graduates also provide regular consultative services to zoos and have provided spectacular healing and behavioral changes to a wide range of animals from injured antelopes to temperamental zebras.

For further information on HTA, KHM, and workshop schedules see Appendix C.

Healing Touch for Babies (HTB): Healing Touch (HT) has become an effective treatment for all babies for optimum growth, health, and well-being. It is especially useful for those babies who are born prematurely or who are critically ill. Healing Touch for Babies was developed by Rita Kluny, RN, a Certified Holistic Nurse with over thirty years' experience, a Certified Healing Touch Practitioner and Instructor, and the 1994 American Holistic Nurse of the Year. She has selected and integrated several of the thirty or so HT techniques into her critical care nursing in the Neonatal Intensive Care Unit (NICU) of her hospital in Austin, Texas.

The Healing Touch for Babies (HTB) program is based on Rita's experience with both healthy and critically ill babies, and provides specific instruction for the application of energy healing techniques on the newborn energy system, which is noticeably different from that of an adult's. The purpose of HTB is to teach both medical personnel and parents specific techniques of healing that are geared toward "new life." Also included in the workshop instruction and training is information relating to developmental issues pertinent to the infant's healing, especially if the birth was traumatic. Participants also increase their awareness of the sophisticated sensory level of the infant and their rich, yet delicate capacity for healing. HTB workshops are scheduled periodically in various locales throughout the U.S. and are usually conducted in hospital settings. Continuing education credits are available for nurses and Massage Therapists. The long-term goal is to integrate HTB into the traditional hospital model to create an exponential leap into the depth and time factors of infant healing on all levels of their being.

Specific objectives of the HTB Workshops include providing information on the difference between the adult and infant energy fields and hand scanning techniques, and to describe and demonstrate specific intervention techniques used in Healing Touch that are appropriate for infants (Magnetic Passes, Hand Scanning, Magnetic Clearing, Chakra Connection, Ultrasound, Laser, Pain Drain, and others). In addition, neonatal development and consciousness and the impact of intentional communication with infants is stressed. Parental guidance in holistic newborn care is also provided for use by parents at home after the infant is released from the hospital.

An example of the ability of specific HT techniques to bring about remarkable healing in a critically ill premature infant is presented in an article by Ms. Kluny that was published in the Exceptional Healing Experience Journal.[8] Gina (not her real name) was two days old when she was admitted to the NICU. She was born at thirty-six weeks' gestation, weighed only 4 pounds, 1 ounce and had Down's syndrome and transposition of the arteries leading from her heart. Following a cardiac catheterization, she developed a clot in her right femoral artery, and soon developed gangrene in her right foot. While doctors were concerned about the possibilities of amputation, Kluny quietly performed Healing Touch; within two days Gina began a remarkable turnaround, recovered enough to permit surgeons to repair her heart by performing an arterial switch, recovered quickly from the surgery, and began gaining weight. Ultimately, she lost only the tips of her big toe and second toe instead of the whole leg, and was able to be discharged and go home within a few weeks.

Many nurses throughout the U.S. are now using Healing Touch for Babies in their own NICUs. Energy healing for infants is often dramatically effective in the treatment of respiratory distress, in calming the baby after a stressful procedure, and in the recovery from surgical procedures and infections. It has also been noted that low birth weight babies who have received energetic interventions have gained weight quickly and uneventfully, against the odds of multiple complications that often plague premature infants.

The National Institutes of Health granted funds for a two-year research project that was begun in 2002 to study the efficacy of HT as a relaxation technique to calm critically ill infants in the NICU. Dr. Sharon McDonough Means heads this study at the University of Arizona Medical Center in Tucson, Arizona, and Rita Kluny has been on the advisory board of this project from the outset. Contact information for further details about the Healing Touch for Babies program is provided in Appendix C.

Healing Touch for Caregivers (HTC). Healing Touch for Caregivers is an introductory program that teaches several basic Healing Touch techniques that can be easily learned and used by nearly anyone. Those who have received HTC training range from professional Registered and Licensed Practical Nurses in acute care facilities (hospitals) to mothers and fathers for care of their children or other family members at home. HTC is an exceptionally convenient way to become familiar with the effectiveness of several easy-to-learn and easy-to-use energy techniques that are practical and useful in an extremely wide range of situations from hospital operating rooms to everyday cuts and bruises.

HTC is the result of a year-long pilot program to determine the effectiveness of several nondrug therapy techniques when used to address the four primary day-to-day concerns of residents in a long-term care facility or nursing home:

1. Acute and traumatic pain management;

2. Relief of anxiety and stress, particularly in elderly residents with Alzheimer's disease;

3. Acceleration of postoperative healing and recuperation for residents in Medicare rooms and transitional care units; and

4. Supportive and compassionate end of life care.

The primary differences between HTC and the formal Healing Touch workshops are that the HTC training is normally conducted locally in the HTC teacher's or students' facility instead of at a formally sanctioned HT workshop, only nine basic healing techniques of the thirty or so in the full Healing Touch program are taught, and HTC training can be conducted by anyone who has received formal Healing Touch training through Level 4. In addition, HTC training is open to everyone since no medical background is required to understand and learn these healing techniques. During the pilot program, training in the HTC techniques was provided not only to Registered and Licensed Practical Nurses, but also to the nurses' assistants, the administrative staff, social workers, and even to spouses of the facility's employees. Healing Touch for Caregivers can truly be considered a "Life Skill" such as first aid training.

The nine Healing Touch techniques are taught in three sequential training sessions normally spaced a week apart. The first Level I training session provides three very effective Pain Management techniques, two of which you can use on yourself; the third technique must be provided to someone else. These three techniques are very effective for quickly reducing or eliminating pain from minor traumatic injuries such as bumping your shin or hitting your thumb with a hammer, and also for severe, chronic pain associated with serious diseases such as cancer.

Level II provides three additional HT techniques that are very effective for reducing stress and anxiety. One technique is excellent for headaches due to stress and tension, another has consistently reduced the anxiety and stress in elderly Alzheimer's patients, and the third technique is for reducing your own stress and anxiety after a long harrowing day, for balancing your chakra system, and for returning yourself to a state of inner calmness.

Level III training provides exercises to develop your sensitivity to energy fields and chakras. The ability to sense energy is used in three advanced techniques that allow you to:

1. Clear energetic congestion in the chest and lungs due to smoking, environmental pollutants, surgical anesthesia, and chronic diseases such as asthma and emphysema;

2. Significantly accelerate the healing of traumatic injuries such as surgical procedures or broken bones. Broken bones usually heal completely in half to two-thirds of the expected time, and surgical patients recover quicker with less pain and less scarring after receiving Healing Touch; and

3. Induce a feeling of profound peace and relaxation where healing on many levels can occur. This technique is very useful for quieting a patient's anxiety just before surgery and also for allowing those who are nearing the end of their lifetime to prepare more calmly for that event in peace, serenity, and dignity.

The exceptional flexibility of the nine selected Healing Touch techniques to address a wide range of patient symptoms, conditions and diseases makes it a very practical and useful tool that can be used in nearly any acute or recuperative care facility such as hospitals and transitional care units, long-term care facilities such as nursing homes, or even at home when you burn yourself on a hot pan in the kitchen. None of the Healing Touch techniques involve drugs of any kind and are totally non-invasive. This means that no doctor's order is required for anyone who is properly trained to immediately administer them to anyone in need. These energy healing techniques can do no harm, can significantly and quickly improve the patient's well-being and quality of life, and can be provided immediately at no cost. Healing Touch for Caregivers provides a great ray of hope and healing to brighten the landscape of health care in America, or wherever in the world it is practiced.

For additional information on Healing Touch for Caregivers, visit the author's website at www.localaccess.com/healinghands and click on the link for "HT for Caregivers."

Healing Touch Newsletter. A sixteen-page newsletter is prepared and distributed to HT practitioners five times each year. It contains much timely information concerning HT administration, research program progress reports, HT news from Australia, New Zealand, Canada, and other countries, and a comprehensive listing of HT, HTSM, HTA and HTB workshops scheduled by location and workshop level. As the official news dissemination vehicle for the HT movement, it also provides timely updates on the evolving HT educational program, as well as announcing the most recent class of Certified Healing Touch Practitioners and Instructors. For further information concerning Healing Touch and its related programs, see Appendix C.

Color and Sound Therapy

Color and Sound Therapy uses specific colors and sounds to deeply cleanse and balance the energetic vibrations within each of the seven major chakras. When the chakras are cleansed and balanced, they are best able to assimilate from the Universal Energy Field those specific energetic vibrations (frequencies) that the body needs for its maintenance, repair and healthy functioning. If one or more chakras is "not balanced" (energetically distorted so that it cannot efficiently bring in the energies), then the organs and glands associated with that chakra receive less energy than they need for healthy functioning.

Since ancient times sound has been used as a healing and a creative force. According to the ancient mystics, sound is the most powerful force in the universe. Sound healing was practiced in all of the ancient mystery schools such as Egypt, Greece, India, and Tibet. It is sound that creates form. When we learn to direct healing sound into the body, health and harmony are restored. The most effective way to provide the healing energy of sound is to direct it into each chakra to restore its balance and correct rotational vibration. In that way, the organs and tissues associated with each chakra are provided with the full measure of energy they require from the Universal Energy Field.

Of the many techniques to rebalance the chakras, Color and Sound Therapy is one of the most effective and deeply acting energetic therapies available. Often just a single one-hour session will cause significant energetic shifts within the body that can be deeply felt by the client.

The elements of color used during the session include guided visualization by the therapist, aided by olfactory cues provided by specially prepared pomanders (fragrant and aromatic essences prepared from natural plant and mineral sources), which accentuate and reinforce the sense of color being visualized by the client.

The elements of sound used during the session include the use of a separate tuning fork to rebalance each chakra, a soothing and protective sacred mantra provided as a musical background, resonant toning of sacred vowel sounds by the therapist's voice directly into each chakra, and the use of Tibetan singing bowls. The combination of all these sound and color elements provides a very moving experience for the client during the session. However, the real benefit usually continues well after the session, with the client usually feeling a positive difference in the way he or she feels for several days.

There are many different formats and procedures for conducting a healing session with color and sound. The format described here is a summary of that taught at Delphi University.

COLOR AND SOUND PRINCIPLES

Sound.   There are seven principles that characterize sound and that ultimately determine the effect that sound has on the human body and its energy systems. These are the Principles of Pitch or Frequency, Resonance, Rhythm, Melody, Harmony, Timbre, and Toning, and are discussed below.

Pitch or Frequency.   When healthy and balanced, each of the seven major human chakras spins or rotates at a constant and predetermined frequency or vibration. The Root Chakra has a normal resonant frequency of 256 cycles per second, or 256 Hz—Middle C on the piano. The next higher chakra, the Sacral Chakra, resonates at 288 Hz, which is the note D. And, as shown in the table below, each higher chakra in the physical body has a successively higher note on the scale, up to the note B. These seven tones or notes are called "Octave 0" in Table IV, below. Each time you go up one complete octave (e.g., from Middle C, 256 Hz, to the next higher C on the scale, 512 Hz), note that the frequency of vibration exactly doubles. This is a very important characteristic which will be discussed below in the Principle of Resonance.

Note also that, just as the piano has many octaves above this Octave 0, so does the energetic vehicle called our Human Energy Field. Humans have at least six octaves associated with their aura, but only the lower octave 0 is associated with their physical body. The higher octaves establish a person's energetic connection to higher dimensions, but yet within the person's local environment (Octave 1), their connection to Mother Earth in a global sense (Octave 2), to this solar system and in particular to the Sun, the immediate source of all the "physical" energies to support life on this world (Octave 3), to our local galaxy, the Milky Way (Octave 4), and to the life-supporting energies throughout the entire Universe (Octave 5). However, when working with Healing With Color and Sound, we will be concentrating on Octave 0, the octave associated with the physical body and its major energy chakras.

If a chakra is slightly "out of tune" and not vibrating in a healthy, harmonious manner, it can be "retuned" through a process of sympathetic vibration. This is the basic concept of this healing technique. Harmonious vibrations of the correct frequency are provided directly into the rotating field of the chakra by using the proper tuning fork. This has the effect of bringing that chakra's vibrational pattern back to its proper frequency so that it can function more efficiently as a transducer of the energies from the Universal Energy Field required by that chakra's associated organs and glands.

Resonance.   When a chakra resonates with a particular vibration or frequency, it takes in and absorbs energy of that frequency. There is a transfer of energy that takes place from the source of the vibrating

Octave	Note	Freq. (Hz)	Color	Tone	Chakra
5	C	8,192.0			Universal
4	C	4,096.0			Galactic
3	C	2,048.0			Solar
2	C	1,024.0			Global
1	C	512.0	White	Om	Ascension
0	B	439.0	Violet	Eee	Crown
0	A	426.7	Indigo	Ay	Brow
0	G	384.0	Blue	Eye	Throat
0	F	341.3	Green	Ah	Heart
0	E	320.0	Yellow	Oh	Solar Plexus
0	D	288.0	Orange	Ooo	Sacral
0	C	256.0	Red	Uh	Root

Table IV: Color and Sound Relationships

sound energy (instrument, tuning fork, voice, etc.) to the chakra itself. This transfer takes place through the phenomenon known as Sympathetic Resonance.

Sympathetic Resonance can best be illustrated by observing two identically tuned stringed instruments (violin, harp, etc.) that are placed near each other. If any string on the first instrument is plucked, the vibrations of that string are felt by the same string on the second instrument, and it also begins to absorb the sound energy of that specific frequency and will also vibrate at that frequency.

This principle of Sympathetic Resonance is used in Healing with Color and Sound to fill each chakra with sound vibrations of the proper frequency for that chakra. Both the human voice and the appropriately tuned tuning fork are used to introduce sound of the proper frequency into the chakra. By introducing the proper frequency, the vibratory rate of the chakra itself comes into balance and harmony at its proper frequency.

An additional characteristic of Sympathetic Resonance is that strings tuned to exactly one or more octaves above the vibrating string will also begin to vibrate. For example, if one violin has a string tuned to Middle C (256 Hz) and a second nearby violin has a string tuned to one octave above Middle C (High C, 512 Hz), when the Middle C string is plucked on the first violin, the High C string on the second violin will also vibrate. Thus working with tonal vibrations in one octave can also produce vibrations in higher octaves.

This principle is used in Healing with Color and Sound to create overtones that can affect the higher energy bodies of the Human Energy Field. The subtle energy bodies (Etheric, Emotional, Mental, and Spiritual Bodies) can be thought of as "octaves" above the Physical Body. Thus, when we work with the chakras on the physical level, the overtones produced have the same effect, through sympathetic resonance, on the vibrating energy patterns of the chakras in the higher energy bodies. This brings about a deep feeling of healing, serenity, peace, and connection within and among the many energetic levels of the client.

Rhythm. The Pulse of Life is subliminally recognized when a steadily repetitive sound is heard. This accounts for the popularity of drumming circles. The hard, resonant sound of drums repeated continuously for several minutes has the effect of lulling the conscious mind into an altered state. The cadence or rhythm of sound also has a definite effect on the human body. A very slow rhythm has a quieting or subduing effect, whereas a fast rhythm gives the feeling of action and movement.

Melody. Melodies and memories are often intertwined or connected somehow, and often a certain melody will trigger a specific memory. Some melodies make you feel light and bouncy, others make you feel heavy and depressed. Often the melody and tempo ("speed" of the melody) combine in some musical pieces to promote a general feeling of comfort and well-being. This can, in turn, stimulate the release of endorphins by the brain, which will ease emotional and mental stress and reduce tension and pain, especially if the melody triggers a very pleasant memory. Just humming a simple melody is one of the most therapeutic exercises we can perform. It restores balance and helps to cleanse us of negative energy debris.

Harmony. Harmony is the combination of two or more tones in a chord. When the combination has a pleasing sound, it affects both the physical body and its subtle energies in a positive, helpful, healing way, and allows the physical body to align itself with the higher spiritual vibrations. Harmony enables us to transmute major conditions of the body and alter states of consciousness. By finding the right combination of tones and rhythms and their harmonies, we can trigger a dynamic resonance that corrects and eliminates great imbalances.

Timbre. When different musical instruments play the same note on the scale (e.g., 512 Hz, C above Middle C on the piano), the characteristic of timbre makes each one sound distinctive enough to be separately recognized. A flute, a trumpet, a French horn, a soprano saxophone, an accordion, and an oboe can all play the same note, yet each will sound different from the others. One may sound tinny, one soft, one mellow, one harsh, one reedy, one brassy, etc. Each of these interpretations about how that note sounds also affects how we feel about that particular note. We react in predictable ways to differing timbres of the same note or tone.

Toning. As we grow and develop, we learn to respond to the sound of the human voice. And we respond to the sound of a human voice in a different way than we respond to the sound of a musical instrument. The human voice has a presence and a tonality that separates it from all other sounds we hear. It is more personal, more immediate, and commands our entire attention. Because of these factors, when we hear the human voice, we respond on a more emotional level, a more feeling level than when we hear musical tones, even though those musical tones may be mellow and harmonious. Toning with the human voice restores the vibrational pattern of both the physical and subtle energy bodies so that our spiritual essence can manifest more fully within the physical environment.

Vowel Sounds

Also associated with each chakra is a specific sacred vowel sound. During a Color and Sound Therapy session, the sacred vowel sound for each individual chakra is toned or chanted directly into the chakra vortex. This is very effective in restoring the original, natural, and healthy vibrational patterns of both the physical and subtle energy bodies so that our spiritual essence can manifest more fully within the physical environment. In Healing with Color and Sound sessions, these vowel sounds are:

Root Chakra	UH
Sacral Chakra	OOO
Solar Plexus	OH
Heart Chakra	AH
Throat Chakra	EYE
Brow Chakra	AY
Crown Chakra	EEE

Sacred Mantras

By combining sacred names within a musical mantra, the Color and Sound therapist can more directly tap into the power of the Divine. In the inspired work, "The Keys of Enoch," J. J. Hurtak informs us that the mantra "Kodoish, Kodoish, Kodoish, Adonai 'Tsebayoth" (Hebrew for "Holy, holy, holy is the Lord God of Hosts") is the measure of the cycle and the beat of all states of matter and most of all—resonance, which is the common factor uniting the lower vibratory levels with the higher levels of creation. Even the human heartbeat with its biological clocks is set according to the function of "Kodoish, Kodoish, Kodoish, Adonai 'Tsebayoth." It ties together all biorhythms of the body with the spiritual rhythms of the Overself body, so that all circulatory systems operate with one cosmic heartbeat.

In addition, this mantra enables the body vehicle to experience the direct energy of the Masters of Light serving God. It is the central vibration coordinating all other vibrations with the spiritual vehicle of man, and is the highest expression of teamwork in the heavens and the earth. This Kodoish mantra is sung as a hymn in the form of background music during all Color and Sound healing sessions, and provides an energetic environment of protection and very deep healing.

COLOR

Associated with each of the seven major chakras is one of the seven colors of the rainbow. The Root Chakra responds to Red, the Sacral Chakra to Orange, the Solar Plexus Chakra to Yellow, the Heart Chakra to Green (and sometimes Pink), the Throat Chakra to Blue, the Brow Chakra to Indigo, and the Crown Chakra to Violet. When the therapist channels or sends light vibrations of the appropriate color into a specific chakra, that chakra begins to respond to its resonant color and becomes more open, balanced, and in tune with its original natural frequency of health and well-being.

For instance, when the practitioner is working on the Sacral Chakra, the orange pomander is used. Two or three squirts of this essence are sprayed onto the therapist's hands, which are then rubbed to activate the aromatic essence. The therapist will then slowly wave his hands in front of the client's face. As the client breathes in this essence of real oranges, the very clear memory of "Orange" is evoked to further reinforce his or her visualization of the color.

WHAT TO EXPECT

The Color and Sound Healing sessions are conducted with the client resting comfortably on a healing table with the eyes closed. You will be asked to remove your shoes prior to lying down on the healing table. The client is encouraged to remain aware of the guiding instructions by the therapist, to the sounds and vibrations provided during the session, and to the feeling or effect in the body and the mind caused by the combination of color and sound.

The energetic state of the client's chakras on the etheric, emotional, and mental levels is assessed both prior to and after the healing session to determine the extent to which that healing session has produced detectable changes to the chakra pattern of these energy body levels. While each of your chakras is being assessed with both a hand scan and with a pendulum, you may rest comfortably on the healing table and enjoy the relaxing music in the background.

When the healing session begins, a Tibetan singing bowl will be sounded, and the therapist will begin attuning and opening himself. Each session usually begins with a short invocation for the energies of healing and balance, and is then followed by playing the Kodoish mantra to further set the mood and tone for the session. This musical mantra, repeated throughout the entire Color and Sound Therapy session as background music, creates an energy environment of sacred protectiveness in which the client may completely and safely release all limiting thoughts, anxieties, and worries and open themselves to the healing energies being offered by the therapist.

The therapist will then establish an energetic connection between himself and the client at the client's head and feet. During the session, it is not necessary to touch any other part of the client's body. Since you will be relaxing with your eyes closed, the therapist will guide you to visualize each color in turn and see it entering into the chakra being addressed. These Color Elements are aided by olfactory cues provided by the specially prepared pomanders that accentuate and reinforce the sense of color being visualized by the client.

In addition to the use of color and the sound of the human voice, the chakras are further balanced and brought into harmony with their natural vibrational frequencies through the use of tuning forks and chanting of the sacred vowel sound associated with each chakra. The tuning fork that exactly resonates with each chakra's natural frequency is placed directly into the chakra (but several inches above the body), and is then moved in a specific pattern to help bring a distorted or "out of tune" chakra back into its natural vibrational pitch through the principle of harmonic resonance. This is repeated for each of the client's etheric, emotional, and mental energy bodies. The sacred vowel sound is also chanted directly into each chakra at the frequency of the tuning fork for that chakra.

When all chakras have been cleansed and balanced, the client's general energy field is further balanced and smoothed. To conclude the healing session, a Tibetan bowl will be "sung" near each ear to bring the right and left brain centers into balance and harmony. This brings the male-female aspects and the logical-intuitive abilities of the client into a balanced partnership.

After the healing session is concluded, each chakra is energetically reassessed with both a hand scan and a pendulum to determine the energetic changes that have been made to the etheric, emotional, and mental levels during the session. And, as always, the client is encouraged to discuss any sensations felt or insights received during each healing session.

For further information on Color and Sound Therapy, websites and other resources are listed in Appendix C.

Spiritual Surgery (Advanced Healing Touch)

Several Advanced Healing Touch techniques have the goal of repatterning the Etheric Body to a vibrational state of greater health; one of these advanced interventions is called Spiritual Surgery. During this technique, the practitioner is much less conscious of making any specific hand movements to repattern the energy field, and instead simply opens himself to be an instrument of healing from the higher dimensions.

During Spiritual Surgery, the healer begins to actually experience the healing energies and forces working through him. Additionally, the healer begins to sense more of a personalization of the healing energies flowing through him. These energies are no longer strictly universal from some unseen source; instead, they now become to be recognized as the energies of specific higher-dimensional beings and spiritual surgeons who are working through him for the highest good of the client.

It is nearly impossible to describe beforehand what will be "felt" by the healer during such a healing session, simply because the healer is not in charge of who will be working through him and how that work will be performed. Instead, he must be open and available to the healing process for which he is but an instrument, a link between the higher dimensions and our physical world. It may also be difficult for the reader to understand what is happening during such a healing session without a personal framework or background in which to give the experience direct meaning. As I recount my experience during such a session in the paragraphs below, the reader may believe me or not believe me; however, it is only after one actually conducts such a session and experiences these sensations for himself that he will be able to know the truth of what has happened.

Each healing session is unique. What is experienced by the healer and the client is simply what is needed by the client. But it is also influenced by the client's willingness to be healed, and what the client's Higher Self is ready to accept from other sources as being in their highest and best good at that time. Nevertheless, let me describe a series of three healing sessions I conducted for a client. These sessions focused on repair of the Etheric Body, and rapid, positive results were shown in the physical body.

Nancy (not her real name) was a thirty-three-year-old woman who had been diagnosed by her physician with severe endometriosis seven years earlier. During my initial interview with her, she related that each period was very heavy and painful, and was also preceded by extremely painful premenstrual cramps that nearly debilitated her to the point where she could not function adequately at work. She came to me initially for Reiki sessions to help reduce the pain and help her heal. During the first Reiki session, which was about a week after the end of her period, I was guided to suggest to her that subsequent sessions include Healing Touch procedures instead of Reiki. After explaining what Healing Touch was, and what technique I would use (Spiritual Surgery), she agreed. Two Healing Touch sessions using Spiritual Surgery were conducted, two and five days respectively after the initial Reiki session.

The Spiritual Surgery technique is one where, after proper energetic preparation of the client, the healer's hands are placed on the client's body wherever he is intuitively guided to place them. In Nancy's case, my right hand was drawn to her Sacral Chakra, and my left hand to her Solar Plexus Chakra. As I continued to open my heart and send unconditional love to Nancy, I focused my intention on being an open channel of healing for her, and soon I felt my hands slip straight down into her abdomen. Actually, it was only my etheric hands that I felt slip into her abdomen, but the sensation was real, and it felt like my physical hands had gone into her body. In addition, I was unable to move or remove my physical hands from their positions on her body for several minutes. But since I had been trained to expect this, it seemed perfectly natural to me, and I knew this to be but the first step of a miraculous healing process that was about to take place.

During the first Healing Touch session, my hands were literally glued to Nancy's abdomen for about fifteen minutes. Once there, I initially had no sensation or feeling in my hands at all. Near the end of the session, I began to feel several sensations in my hands, and both clairaudiently and clairvoyantly was able to sense what was happening on Nancy's higher energy levels. I had a distinct impression of continuous, soft, angelic music in the background, and in the foreground I "heard" and "saw" a medical operation being performed inside her abdomen with several instruments including scalpels, hemostats, and needle and thread. Although I observed the motion of several pairs of hands working very quickly and precisely, and saw and heard the instruments used, I did not get a clear sense of exactly what was being worked on. Nevertheless, I soon "heard" a voice say very clearly, "OK. That's all for today!" Almost immediately, I felt my etheric hands withdraw from Nancy's abdomen, and my hands and arms had a distinct change in the way they felt as the spiritual surgeons withdrew. I was then able to remove my physical hands from her body and continue closing the session.

During the second Spiritual Surgery session three days later, my hands were again drawn to the Sacral and Solar Plexus Chakras, and I felt my etheric hands again drop down inside her abdomen and just rest there. As before, I was unable to move my hands from her body for several minutes. And although I continued to hear the angelic music in the background, this time I did not see an operation being performed. However, soon I clairvoyantly saw a curious, instant "video clip." A man in white coveralls with straps over his shoulders and a little white plasterer's cap was on a ladder and was using a trowel to patch up some holes in the sheetrock he was working on. He was whistling a happy little tune as he worked away filling in all the big and little holes and cracks. Soon he climbed down the ladder, picked it up, and as he walked off, he tipped his cap at me and said, "OK. We're through now! Have a good day!"

At the same time, I also had a "knowing" that this instant little video clip was telling me that the holes and cracks in Nancy's uterus, which had allowed the endometrium cells to enter her abdominal cavity and cause so much pain, were now all "patched up." Several weeks later, Nancy called me joyously to say that for the first time in seven years, she had not had any premenstrual cramps, and had just completed a normal, painless period.

What had actually occurred during the Healing Touch sessions was a repatterning of her Etheric Body blueprint to its original and natural state of health. This healthy vibrational pattern in her Etheric Body in turn caused the corresponding changes to become manifest in her physical body, and she proceeded through a normal menstrual cycle with no pain. The "operation" that I clairvoyantly saw was the metaphor for the changes taking place in her Etheric Body.

Although I suggested a follow-up combination of Ro-Hun and Regression Therapy sessions to investigate and release the original cause of the endometriosis, Nancy was not emotionally ready to address the issues that might arise, and she elected to terminate her healing process at this point. It is not known whether her healing was permanent. Still, the knowledge that her symptoms had at one point been successfully addressed sent a powerful message confirming the effectiveness of these energy-healing techniques. Additionally, even though Nancy had terminated her healing process prior to receiving maximum benefit, the seeds of awareness of how to complete the process had been planted, and these seeds will grow when she is ready to proceed.

Reflective Healing

The purpose of Reflective Healing is to replace the vibrational pattern of a diseased organ or tissue in the etheric body with the pattern of a normal, healthy, and perfectly functioning organ. This healthy pattern will ultimately be reflected into the physical body and replace the diseased organ or tissue. Reflective Healing is an advanced healing technique that requires significant training and development on the part of the healer. In particular, highly developed intuitive abilities and the ability to precisely sense and recognize energy fields are necessary.

Reflective Healing is taught by Marshall Smith, codirector of Delphi University in McCaysville, Georgia. He has developed this remarkable healing process through his study and application of Spiritual Anatomy, and his extensive background and knowledge of metaphysical healing techniques gained from historical writings, more current research, and inspired guidance. This technique directly addresses the etheric body in a combination of guided imagery techniques and energy body manipulations.

Marshall Smith is an accomplished teacher, author, and speaker, and has done extensive biblical and comparative religion studies. He has also held a pastoral position in a nondenominational Christian church. His work in harmonizing spiritual studies with transpersonal and alternative medical therapies has resulted in a unique blend of left brain analysis and right brain intuitive abilities.

Marshall is a retired vice president and Corporate Officer of the Kimberly-Clark Corporation. He received a Bachelor of Science Degree in Electrical Engineering from the University of South Carolina, and has a doctorate in Alternative Medical Therapies, Intuitive and Spiritual Sciences, and Transpersonal Psychology.

In his studies of Spiritual Anatomy, Marshall has identified four distinct layers within the etheric body; each with a specific function and purpose. The four layers are the outer Reflective Layer of the etheric body, the Light-Sensate Layer, the Life Layer, and the Chemical Layer. The Light-Sensate and Life Layers are between the outer Reflective Layer and the surface of the skin. The skin is, in fact, the Chemical Layer of the etheric body. Knowledge of these layers and their functions is combined with a guided imagery process that directly involves both therapist and client to produce changes in the client's etheric and physical energy bodies.

The guided imagery facet of this healing technique involves bringing forth the two necessary ingredients to cause physical manifestation: the thought or idea of what it is we want to create, and the deep desire and passion to bring that idea into reality. It also forces the healer to be very specific in the way the client's anatomy is addressed. The healer cannot rely on general, universal healing energies such as those provided during a Reiki session. Here, a detailed knowledge of anatomy and, in particular, the organ or system the client wants addressed, must be available to the healer so that the healing process within the client can be properly visualized and guided.

Both thought and energy-passion are absolutely necessary for anything to be created or changed in the physical. Without the thought, there is no direction or goal for what is to be created. Without the passion, we might know what we want to create, but have no desire or conviction that it would or could happen. But when the two are combined, the creative energies of the universe are brought into play and the thought quickly becomes reality. Such is the power of creative thought, and it can be used for either good or harm. In Reflective Healing, we use our energies creatively for the assistance of the client; our intentions must be pure and our hearts must be open with universal love for the client. The Reflective Healing therapist must also be able to sense and selectively repattern each of the four separate layers of the etheric body.

REFLECTIVE HEALING SESSIONS

When Reflective Healing is indicated, each session proceeds in the exact sequence discussed below. However, the specific procedures used while repatterning the etheric body will be determined by the client's needs and the organ or system being addressed during the session. Normally, a series of three Reflective Healing sessions are scheduled on each of three successive days. Each healing session is conducted with the client relaxing on a healing table, and may last from about twenty minutes to over an hour, depending on the extent and complexity of the healing required.

Relaxation of Client. After the client interview, the client is asked to remove his shoes and lie down on the healing table. The healer then talks the client through a relaxation exercise that starts at the feet and ends at the top of the head. A number of different guided exercises are available to progressively relax the client. One such exercise is to imagine a golden ball of relaxing light entering and relaxing the feet, ankles, calves, knees, etc. under the guided direction of the healer until the client's entire body is peacefully relaxing on the table.

Healer Preparation. When the client is in a relaxed state, the healer begins by moving to the client's side with his hands in an upturned position. The healer silently asks for Universal Healing Energy to come into his hands, and for the assistance of the higher dimensions as appropriate. When this energy is felt in the hands, he begins a specific breathing exercise to raise his own energy to the highest possible level. His energy field is then expanded to totally enclose the client on the table as well as himself.

Energize Brain Centers. Using a series of specific hand positions and motions on the client's head, healing energy is moved into the medulla and brain ventricles. This energizes and activates several energy centers within the brain, including the pineal and pituitary glands of the endocrine system. These centers are sometimes called the spiritual centers, and are directly associated with the crown and brow chakras, respectively.

Scan and Repair Etheric Body. The next step is to expand the volume of the client's etheric body so that its four separate layers can be individually discerned and sensed with the hand or fingers. Through intention and a specific breathing process directed at one of the client's major chakras, the client's etheric body is expanded from about an inch to about a foot or so above and around the client's physical body. This expanded etheric body is then scanned with a sensitive hand to locate any energy holes, tears, or leaks. These are areas where energy is literally pouring out of the client's energy field, and can result in pain, distress, or an overall feeling of "no energy."

These areas may be felt by various sensations in the healer's hands or fingertips; one common sensation is that of air escaping from a hole in a bicycle tube. Others include scratchiness, vibration, or a sense of hot or cold. When any disturbance in the pattern of the etheric body is detected, it is immediately repaired by placing the healer's hand directly on the client's body over the disturbance, or by placing the client's hand on the disturbance and then the healer's hand on the client's hand. Such healing techniques are also taught in Healing Touch, "Sealing a Wound."

Repattern Etheric Body.   After all holes, leaks or tears have been repaired in the client's etheric body, the real work of Reflective Healing can be initiated. Using the knowledge of the function of each of the four layers of the client's etheric body (Reflective, Light-Sensate, Life, and Chemical), the healer and client enter into an interactive dialogue to visualize the perfect organ that will replace the diseased one, energetically bring it to life, and introduce it into the etheric vibrational pattern of the client. A combination of guided imagery, visualization, and specific breathing techniques are used to bring about this replacement of the organ's pattern in the etheric body. When this has been accomplished, the diseased organ in the physical body begins to realign itself with the perfect, healthy etheric blueprint. As mentioned above, this entire process is repeated on two successive days for a total of three sessions.

Ground Client.   After the client's etheric repatterning has been completed, his overall energy field is then balanced. The client is then grounded and requested to slowly come back to full conscious awareness in a few minutes. When the client is ready, he is helped to an upright position so he can sit on the edge of the table and receive a glass of water. This helps the grounding process.

For further information on the Reflective Healing process or inquiries regarding training in Reflective Healing, see Appendix C.

Chapter Three

Healing the Emotional and Mental Energy Bodies

The thoughts that one creates generate patterns at the mind level of nature. So we see that illness, in fact, eventually becomes manifest from the altered mind patterns through the ratchet effect— first, to effects at the etheric level and then, ultimately at the physical level [where] we see it openly as disease.

—William Tiller, quoted by
Michael Talbot in
The Holographic Universe

IN EARLIER CHAPTERS, WE HAVE seen that our physical health is significantly influenced by our emotional reactions to the thoughts we think and the belief systems to which we subscribe. If we hold positive, uplifting thoughts as healthy vibrational patterns in our Mental Body, the Mental Body will then affect the Emotional Body in a constructive manner, and we "feel good" about ourselves and radiate positive, charismatic qualities in the energy of our aura. However, if we have limiting or negative beliefs or perceptions about ourselves, the vibrational pattern of our Mental Body causes a corresponding negative reaction in our Emotional Body, and we feel limited, helpless, fearful, cynical, unworthy, etc.

Since the Mental and Emotional Energy Fields are so closely intertwined, this chapter will deal primarily with Ro-Hun, a remarkable new healing method that specifically addresses both the Mental and Emotional Bodies within our auric field. Ro-Hun looks for limiting or faulty thoughts in our Mental Body as the source cause of our negative emotional reactions and feelings. However, to highlight the strengths of Ro-Hun without a comparison to more conventional approaches for dealing with emotional problems would be telling only part of the story. Therefore, a brief discussion of the more traditional approaches for dealing with emotional issues is provided to contrast with the depth and breadth of Ro-Hun. Ro-Hun clearly goes beyond these other therapies and is much more effective in releasing the source cause of negative thoughts about self and emotional blocks held in the Mental and Emotional Energy Bodies, respectively.

Traditional Therapies

Two broad categories of traditional methods for dealing with emotional issues and mental belief systems are examined: counseling and hypnotherapy (including Regression Therapy). The capabilities and limitations of each approach are then used to formulate the requirements for the "ideal" emotional therapy.

COUNSELING

The process of counseling to recognize, deal with, and release emotional issues can be effective when the issues being dealt with are easily recognizable and manageable. In counseling, whether conducted by a social worker or a psychiatrist, the client is usually awake and alert, as opposed to being placed into an altered state. Therefore, the therapy is conducted at a mental level. The client is urged to talk about his or her own problems so that the counselor can understand the problem, identify "abnormal" behavior patterns, and recommend a potential solution.

However, there are three things in this scenario that limit the effectiveness of counseling for removal of deep emotional issues. First, the client can tell the counselor only that of which he or she is consciously aware. Second, the client will tell the counselor only what the client wants to talk about. And third, the recommended solution usually comes from the perspective of the counselor, not the client. The ability to understand the surface symptoms of an emotional issue does not necessarily mean that they can be dealt with effectively through simple logic and knowledge. Further, many sessions over a period of months or years may be required for "... psychoanalytic methods of treatment, which are often slow because they fail to engage experientially and remain at an intellectual and interpretive level only."[1]

Occasionally, improper behavior may be a manifestation of some suppressed traumatic experience, and the client may not consciously be aware of the root cause of his or her behavior. On a purely mental or logical level, counseling and talk therapy in general just simply cannot uncover the reason for this behavior. "Only a remembered trauma can be let go of."[2] Therefore, for deep emotional issues and problems, counseling usually provides little or no reason for changes in behavior.

HYPNOTHERAPY

Hypnotherapy is a form of psychotherapy that directly or indirectly induces an altered state in order to gain access to the subconscious mind in order to alleviate subconscious conflicts and buried traumas. It is generally a very effective technique for reprogramming the subconscious mind to break old habits and substitute new ones. Smoking cessation, weight release, removing anxiety, and building self-confidence are typical applications that usually result in positive changes in the client's behavior. If prescribed by a medical doctor, hypnotherapy may also be used effectively to treat some medical conditions such as asthma, allergies, constipation, hemorrhoids, and others.

Hypnotherapy is also very useful in dealing with some emotional problems because when the client is in an altered state, the experienced hypnotherapist can gain access to the client's subconscious memories. Memories of a traumatic experience may be too terrible to be dealt with and comprehended by the conscious mind, so they are suppressed below the threshold of consciousness. By gently guiding the client, the hypnotherapist may gain access to such memories and bring them up safely to be recognized by the conscious mind.

Hypnotherapy is a very effective tool in uncovering suppressed memories, emotions, and feelings; however, the client may only be required to understand and "forgive" the situation on only a Mental level. But the deep pain and hurt, the emotional reaction of the experience, may still be affecting the client's Emotional Energy Body. The client understands what happened, but it still affects the way he or she feels about what happened. Complete release of the underlying emotional issue can occur only when the client's energetic connection to that experience has been completely severed. Only then will that experience cease to affect his or her life on either a Mental or Emotional level.

REGRESSION THERAPY

Regression Therapy is a subspecialty within the umbrella of hypnotherapeutic techniques. In regression therapy, the client's awareness or consciousness is directed back to a point in time to fully understand the details of a previous experience. The distinct difference from traditional hypnotherapy is that we may now investigate not only repressed memories from childhood, but also experiences prior to the client's birth. Controversial as this may seem to some, there is a rapidly growing body of knowledge and documentation that deals with experiences felt within the mother's womb prior to birth, and even with experiences prior to conception (prewomb). Each of these is discussed below.

The Womb Experience. My own work and that of many other hypnotherapists has convinced me that our awareness or consciousness extends back in time well before we learned the language of our parents, and could describe what is happening to and affecting us on our physical, emotional, and mental levels. It can be stated with certainty that human consciousness is not limited to the five human physical senses, nor is our capability for awareness limited to only these senses. We are much, much more than what we physically perceive ourselves to be. Our awareness exists well before we are born, as evidenced by the growing number of transcripts of sessions wherein clients have been regressed back to a time when they were in their mother's womb. These sessions are exceptionally useful in investigating and resolving emotional issues existing between a client and his or her mother or father.

For instance, a client's feelings of rejection or unworthiness may often be traced back to a womb experience where the unborn child was not wanted by the mother. The unborn child grows to term in the mother's total energy environment, not just her Physical Body. The mother's total energy field, including her mental thoughts and belief systems, as well as her emotional reactions to these beliefs, determines the energy environment in which the unborn child develops and grows. If that energy environment includes feelings of guilt, shame, or anger at being pregnant, the child within her also feels those feelings in her Emotional Energy Field.

The unborn child has little analytical ability since that comes after the brain is developed well after birth. Therefore, the unborn child can only receive these repeated emotional feelings of the mother and begin to incorporate them as a part of its own developing energy patterns. If the mother's thought pattern is "I don't want this child," the unborn child may begin to form an energetic Mental Body with the thought pattern "I am not wanted" or "I am unlovable." The unborn child has taken on the faulty thoughts and mental patterns of its mother.

"There is now a growing consensus among therapists doing deep experiential work involving prenatal and birth memories that even if the fetal infant has no ego consciousness—i.e., an identity—before or at birth, the subconscious mind of the fetus is very much awake. . . . What this means psychologically is that in the absence of an ego to discriminate, the child cannot distinguish between its own feelings or ideas and those of its mother."[3]

The unborn child's own energetic Emotional Body may be forming with feelings of rejection, anger, helplessness, unworthiness, or a host of other negative reactions. It is essential to release these faulty emotional and mental patterns imprinted from our past or from within the womb in order to move ahead in the present with joy, love, balance, and harmony.

Dr. Michael Gabriel, a hypnotherapist in San Jose, California, uses four processes to investigate and heal prenatal emotional stresses and traumas: Recall, Reframing, Releasing, and Rescripting.[4] During Recall, the client simply observes and gives words that objectively describe, but do not necessarily interpret, their prebirth experience. During Reframing, the client calls on his or her adult perspective, knowledge, and experiences to give an understandable meaning to what has been described during Recall. During the Releasing process, the client lets go of the negative emotional connections absorbed during the prebirth experience. And through Rescripting, an active imagination and guided imagery process is used to relive the prebirth experience in a positive, supporting manner. In this way, positive memories can be imprinted into the client's memories to replace the previous negative memories.

Dr. Gabriel's processes are a major leap forward in the investigation, understanding, and release of negative emotional memories formed during the womb experience. These same processes can also be used in the healing of emotional issues that develop during childhood and which may have been suppressed.

Prewomb Experiences. During many regression cases, experiences are described that are clearly not part of the client's adult, childhood, or prenatal experience. It is clear that our awareness extends to realms and times which we do not consciously consider part of our current lifetime experiences. Yet these glimpses into these other dimensions are repeatedly encountered during hypnotherapeutic sessions that involve regression. Therefore, we also need to be able to understand what is happening during such a regression and why, so that our rational mind can make sense of this new information and process it in a way that does not confuse us, and which aids the greater understanding of ourselves and the world we perceive.

During regression sessions where prewomb experiences are clearly described in detail by the client, both the client and the therapist need to have a framework in which to understand what these experiences mean and how they are related to the client. I have conducted numerous sessions in which the client described participating in a chariot race in ancient times or described in detail how he or she died at the sword of a Russian soldier hundreds of years ago, and other scenes quite vivid and real to the client. I myself have physically cried out in agony as I described in detail a scene where I was speared in the chest and died in front of my Stone Age cave. So how do we make sense of these experiences? Obviously, we must first broaden our beliefs of what we perceive as reality and how we participate in our reality. Is reincarnation real? If so, what is the reason it exists? Must I accept that concept to make sense of my world?

To answer these questions in a framework that contributes to our understanding of emotional and mental healing processes, we must first understand that in order to repattern our energy field so that faulty thought forms are released completely, we must first know what pattern is there and why it was created. Every thought form or belief system in our energy field is there as a result of some previous experience. If a previous experience resulted in a faulty thought and a negative emotional reaction, these cannot just go away on their own. They will stay there in your field until they are forgiven and released through some process. You created them, and only you can release them.

There are at least three processes which may accomplish this: Divine Forgiveness, release through karmic repayment, and release by repatterning the energy bodies. Depending on your beliefs, Divine Forgiveness may be given to a person as a result of living a particularly pious or self-less life of service to others. However, a debate on the relative merits of the beliefs of different religions is not the purpose of this book. Further, I prefer to believe that our sojourn on earth is a continuing series of learning experiences, ones wherein we learn about our true nature through interactions with others and, ultimately, of our own place in this universe we inhabit. But the pressing questions here are "What am I supposed to learn here?" and "How does this knowledge help me understand who and what I am in my universe?"

For many centuries, Eastern philosophies that embrace the concept of reincarnation have recognized that one of the Universal Laws that governs this universe is the Law of Karma, or the Law of Cause and Effect. The central Truth here is that whatever you do is ultimately returned to you in kind. This is stated very succinctly in the Golden Rule: "Do unto others as you would have them do unto you." Notice, however, that is does not say that whatever you do unto others will be returned to you in this lifetime.

The karmic notion allows for the fact that it might not be in your best interests (i.e., for the evolvement of your highest understanding) that a negative, hurtful, or unkind act be repaid in this lifetime. To do so might interfere with the learning of the lesson you came here to learn the time around. But at some point, you will be given the opportunity to experience exactly what you have previously projected into your world. That may be loving kindness, compassion, and understanding; or it may be prejudice, hatred, disease, or greed. Ultimately, each person is totally accountable and responsible for his or her own situation and circumstances in life. This is determined by the nature of the previous actions and what each soul has agreed to experience in order to learn the lesson of those actions.

It is believed that many hundreds, or perhaps thousands, of lifetimes are experienced before the balancing effect of karma is erased and the soul record of Earthly incarnations is cleansed to the point that the soul begins to become aware of its true nature as an evolving, spiritual being. In this Earth experience, its actions in the denser third dimension reality are set into a progressive timeline from past through present to future;

this permits the evolving soul to become experientially aware of the results of its actions. There is no judgment in this process at all; it is merely an opportunity for each person to necessarily experience both sides of the coin for each of his or her actions, and thereby gain a greater understanding of the most productive manner in which to exercise free will/choice for subsequent actions.

Although it may be easier to explain and discuss previous life experiences in terms of reincarnation, it is, however, not absolutely necessary to believe in that concept. As suggested in chapter 1, if reincarnation is difficult to accept, one may think in terms of previous experiences instead of previous lives. Carl Jung, the renowned psychiatrist of the early 1900s, theorized that all human thoughts and beliefs are somehow collected into a vast universal storehouse that he called the Collective Unconscious. Further, he taught that, at some higher level of awareness, all human consciousness is connected in a way that allows each person to access this storehouse under the right conditions. Therefore, experiences recorded by one individual in 1600 may be available to another individual in 2000, even though the reason the two lifetimes may be connected is not obvious.

However, Jung resisted the idea that these different people were separate incarnations of the same spirit. Nevertheless, this Jungian philosophy allows one skeptical of reincarnation to accept the possibility of previous experiences affecting the current lifetime. Dr. Woolger takes the position that "it doesn't matter whether you believe in reincarnation or not. The unconscious mind will almost always produce a past life when invited in the right way."[5] He also continues that "For the therapist, what is important is not the literal truth of a story but its psychological truth."[6] With this as background, it may be easier to accept and understand how to deal with the previous lives that are repeatedly encountered during hypnotic regression sessions.

THE IDEAL EMOTIONAL/MENTAL THERAPY

The Law of Cause and Effect may require many life experiences before the soul "gets it" and has paid back all the karmic debts it has incurred to date. The ideal emotional/mental therapy should be able to shorten the number of learning experiences (lifetimes, if you accept the concept of reincarnation) required by a soul to clear its karmic slate. This would allow more enlightened choices to be made, and the soul's evolvement process would be thereby accelerated. It would permit removal of the negative energy patterns resulting from previous harmful actions, both to the client and by the client, and which have been carried forward to the present life experience. Removal of these negative patterns would enable the client to attract and enjoy an entirely new and different reality that allows rapidly accelerated self-growth and inner awareness of his or her true nature.

The ideal emotional/mental therapy then is one that includes the use of hypnotherapeutic techniques that can access: (1) suppressed memories in the current lifetime, (2) faulty thoughts and beliefs about self that were erroneously taken on during the womb experience, and also (3) previous experiences that are still affecting the client's day-to-day behavior and perception of him- or herself. This ideal therapy must also be capable of completely breaking and releasing for all time the energetic connections between the client and the negative experiences that have been affecting his or her life. Further, energetic repatterning of the Mental and Emotional Bodies must be done in a way that the conscious mind understands and can rationally process. Last and most important, all these requirements must be blended into a technique that recognizes that we are, first and foremost, truly spiritual beings who have chosen to have a human experience. This technique must also recognize our energetic nature as the framework and blueprint for what we express as our physical existence. Ro-Hun Transformational Therapy has been specifically developed as the single, comprehensive therapy to meet all these needs.

Ro-Hun Transformational Therapy

The two goals of Ro-Hun are to quickly and permanently release *all* major negative emotional energy (your emotional issues and "baggage") from your energy field, and to awaken your intuitive and creative abilities. Release of emotional issues is accomplished by a structured, yet flexible, approach that allows the client to systematically locate, identify, understand, own, forgive, and completely release all the major negative emotional issues that may have resulted from previous emotionally traumatic experiences or faulty thoughts and belief patterns. Intuitive awakening nearly always occurs as the client progresses through the very powerful and effective transformational processes that are an integral part of the Ro-Hun sessions.

Ro-Hun is a very rapid-acting psychotherapy that incorporates hypnotherapeutic techniques into a unique, spiritually oriented process of healing old emotional wounds, letting go of the negative energy in your field, and attracting positive experiences. Ro-Hun therapists all receive special training in the development of their intuitive abilities and also their ability to sense and repattern their clients' energy fields.

OVERVIEW

The basic philosophy of Ro-Hun is that emotional issues and negative emotional energy are ultimately caused by negative or faulty thought patterns and beliefs in the Mental Energy Body. Examples of faulty thoughts include "I must always be perfect"; "If I love completely, I'll be hurt"; "I'm unworthy of success and abundance"; and "I'm abandoned and am all alone." The negative emotional reactions to these faulty thoughts are stored in the Emotional Body and might include anger, frustration, fear, isolation, etc. The systematic Ro-Hun processes allow the client to come to terms with and release these negatives thoughts in the Mental Body and their damaging reactions in the Emotional Body. By repatterning these higher energy bodies to contain more constructive, loving, and helpful patterns, there is less negativity that might subsequently affect the Etheric Body and ultimately the Physical Body. In several instances, removal of negative belief systems has caused a dramatic shift in the energy patterns in the Etheric and Physical Bodies. In my own experience as a therapist, this has occasionally resulted in a complete release of physical symptoms such as pain or soreness in the lower back within a period of just a few hours or days after a Ro-Hun session.

The therapeutic power of Ro-Hun comes from realizing that most mental and emotional baggage is usually associated with a specific chakra. Ro-Hun provides a systematic process for locating and dealing with these chakra-related energy patterns so they can be released forever. Table IV shows the general type of issues associated with each chakra, and an example faulty thought pattern that might be stored in the Mental Energy Body near that chakra.

The Ro-Hun process addresses not only the issues in each chakra, but also the entire energetic envelope of the Human Energy Field. Although most of the initial Cleanse and Purification table sessions described later deal with the thought forms and energy patterns of the Emotional and Mental Bodies, much work is also done in the higher vibrational bodies above the Mental Body, collectively called the Spiritual Body. In particular, the Advanced Processes bring an awareness of self as a spiritual being in a multidimensional existence. Repatterning the Spiritual, Mental, and Emotional Bodies to higher states of functioning and harmony ensures that negative influences cannot be impressed downward into the Etheric Body and ultimately manifest in the Physical Body as disease or a set of unhealthy symptoms. Therefore, Ro-Hun is a very powerful, holistic process, which improves one's life on all levels.

Ro-Hun incorporates hypnotherapeutic techniques and processes in each session so that the Ro-Hun therapist can effectively guide the client to look at issues presented from the client's subconscious mind. Therefore, there are certain considerations to be observed when providing Ro-Hun or any other form of hypnotherapeutic services. First, if the potential

Chakra	General Issue	Typical Faulty Thought
Root	How I See Myself	I'm not worthy of abundance
Spleen (Sacral)	How I Feel About Myself	I'm afraid of making a mistake
Solar Plexus	How I Think About Myself	I'm not in control of my life
Heart	How I Care About Myself	If I love, I'll be hurt
Throat	How I Express Myself	If I speak out, I'll be ridiculed
Brow	How I Perceive Myself	I must always be perfect
Crown	How I Feel My Purpose	Life is an exercise in futility

Table V. Chakras and Typical Faulty Thoughts

client has previously been treated for mental illness, psychosis, or depression, a statement of satisfactory treatment of that condition should be provided by the attending psychiatrist, clinical psychologist, etc., before the client begins any Ro-Hun sessions. Second, if the client is currently being treated for mental illness, psychosis, or depression, the Ro-Hun therapist should gently decline accepting that person as a client until that condition is successfully treated. These precautions protect both the therapist and the client from situations wherein psychological damage might unwittingly be done by having issues arise from the client's subconscious mind that the client is not able to handle.

When dealing with emotional issues that are very personal and sometimes quite traumatic, it is very important for the client to understand and know he or she is not alone in this process of emotional healing. Not only is the therapist there to guide them, but also his or her own Higher Self is ever present to ensure the client's emotional and mental safety is protected at all times. If the client is mentally and physically prepared, his or her Higher Self will always make sure that no emotional issue will surface that the client is not ready to safely face. On the other side of the coin, however, each issue that does come up in a Ro-Hun session is being presented by the client's subconscious mind as one which needs to be dealt with at that time, no matter how painful it may be to look at and work through. The client's subconscious mind understands completely what emotional baggage is present and what parts of that baggage must be released during each session.

However, in order to completely release an emotional issue, the client must first understand how it and the negative thought pattern causing it were created in the first place. Again, only a remembered trauma can be let go. Because of negative patterns in one's mental and emotional bodies, an individual's personality and outward life might reflect insecurities, fears, and assumed limitations. But if these negative patterns are removed and replaced with positive beliefs, the person's aura will then project a completely different energy quality that will attract positive experiences instead of negative ones. For instance, the faulty thought "I must always be perfect" could be replaced by "It's OK to make a mistake—that's one way of learning new things." And the thought "I'm not worthy of love" could be replaced with "I have an infinite supply of love and can give and receive that love unconditionally."

When a faulty thought form is reprogrammed or transformed into a positive thought form, the effect is immediately felt in the Emotional Body as well. Remember that the Emotional Body contains the reactive emotional energy resulting from higher thoughts. Therefore, if a belief such as "I am unloved" is held in the Mental Body, the person may have an emotional reaction to that belief such as anger, frustration, or a feeling of worthlessness. These negative emotions are particularly powerful and cause us to act or react in ways that attract similar negative energies through the universal Law of Attraction, sometimes stated as "Birds of a feather flock together."

If your Emotional Body is radiating anger, you will naturally attract situations that allow you to express your anger. If you radiate helplessness, you may attract situations in which you may be dominated. If you radiate unworthiness, your lifestyle can quickly become one of hardship, perhaps financially, healthwise, or in terms of less-than-fulfilling relationships. Basically, we attract what we radiate energetically from our own Human Energy Field. If our field is filled with negative emotional energies, we will have a very difficult time attracting positive, loving, empowering situations.

When a person becomes aware that his or her own self-growth is being held back because of false beliefs and emotional baggage, a giant step has been taken toward further evolvement as a spiritual being ("ascension" if you will). However, in order to release this baggage and move forward, one must first understand not only the emotions and feelings involved (anger, hate, fear, etc.), but also why and how these emotional patterns came to become imbedded in the energy field. All significant previous experiences that caused you to take on faulty beliefs and limiting emotional patterns must be revisited; only then can you fully understand why and how that experience happened.

During this process of reliving an experience, the negative emotional reactions that resulted from that experience are also usually felt or re-lived as well. Whether that experience actually happened to you in a previous lifetime or this lifetime is not of importance. What is important is that somehow your subconscious mind has made an energetic connection with some previous experience. So now, that experience must be understood and released so that the energetic connection to those previous events can also be permanently severed.

Once the energetic connection to a previous set of events has been released, it can no longer influence one's energy field. At this point, or whenever a faulty thought or belief has been removed from the client's subconscious memory, a positive belief must always be substituted for the released negative one. When "I must control others to protect myself" is released, it could be replaced with "I respect the rights and ideas of others." When the negative energy of a past experience has been removed, that energy is no longer able to roll forward in time and influence the current life experience. This deep emotional healing results in very powerful self-forgiveness and shifts your entire perspective to one of self-confidence and inner strength. As you keep shedding your emotional baggage, you learn to love yourself unconditionally, become increasingly more self-confident, and begin to radiate a new sense of optimism, adventure, and inner peace, which others can sense and readily react to, even if only subconsciously.

A significant difference between Ro-Hun and the more traditional emotional therapies discussed before is that the Ro-Hun therapist receives instruction and training in the development of the ability to sense and work with the energy fields surrounding the client's body. Since the vast majority of people cannot visually see energy fields, Ro-Hun therapists included, it is important to be able to sense or feel the energy field boundary layers and energy qualities with the hands. By scanning the hand through an area near a chakra but within the Emotional Field (as opposed to the Etheric or Mental Fields), the therapist can detect stagnant or disturbed Emotional Energy patterns.

In a hypnotic state, when the client is directed to focus attention on a chakra and describe how it "feels" to him or her, the client may say "Like a volcano ready to explode!" or "heavy and dense" or "cold and hard." The therapist is also scanning the energy field at the same time to confirm what the client is saying. If the client says the chakra is "nice and clear" but the therapist feels a definite area of sluggishness, it may be that the client does not want to consciously recognize what is there. But since the client's field has presented that sensation, it is obvious to the therapist that an issue needs to be dealt with in that chakra.

In addition to being sensitive to energy fields, all Ro-Hun therapists are trained in intuitive skills. Many are able to clairvoyantly see what the client is seeing in his or her own mind and to empathically feel what the client is feeling. This additional source of information about the client's experience can then be used to guide the client to discover new truths about themselves. Experienced Ro-Hun therapists are both intuitive and sensitive to clients' energy fields, and they receive a wealth of information from the clients that can be used to help guide the healing and release processes.

Two basic types of Ro-Hun sessions are practiced: Card Sessions using a specially developed set of 177 cards, and Table Sessions, which allow the client to rest comfortably for an extended period of time. Each Ro-Hun Table Session usually lasts from two to two-and-one-half hours, so client comfort is especially important. Each type of Ro-Hun session is discussed in depth below.

Card Sessions. The goal in a Ro-Hun Card Session is to locate and release the single most important emotional block that is holding the client back at that time from expressing his or her full potential. The Card Sessions are particularly appropriate when dealing with a specific emotional issue (e.g., "Why don't I get along well with my mother?") Card Sessions have also been used very successfully by some Ro-Hun therapists with children as young as five or six. Since children this young still have very active imaginations and intuitive abilities (they have not yet learned that they are not intuitive), the Card Session can be turned into a "Let's Pretend" game with excellent results.

In a typical Ro-Hun Card Session, which usually lasts about an hour, the client and therapist sit side by side in comfortable chairs or on a sofa. As in the Table Sessions described later, it is important that the therapist be within the energy field of the client in order to intuitively receive additional information. A specially designed set of "Ro-Hun Therapeutic Cards" has been devised for these sessions. This deck of 177 cards has five "sets" within it: fourteen Chakra Cards, eighteen Self

Cards, fifty-three Life Cards, fifty-four Thought Cards, and thirty-eight Message Cards.

Since each Ro-Hun Card Session will address only one emotional block, it is necessary to first locate the particular chakra with which that issue is associated. The Chakra Card does this. There are two cards for each of the seven chakras, and each has an opposite aspect of the emotional block. For instance, the two cards for the Heart Chakra say: "The block is in your Heart Chakra and inhibits your ability to love yourself"; and "The block is in your Heart Chakra and inhibits your relationship with others."

After each set is shuffled separately, the client draws one card, facedown, from the location set and turns it over. The card selected will be the one intuitively known by the client's subconscious mind that relates to the most important emotional issue that needs addressing at that time. A different card may be drawn in a session at a later time when the emotional needs of the client have changed.

Both to illustrate what to expect in a Card Session and to demonstrate how accurate and useful these are, I will describe an actual session. Jill (not her real name) came to me in a very upset and disturbed frame of mind because she was now in the position of having to care for her invalid mother for an extended period of time. Since her teen years, she had bitterly resented having anything to do with her mother. During the presession interview, I found that, as a teenager (she was now in her early sixties), Jill had wanted above anything else to become an artist. However, her mother had said, "No, you can't do that. There's no money in being an artist. Be a secretary and you can always support yourself." Jill's father also took her mother's position. After many frustrating years of trying to convince her parents she could still become an artist, she was told that if she did, she would be disowned and asked to leave the house forever. So she relented but since then had always suppressed a deep anger at her parents for keeping her from her life's passion. She also admitted that as a result of this anger, she had become a bitter and complaining person, and she was very judgmental and critical of others.

With this background, we began the Card Session, and she drew a face-down card from the Chakra set. As soon as she turned the card over, she saw that it read "The block is in your Brow and causes you to judge people" and immediately saw the connection to her present personality.

The next card drawn was the Self Card. The Reactive Self Card is best explained as that aspect of your personality that is created by the emotional block and is how you see yourself or how others see you. For example, because of a block in a chakra, you might react toward yourself or others in an angry or confused manner; you may have created an Angry Self as a part of your personality because of the block, or a Confused Self, a Frightened Self, an Isolated Self, a Controlling Self, etc. When she drew and turned over the Self Card, Jill saw that it was the Complaining Self. This obviously reinforced the emerging story line as a parallel to her own situation. Up to this point, her story line was "At some point, you created a block in your Brow Chakra, which causes you to judge people; this resulted in the creation of an aspect of your personality wherein others see you as a complaining person."

The third card drawn facedown by the client was the Life Card. The fifty-three Life Cards include various professions or family relationships that may pertain to the present life or a past life. Present Life Cards include Father, Mother, Sibling, Peer, Grandfather, Grandmother, Lover/Friend/Spouse, and the Abuser. Past Life Cards include occupations such as the Monk, Beggar, Slave, Queen, Judge, Warrior, Priestess, etc. Of the fifty-three Life Cards, Jill drew the Past Life Card "Artist"! Jill's story line had now become, "In some previous experience you were an artist, and you created a block in your Brow Chakra, which causes you to judge people; this resulted in the creation of an aspect of your personality wherein others see you as a complaining person."

Now we know who (what character) created the block, where the block is located in Jill's energy system, and its effect on her current life. But we still need to know WHY the block was created. All emotional blocks are caused by our reaction to the acts or ideas of ourselves or others; we then take on a faulty belief about ourselves that is not in our highest interest. After shuffling the fourth set of fifty-four Thought Cards, Jill drew the Faulty Thought Card "I am unable to forgive my parents." Both fascinated and unnerved that she had drawn this specific sequence of cards, Jill began to understand her story line more completely now: "In some previous experience as an artist, you had the faulty thought 'I am unable to forgive my parents', and this faulty thought created a block in your Brow Chakra, which causes you in this lifetime to judge people. This has resulted in the creation of an aspect of your personality wherein others see you as a complaining person." The final piece of the puzzle to understanding and releasing the faulty thought and its emotional block is to learn why the artist had that particular faulty thought and such a strong negative emotional reaction to that thought.

After a short induction to place the client in a relaxed state, we began working to release the Complaining Self energy, which had been made a part of her current personality. By understanding how this negative aspect of personality had been keeping her from enjoying the fullness of life, Jill was ready to release that part of her. A very specific healing process was used to accomplish this very quickly. When the Complaining Self energy had been released from her current life energy field, she was then able to be guided to "look deeper" into the more subtle energy patterns associated with previous memories that were still being held in her field.

With this preparation, we began to investigate the story line she herself had built by allowing her subconscious mind to guide the selection of each card. Since a Past Life Card (the Artist) had been drawn, Jill was regressed to that previous experience in which she was an artist; we looked for the very special artist who had the specific faulty thought, "I am unable to forgive my parents." Very quickly, she began describing a scene in which she was a poor, starving, destitute male artist about thirty years old, barely able to survive on the little money he made. However, being an artist was his dream, and he was not about to get a regular job, no matter what hardships he had to endure. Yet he was also very bitter about his destitute condition; he was a complaining man with no friends. He also harbored a deep hatred for his parents.

To understand how this hatred had developed, it was necessary to regress the thirty-year-old artist to an earlier time in his life before he had the faulty thought, "I am unable to forgive my parents." As the artist was regressed in Jill's mind, she described a scene at the kitchen table when the young boy was about ten. He was telling his parents that he had developed a real love of art and wanted to be an artist when he grew up. His mother told him, "No, you can't be an artist. They don't make any money. Be a carpenter and you can always support yourself." The lad's father also took the mother's side. We then brought the young boy forward in time a few years, and he still wanted to be an artist; by this time, the tension was running very high in the family, with the parents still objecting strongly. Again the boy was progressed until he was nineteen. At that point, he flatly told his parents he was going to be an artist, regardless of what his parents thought. His parents immediately and summarily disowned him. He was told to leave the house, to never return, and that they no longer considered him to be their son. Of course, he felt totally and completely abandoned, and vowed that he would never forgive them for withdrawing their love from him.

With this knowledge, Jill immediately saw not only how and why the block was created in a past lifetime, but also how that hateful emotional energy had become a part of his energy system. This negative emotional energy had not yet been addressed and released, so it had become a part of his soul record and would continue to be brought forward with each incarnation until it had been released. The particularly powerful healing and releasing processes of Ro-Hun were then used, and Jill immediately released this negative subconscious energy pattern from the artist's energy field in that past life. This, in turn, rolled forward in time into all subsequent incarnational patterns to immediately release Jill from that pattern in her current life as well. It was a profound session with deep insights for Jill, not only for uncovering and releasing her most pressing emotional block at that time, but also for an exciting, new insight about the nature of her own reality.

Following the release of the emotional block, the Ro-Hun Card Session is concluded by gently bringing the client back to full awareness and asking him or her to draw a card facedown from the thirty-eight Message Cards. These cards are the "Chinese fortune cookie messages" of the session—a positive affirmation that the client can take home. As Jill drew the Message Card and read, "You are artistically inclined and will benefit from your hands," she nearly dropped off her chair!

As a postscript, Jill later told me that she and her mother had finally arrived at a mutually agreeable understanding and appreciation of each other. There was not total forgiveness on Jill's part of her mother's attitude and actions of nearly fifty years ago, but there was a definite acceptance of each other and a new insight into what was important to each. For even that much, Jill was very thankful for the Ro-Hun Card Session. It had at least paved the way for her to make peace with her mother in this lifetime. She has also invested in some art supplies and has begun to paint, something she had never allowed herself to do since childhood, and has found a wonderfully new creative outlet through which she now enjoys expressing herself.

What are the odds of a particular combination of cards coming up in a single drawing? Only 27,406,512 to 1!! And then what are the odds that this particular set of five cards was drawn by the one person who needed to remove this particular emotional block and receive this particular inspirational message? Astronomical, to say the very least. Yet the unique and specific combination of cards needed by each different client keeps coming up time after time. There is no doubt whatsoever in my mind that these cards, and the Ro-Hun process itself, are guided by a wisdom and intelligence from dimensions and levels of consciousness far above our normal, mundane awareness. And it continues to be a humbling experience to be able to participate in the healing of others with the certain knowledge that such help is always available. We only have to stop and ask for it!

Table Sessions. Ro-Hun is a very rapid-acting psychotherapy. For example, the goal in a series of four Ro-Hun Purification Table Sessions held over a period of less than two weeks is to locate and completely release forever all the major negative emotional "victim" energies and issues that are holding the client back from expressing his or her full potential. During this "thought surgery," the Mental Body is energetically repatterned by removing faulty thought forms and belief systems and replacing them with positive beliefs about self, and the Emotional Body is repatterned for more harmonious energy flow by releasing all the negative reactive energy associated with the released faulty thoughts.

All Ro-Hun sessions except the Card Session (described previously) are conducted with the client lying comfortably on a healing table. Only the shoes need to be removed for a Ro-Hun session. The client is first hypnotherapeutically relaxed into a light or medium altered state similar to meditation. In this state, the client's conscious mind can be gently moved aside for a while and become an observer (rather than an analyzer) of the Table Process. However, the client will be fully aware of everything happening and able to interact with the Ro-Hun therapist. In this state, the therapist can access information from the client's subconscious mind without the personality and ego filters of the conscious mind coming into play.

Interaction with the client's subconscious mind is necessary for two reasons. First, the subconscious mind has access to all knowledge and experiences of the soul on the table; to the subconscious mind, it does not matter whether those previous experiences were actually from past lives of that soul or gained through some connection to the Collective Unconscious. The experiences seen by the subconscious mind are somehow relevant and are energetically connected to the current lifetime. Second, the subconscious mind has no agenda other than to protect the safety and allow spiritual growth of the client. All experiences from the subconscious mind are treated as real and true; it is the conscious mind that makes judgments as to the reality or degree of truth that it wants to assign to an event. But once the conscious mind has made this judgment, the subconscious mind accepts that as fundamental truth and incorporates that "truth" into its greater belief systems. This is why it is so important to bypass the personality and ego agendas of the conscious mind—we need to get at the origin of those faulty beliefs imbedded in the subconscious mind in order to remove them.

However, interaction with the client's subconscious mind has its challenges, as well as its rewards. The therapist must be well aware of the linguistic implications of each word used while the client is in a suggestive state. Obviously, a deep sense of trust between client and therapist must be established before the process is even begun, and the therapist must be specifically suited and trained to become proficient in the Ro-Hun process. It is decidedly different than many traditional therapeutic techniques that involve hypnosis. While other hypnotherapeutic techniques are more mental in their approach to an emotional issue and its resolution, there is a strong energetic and empathic attunement between the Ro-Hun therapist and his or her client during each session. Indeed, the therapist may become so closely attuned to the client that many of the visions seen in the client's mind and feelings felt by the client are also seen and felt by the therapist. This is due, at least in part, to the development of the intuitive faculties that is integral to the Ro-Hun training.

From my own personal experience during the conduct of Ro-Hun Table Sessions, there is also a very strong awareness on the part of the Ro-Hun therapist that much unseen help and advice is constantly available from higher dimensions. During a smoothly flowing Ro-Hun session, the therapist may be guided to steer the conversation with the client in a particular direction without knowing why, only to find that, unknown to the therapist's conscious mind, the client's subconscious mind needed that specific question to allow a repressed, traumatic experience to be brought forward.

The second challenge that the Ro-Hun therapist has to deal with when interacting with the client's subconscious mind is that the subconscious mind communicates not in the words of the conscious mind, but with its own symbolic language. The subconscious mind has access to all knowledge and information in the client's soul record—the totality of all experiences, actions, words, and thoughts of that soul—that are energetically connected to the present lifetime or previous life experiences. However, this information is communicated to the client's conscious mind in symbolic form and images instead of words. The challenge for the therapist is to gently and supportively guide the client to understand what each symbol means as it comes up from the subconscious mind. Again, the words used in the interactive dialogue between client and therapist are very important, and the Ro-Hun therapist is specifically trained to be able to guide the client to his or her own meaning and understanding of each symbol.

The basic systematic processes that have been developed for Ro-Hun include the Cleanse Session, the Purification Series, the Skim Session, and the Shadow Self Series. In addition, several advanced processes are discussed below. These address further transformation and integration of all aspects of your multidimensional being and realization of the abilities within your Cosmic Self. Each session is conducted using a healing table since each session will last from two to two-and-one-half hours, and client comfort in an altered state can be maintained much more easily on a table than reclining in a chair. Additionally, with the client on a table, the therapist has convenient access to each of the client's major chakras.

Cleanse Session. The Cleanse Session is a single Table Session that allows the curious client to experience the gentle, supporting, loving nature of Ro-Hun without getting into deep, and possibly uncomfortable, emotional traumas. Essentially, it is a good way to dip your toe into the waters of Ro-Hun to see if you want to proceed with the more in-depth Purification Series. That is not to say that the Cleanse Session is not very powerful and effective; it just deals with fewer negative issues. The essential processes within the Cleanse Session are:

- Client Interview—Development of an emotional and mental profile of the client.
- Hypnotherapeutic induction into a relaxed state of awareness.
- The Womb Process—Deals with and heals issues surrounding your mother and father.
- Release Reactive Selves—Release those aspects of your personality that make you feel unworthy, fearful, helpless, and judgmental/critical of yourself and of others.
- Inner Child work—Meet your Inner Child and increase the enjoyment, fun, and spontaneity in your outer life.
- Temple/Sanctuary Experience—A very personal, sacred experience in the high vibrational energies of your inner being.

The Purification Series. The Purification Series is the beginning of the self-transformation process; this is where the main emotional healing work is done to release negative thought patterns and their emotional reaction from one's field. The great majority of issues dealt with here will be those wherein you were a victim of someone else's negative actions, and you took on a faulty thought or belief about yourself as a result. These sessions may be intense and emotional, and the client must be willing to look at issues that may be painful to address. However, remarkable benefits are received by those who do.

Usually three Table Sessions, each about two-and-one-half hours long, are required to complete the Purification Series. The first session concentrates on the Root and Sacral Chakras, the second session looks at the Solar Plexus and Heart Chakras, and the third session deals with the Throat and Brow Chakras. Each Ro-Hun session ends with a Temple Experience, which corresponds to the Crown Chakra. The essential processes within the Purification Sessions are:

- Client Interview—Review and update of the emotional/ mental profile of the client.

- Hypnotherapeutic induction into a relaxed state of awareness.

- Male-Female Balancing—Integrate both the analytical and intuitive aspects of the self.

- Release Emotional Issues—Understand, forgive, and release completely the negative emotional energy associated with why faulty thoughts and beliefs were taken on. These faulty thoughts and beliefs about the self are then replaced with positive, empowering beliefs.

- Inner Child work—Meet your Inner Child and increase the enjoyment, fun, and spontaneity in your outer life.

- Law of Attraction—Be OK with the fact that not everyone is going to like you. You only want to resonate with and attract those people and opportunities that will best allow you to express your love and your wisdom, and that will unconditionally let you be yourself.

- Connect with the Higher Self—Recognize and merge with your own higher aspects.

- Temple/Sanctuary Experience—A very personal, sacred experience in the high vibrational energies of your inner being. Discover your purpose in this life, and meet your higher-dimensional guides and angels.

Skim Sessions. Each Skim is a single Table Session lasting from two to two-and-one-half hours. As each emotional issue is removed during the Purification Series, other issues that may be buried more deeply are then allowed to surface and be dealt with. Like peeling the layers off an onion, during each Skim Session, issues are identified and removed using the same processes of the Purification Series. Skim Sessions are similar in format to the Purification Series sessions, except that work is done in only the three chakras most in need of being addressed at that time. Skim sessions are usually held at approximately one-month intervals after the final Purification Session and continue until all the significant issues are cleared. Usually only one or two Skim sessions are required.

The Shadow Self Series. Following the full Purification Series and at least one Skim Session, the client can elect to begin the Shadow Self Series, sometimes called the Caged One Series. Recall that in the Purification Series discussed above, the client is releasing "victim energy" where faulty thoughts or beliefs have been taken on as a result of someone (or themselves) abusing them in some way. In the Shadow Self Series, the Ro-Hun therapist will look for and remove faulty thoughts and emotional issues that were created when you were the abuser instead of the one being abused. This is the deep, dark, secret side of our psyche we usually refuse to admit exists. Yet each of us has that dark side where malevolent or destructive thoughts and actions are contained in a corner of our mind below the conscious level. We purposely put them there below the threshold of consciousness because we do not want to admit they are a part of our being. The emotional release work done here can be as intense, or more so, than that done in the Purification Series; therefore, dealing with the abuser issues is always done after the victim issues are satisfactorily resolved in the Purification Series and Skim sessions.

The Shadow Self Series usually takes four Table Sessions. The first three sessions deal with removal of the abuser energies, and with the guilt, remorse, shame, and other emotional reactions accompanying the issues. By the time the client has released his or her victim energies and memories (Purification and Skim Sessions) and the abuser energies and memories (Shadow Self), he or she is energetically a completely different person and radiates new and purer vibrations from all levels of his or her aura. The final Shadow Self Table Session is designed to provide a solid transition from his or her old views of self and the world into this new and more vibrant way of looking at and interacting with others and with him- or herself. Instead of a therapeutic session to root out issues, it is a beautiful building and growing experience, using guided imagery and meditation techniques to allow the client to comfortably adjust to this exciting, new reality.

PURIFICATION SESSION EXAMPLES

To best illustrate what to expect during a Ro-Hun Purification Session, a portion of three separate sessions are described below. These illustrate how the client is gently guided to comprehend the symbolic language of the subconscious mind and to discover his or her own truths on the Ro-Hun table. They also illustrate the three reasons I have found that a scenario might be presented and described by the client during a session: (1) to permit emotional release of negative energy associated with a previous experience, (2) to allow experience rescripting so that the negative energetic results of a previous experience can be altered to a positive situation, and (3) to provide inspired guidance and direction to prevent a future action that would negatively affect one's energy bodies.

Case #1—Emotional Release. Sue (not her real name) came to me with feelings of total frustration in her life. No matter how hard she tried to be perfect and do things right, it was never enough in her eyes. She also felt that her husband was continually observing her lack of perfection and was withdrawing emotionally from her because she was not a perfect wife.

In the Womb Process during the Cleanse Session, I asked Sue (as an unborn child) to telepathically look into the eyes of her mother and describe her mother's thoughts and feelings. Sue said that her mother was not very loving and did not want any children. She was willing to go along with the pregnancy only because her husband wanted a child so much. We then regressed Sue's mother to find out why she did not want children, and discovered that when Sue's mother was three years old, she and her two sisters had been abandoned by their mother, and were being raised by another family member. Sue's mother felt totally rejected and unloved by her mother and had taken on the faulty thought "I am unloved." That pattern had become ingrained in her energy system, and now that same pattern was also becoming a part of the unborn Sue's energy environment.

When she telepathically looked into the eyes of her father, Sue initially saw a lot of love and affection for herself as an unborn baby. But when she was born and he saw it was a girl, Sue's father became very angry—he had wanted a boy very much to carry on the family name. The act of withdrawing his love from Sue reinforced her faulty thought "I am unloved." During Sue's childhood, the father kept pushing her to be the perfect son he never had. And when she could not measure up to his standards, he repeatedly drummed into her that she must try harder and be perfect. By regressing her father to his childhood, Sue learned that he had grown up in the same environment of being continually pushed by his father, who was not only a perfectionist, but was also cold and unloving. Sue's father had taken on his father's faulty thought "I must be perfect to receive love," and he was now energetically passing that same memory on to Sue.

In this energy environment, both as an unborn child and during childhood, Sue naturally took on these faulty thought patterns and belief systems as her own during her development and retained them into her adulthood. During the Womb Process, however, she was guided to understand the difference between her parents' limiting beliefs and her own thoughts. She was then able to understand and forgive each for contributing to her faulty thoughts now. And, more importantly, she was able to forgive herself for erroneously taking on the beliefs of others as if they were her own beliefs. This process of forgiving herself resulted in a significant emotional release in itself.

Later, when I was systematically scanning Sue's chakra system with my hand, I detected a dense field of energy surrounding her Spleen (Sacral) Chakra and began mixing the energy patterns there. I asked her to describe what she was feeling or seeing while I was mixing, but she said it felt nice and smooth to her. She was obviously resisting looking at what caused the energies there, which I felt as a sharp scratchiness in the tips of my fingers. However, I knew that those energies would not have been presented unless Sue needed to deal with them at that time. I asked Sue to get in touch with all her feelings of resistance and to project them out in front of her and give them form as a smaller image of herself, that resistant part of her whole personality. When I asked her to look into the eyes of her Resistant Self and describe the feelings she saw there, she began to feel fear, a fear of seeing who she really was underneath—she might not like herself! I had her surround the Resistant Self standing in front of her with light and love and slowly begin to see there was no need to fear herself.

When the Resistant Self energy was released, she was then able to look more deeply into her subconscious mind and begin to describe the symbols she saw there. Very quickly, a devil face appeared full of gloom, destruction, and unhappiness at being discovered. As we investigated the feeling of destruction, Sue began to understand that her own self-destructive beliefs and thought patterns had been destroying her self-esteem and denying all hopes of coming to know inner happiness and joy. As I carefully guided her through this discovery, she began to understand that only she was responsible for buying into the false thoughts from her father ("I never measure up" and "I'm not good enough") and from her mother ("I'll have a hard life" and "Nothing good will ever come to me").

Then I asked Sue to visualize her mother and father (one at a time) standing in front of her as an adult, and declare to them that she understands that their faulty thought patterns have been controlling her life, and that she now intends to take back control of her own life from them. With compassion, Sue was able to forgive and accept each of her parents without condoning their actions. Then she informed each that she now knows that only she is responsible for the way she feels, and that they no longer have control over her life and her feelings. She also released back to each of them all the limiting thoughts and beliefs she had grown up with, recognizing that they were her parents' thoughts, not her own thoughts. Sue immediately had a major emotional release, and began crying great tears of joy at having taken control of her life.

However, when I rescanned the chakra with my hand, I still sensed a dense cord of energy that was leaving her Spleen Chakra and connecting to her father's Solar Plexus Chakra. I asked Sue to look down at her chakra with her mind's eye and describe what she saw there. She said it looked like "a rope coming out of her belly." When I asked her to follow the cord of energy and see where it was going, she saw it going over to her father. When I asked her which of her father's chakras it was attached to, she responded the Solar Plexus Chakra. So she understood that there was still an energetic link between herself and her father that needed to be released and that this link was from his power or control center (Solar Plexus Chakra) to her Spleen Chakra, the center of how she felt about herself. Simply understanding her father's faulty thoughts and declaring that she no longer wanted him to control her was evidently not enough to completely sever this energetic connection. What we needed was an additional process that would unquestionably communicate to Sue's subconscious mind that the energetic connection had indeed been severed.

I then asked Sue to again state her intention to the image of her father standing before her that the negative energetic connection between them be dissolved for all time. I had Sue ask her father for his participation in helping to sever this cord, and he reluctantly agreed. Then as I guided Sue to take a sharp knife and her father to put his hand on Sue's, I had them both cut the energy cord and it immediately dissipated. I then had Sue thank her father for his cooperation, and then stand tall and straight in her own energy and affirm that she and only she was now in total control of her life and her feelings. When I rescanned the chakra, it felt smooth and clear to both of us. Sue had another very positive emotional release.

Case #2—Experience Rescripting. Jane (not her real name) came to me for Ro-Hun sessions to release many emotional issues that had been plaguing her. During the initial interview, she said that among the many issues she wanted to address was her relationship with her teenage son; he seemed to do everything possible to annoy, irritate, and anger her, with no reason which was obvious to her.

During the second Purification Session, I was loosening and stirring up the energy patterns in the emotional layer above her Solar Plexus Chakra, when Jane "saw" a large, heavy box on her chest and "felt" it pressing down terribly hard and crushing the breath out of her. From her wincing grimace and labored breath, she was obviously experiencing these feelings in her mind. However, I recognized that the box was only a symbol representing something else in her subconscious mind. When I asked her to let the pain go away and to look inside the box, she saw "two round things" there. I asked her to take the first round thing out and look at in the light so she could see what it really was. As she did so, she said it was a large wood screw about two inches long, but all of a sudden she felt it buried in her neck and she was bleeding severely. She also felt the pain in the side of her neck very clearly, so I again suggested that the pain would go away and the bleeding stop for now, but all other details would remain very clear so we could understand them. She felt that she was dying and was very confused, upset, and angry.

Then I calmed her and asked her to look at the box on her chest again, and take out the second round thing so we could see what it was. As she brought the round thing out into the light, she said it became a small statue of a horse-drawn chariot. I then asked her to move her awareness into the chariot, feel herself holding the reins of the chariot, and to look around and tell me what she was seeing. Immediately, she started describing a chariot race in which she was a man about twenty-two years old, racing with seven other charioteers in an oval open-air amphitheater. She described in detail the smell of the dust and the sound of the horses' hooves as they raced around the course. In her mind, she was experiencing this race firsthand, and to her subconscious mind it did not matter whether it was one of her previous lives in which she incarnated as a man, or whether she connected with a remote event in someone else's life. For some reason, her subconscious mind had connected with this particular experience from the past and was now replaying it for her. And she was actually reliving that experience now on the table in the sense that she was able to describe the smells, hear the sounds, and see the events as clearly as if she were really there in person.

As she/he rounded the pylon at one end of the race course, he saw he was swiftly coming up on the chariot of his friend, and he planned to sideswipe his friend, cause him to crash, and then go on to win the race. As we examined this, Jane came to understand that his faulty thought was "I can control others to get what I want." But as he rammed his chariot into that of his friend, his own wheel cracked instead, and he was thrown from his chariot, which then fell on top of him, crushing his chest. The chariot was, of course, the large heavy box that Jane had felt was crushing her chest. Also, as the chariot fell, a large metal screw was loosened and was rammed into his neck and tore it open. As he lay dying under his chariot, his last thoughts were, "I'm better than this! This isn't supposed to be happening!" I then asked Jane what she would like to do next about this scene, and she immediately said, "I need to change what happened." So I took her back into the race just before he ran into his friend, and asked her how she would now like to change the events. She responded, "Don't run into my friend!" So I then had her watch as they both raced side by side toward the finish line. However, neither he nor his friend won the race, so sideswiping his friend would have been in vain anyway.

After the race, I was intuitively guided to ask the young man and his friend to embrace in friendship as gallant competitors and go to the local tavern to celebrate with a little ale. While they were laughing and talking with each other, I was again guided to ask the young man to look deep into the eyes of his friend, and I asked Jane if she recognized the friend. She shouted, "Oh, my God! It's my son!" The next day, Jane called to say that there had been a remarkable turnaround in the attitude of her son toward her, and that he had actually sat down with her and discussed how he felt about himself with her! When the negative patterns in her own energy field were removed, the way her energy field interacted with that of her son's changed significantly!

Case #3—Inspired Guidance. Whether one believes in past lives or not does not alter the reality presented from the client's subconscious mind. But while there may be several different interpretations of what is observed, there is usually one or more underlying Universal Truths with a capital T that cannot be denied. Many times these Universal Truths come through on the Ro-Hun table. One such Universal Truth is "Do unto others as you would have them do unto you": the Golden Rule, the Universal Law of Cause and Effect, the concept of Karma.

Let me illustrate how this Universal Law works with another example. During the second Purification session, I was stirring up the energies in the emotional layer of Sally's (again, not her real name) Heart Chakra, and she began to see a sailboat on a lake. When we zoomed in to see who was on the sailboat, Sally began to describe two people: one was a small Asian woman whom she knew to be herself, and the other was a hideous, mean, and loathsome bald man wearing a blue shirt.

I asked Sally to describe what each of them was doing, and she said that the ugly, hateful man was tying a rope very securely to the end of the boom to which the sail was attached. Then he was wrapping the other end of the rope around her body, and she was not strong enough to prevent it. Then he said, "It will look just like an accident. The next time the boom swings out, it will choke her and drag her overboard." He said it with a lot of malice because he hated her and Asians in general. To him, it would be just like killing a rat. He thought, "There are too many rats, and they must all be killed."

The woman was screaming in terror and knew he was completely crazy, but she was not strong enough to prevent what she knew was going to happen. Then all of a sudden, the boom swung out as the wind shifted, and it hit her in the head, mouth, and shoulder. As Sally watched the scene unfold, I suggested that she would feel no pain, and that she could continue to describe what was happening. Sally said that there was "a lot of red goo" coming out of her throat and shoulder area, and then she was carried out over the water and then slammed back into the side of the boat, breaking her neck. The Asian woman then died, hanging tangled in the rope.

On the table, Sally was sobbing and visibly upset, and I calmed her quickly with a few positive suggestions. I then asked Sally to take her awareness back into that Asian woman and describe what was happening as she died. She described going into a "spiritual place" where everything was light and bright. When I asked how she felt there, Sally replied that she felt "ecstatic," beyond joy and happiness. She said, "I feel just great! The payback went perfectly!"

Well, that was the last thing that I as a therapist had expected her to say, and I felt we both needed to understand more of what had really happened at the end of that lifetime. So I guided Sally's awareness back to the Asian woman, had her look into the eyes of the loathsome man, and then follow the energy of that hate in his eyes back, back, back to its source. Very soon, Sally began to describe a primitive farming community where all the townspeople were gathered around at some sort of meeting. When we looked closer, Sally described a trial being held out in the open with a judge pronouncing sentence for all offenses that came before him. Sally knew that she was that judge and saw herself looking out at the accused from a sort of raised dais.

The next person to come before him was a small Asian woman who had been accused of stealing some sweet potatoes. With no defense, the woman was found guilty, and the judge sentenced her to be tied by the hands behind a cart and dragged in the dirt until she died. Everyone thought that the sentence was unusually harsh, but no one dared oppose the judge, so the sentence was carried out. The judge felt no remorse or compassion, and he did not care that the punishment was out of proportion to the crime.

When I asked what the connection was between these two lifetimes she had witnessed, Sally replied that in the earlier lifetime she had been the judge and had unnecessarily caused the death of the Asian woman accused of stealing sweet potatoes. Therefore, she (the judge) must also experience a brutal death as an Asian woman to fully understand, on a soul level, both sides of what she had caused as the judge. The second lifetime as the Asian woman on the ship was that "payback" experience!

Also of interest was Sally's great joy at seeing that "the payback went perfectly." Sally expressed great relief and happiness that the slate was now clear of that one karmic debt. I then asked Sally to obtain the meaning of these two lifetimes from her Higher Self, and she replied, "The Law of Cause and Effect is eternal. Speak from your heart, not your mind!" After the session was over, Sally admitted that, although the karmic slate was clear with respect to these two specific previous experiences, she had recently been considering taking action against one of her coworkers, which, under this broader perspective of the Law of Cause and Effect, probably would have required a future karmic payback. In this case, Sally had been given a generous gift—a gentle reminder that she should not create a situation that would require a future "payback." And yet the choice as to what course of action she should take was still left to her, so her own free will had not been restricted.

Advanced Processes

When Ro-Hun clients finish the Purification Series, one or more Skim Sessions, and the Shadow Self Series, there are several additional advanced processes available for further enlightenment. These complete the emotional release and transformation sequence in a manner that gives the client an enlightened view of the self as a spiritual being, and also permits him or her to be placed in proper perspective as a Cosmic Being and citizen of this universe. These include the Inner Child Healing Series, the Origin Process, the Seven Visions Process, the Divine Mother Process, and the Male/Female Analysis Process. Each is discussed below.

Inner Child Healing Series. This process heals and releases the mental "constructs" we create to get through intolerable situations; the "vaults" or rooms where we keep our four primary fears (abandonment, failure, nothingness, and death); and the "tanks" in our lower three chakras where mortally damaging emotions of abuse, deception, hatred/rage, and death wishes can be found.

When we experience trauma in our lives, we create what we need to feel better or avoid the pain of the situation we are in. For example, if a child is in an abusive situation, he or she will create whatever it is that he or she needs to survive. It may be an alternate personality or behavior that the child believes may be acceptable to the abusive parent, or it may be an imaginary theater room or costume department that has all the different masks and makeup he or she believes is needed to survive. Alternatively, if the child is not allowed to express anger, he or she may then create a safe space in his or her mind where he or she can enter and flail and scream. If the child needs to take that anger out on Mom and Dad, he or she might even find them in that room tied to a tree and the child is poking them with pins.

These are, of course, all imaginary escape mechanisms or mental constructs used by the child to deal with an intolerable set of reality circumstances. Usually, only a few mental constructs are created. Examples might include the Chameleon, who becomes what others want him or her to be; the Punisher, who wants to get back at someone (or him- or herself) for some wrongdoing; or Pollyanna, who creates a loving, nurturing place for him- or herself because the child does not have any love in the real world. This session deals with identifying the mental patterns and the real-life situations that send a person into that construct, and shows how these constructs affect that person's daily life. Then the Inner Child that created these constructs is located and comforted. The child created these constructs, and the child is the only one that can dismantle them. After all constructs are dismantled, and the Inner Child is empowered; the Inner Child is then taken to the Garden of the One Who Cares (the Higher Self) until the next session. All of the energy work is done in the Brow Chakra during this session.

The second session deals with the vaults (fears) that the child would have dropped into if he or she went into each mental construct. Here, the energy work is done in the Heart Chakra. Four primary fears have been identified, with all other fears coming under one or more of these: fear of abandonment, fear of failure, fear of nothingness, and fear of death. Each of these fears is portrayed during the session as a room into which you must enter. The client must name it and claim it as his or her own, and with the help and guidance of the therapist, release that fear by completely understanding how that fear was created and what effect it has on his or her daily life. Only then will the room be destroyed by the client's Inner Child. The room and the fear are an illusion, a *maya,* that was created by his or her own Inner Child, and only that Inner Child can eliminate it. After all rooms are eliminated, the Inner Child is again taken to the Garden of the One Who Cares. After the session, the therapist and client will match up which mental construct leads to which vault. Invariably, there is a clear one-to-one matching pattern presented.

The third and fourth sessions deal with the emotional "tanks" found in the lower three chakras that correspond to the mental constructs and vaults discovered in the first two sessions. The tanks are those of Abuse, Deception, Hatred/Rage, and Death Wishes. Each tank has an inner and outer chamber that represents the other-directed and self-directed aspects of each damaging emotion. For example, the outer chamber of the Deception Tank represents how I deceive others and how they deceive me; the inner chamber represents how I deceive myself. Each chamber of each tank must be entered, owned, understood, and ultimately destroyed by the client's Inner Child.

Of particular attention is the inner chamber of the Death Wishes tank. When we get into a situation that is really intolerable (e.g., a failing marriage, never taking the time to nourish one's self, an abusive relationship at work, etc.) and we do nothing about it, we may begin to think, "I wish I were dead!" or "I can't live like this!" If that thought persists, it becomes a belief, and the body may soon obey by developing a life-threatening disease such as cancer. Each Death Wish thought that the client has ever held is dealt with. As each inner and outer tank for each Death Wish thought is entered, understood, and destroyed, the client is healed, and the client is strongly empowered to take back control of his or her life and to restore the will to live a positive, fulfilling, and happy life.

At the end of the fourth session, the therapist and client match up each tank to each mental construct and vault. This discussion serves to crystallize in the conscious mind all the discoveries the client has made about him- or herself during these four sessions, particularly in how the client's own beliefs and thoughts have been influencing or affecting his or her life.

Origin Process.   The purpose of the Origin Process is to understand how Archetypal energies affect your daily life. In the spiritual realm, the Divine Male (Father of Manifestation) and the Divine Female (Mother of Life) come together as a single energy and create a Divine Child (Mission or Purpose) for the purpose of expressing themselves in the physical world. The Divine Child is expressed as the male or female energies in the Earth plane. This allows it to acquire additional experience and information, particularly with regard to dealings and relationships with others. How that Divine Child expresses itself is chosen through its occupation, interests, and interactions that are set up for the lifetime before incarnation.

We have seen earlier that the beliefs and emotional patterns taken on *in utero* by the developing fetus are very strongly influenced by the mental and emotional energy fields of the mother. The reactive patterns of the Divine Child are similarly determined by the intentions and beliefs of the Divine Male and Divine Female archetypal energies. As the Divine Child archetypal energy becomes associated with an individual soul expression, God's light, love, and energy are often perceived as not being fully present—the soul expression takes on a feeling of separation from its Source. This feeling of separateness may leave the client in a state of suffering, terror, rage, hopelessness, or guilt at being "abandoned" by God. This is the drama so often referred to as the "Garden of Eden" experience.

In the Origin Process, the Ro-Hun Therapist guides the client from the Garden of Eden into the world and feelings of separateness from their Source, and assists them to remember his or her Source. In this way, the separation feelings and the reactions to these feelings are healed, and the Divine Child within the client can forgive and release these erroneous beliefs and feelings and can then return the Divine Father, Divine Mother, and Divine Child energies to the Source and satisfactorily reconcile the separation experience.

During the second session of the Origin Process (clearing the ego), additional energy work is done to determine where any patterns of abandonment may be stored in the client's energy field and to release that energy. Each chakra is scanned with the hand, and when an issue of abandonment is found, the client is regressed to the point in time when he or she felt separated from or abandoned by someone or something.

Many experiences of abandonment may be found in the lower six chakras; each is systematically investigated and released. At the conclusion of the session, the client is guided into a Sanctuary experience where he or she may listen to the wisdom of his or her guides and remain in the comforting healing energies for a while.

Seven Visions Process.   This is a three-session series that cleanses and purifies all the energies in each chakra on a very deep level. Beginning with the Heart Chakra, the client gets in touch with the One Who Cares, his or her Higher Self. This pure, unconditionally loving energy is then used to cleanse the Heart Chakra and each of the lower and upper three chakras. A guided imagery process is used to introduce and heal the primary personality present in each chakra: Root Chakra—Presence; Sacral Chakra—the Emotional One; Solar Plexus Chakra—the Achiever; Throat Chakra—the Expressor; Brow Chakra—the Visionary; and Crown Chakra—the Angel.

The Heart, Root, Sacral, and Solar Plexus Chakras are visited and cleansed during the first session, the Throat Chakra is addressed during the second session, and the Brow and Crown Chakras are addressed during the third session. As in the Purification Series, past life experiences may be encountered in any of the chakras during the cleansing and healing processes.

Divine Mother Process.   This process deals with your relationship with your mother and any negative effects this relationship has on your daily life. If after the Shadow Self series there are still significant mother issues remaining, they can be resolved here. An example of a contract you may have made as a child with your mother is that you would always be quiet and obedient and never tell your mother your problems, and she would not scold you for having to take time from her hectic day to deal with your feelings and problems. In this kind of a contract, you both get something positive out of it, but there is also a negative energy sent and received by both sides.

This negative energy is felt by the therapist as a cord of energy between a specific chakra of the client and the client's mother. This energy cord binds them together until the contract is broken by both client and mother; the energy of the contract (the cord felt by the therapist) then dissolves and is released. Contracts made during the womb experience are found in the first and second chakras, and contracts made when the client was five years old are found in the Solar Plexus Chakra. Contracts of the ten-year-old are found in the Heart Chakra, the fifteen-year-old's are in the Throat Chakra, and the twenty-one-year-old's contracts are in the Brow Chakra.

After all the energetic cords are cut in each chakra, the client is then guided to find the Divine Mother and examine all the aspects of the Divine Mother that appear fearful. She may be overpowering, controlling, or manipulative. Once these aspects of the Divine Mother have been healed and released, any unhealthy contracts that the client may have made with Mother Earth are healed and released. The client is then free to claim his or her space on the earth and stand in his or her own power to fulfill his or her true purpose on Earth.

Male/Female Analysis Process.   This process addresses potential imbalances in the male and female energies within the client. As a rough rule of thumb, each woman's energies are about two-thirds female and one-third male, and each man's energies are about two-thirds male and one-third female. When these energies become significantly unbalanced in one direction or the other, the people and situations we attract usually contribute to an unbalanced relationship with others. However, when the desired balance of male and female energies is shown by both partners, relationships are healed and transformed since there is love, value, and respect not only for your partner, but also for your own inner male and female selves.

Here, the client learns that he or she must reach out to the opposite side of his or her own personality (male for women, female for men) and be OK with the fact that he or she really does really need the opposite aspect to be complete and whole. Metaphorically, each sex needs to see the other as the opposite side of the same coin and not as separate coins.

Up to three sessions are required for the Male/Female Analysis Process due to the time required to deal with several levels of issues in each of the chakras. The guided imagery begins, as all Ro-Hun processes do, in a relaxed state. Here, the client sees the male and female aspects of themselves and begins to describe what each is doing. If the female is lying in the bed waiting and the male is sitting reading the paper, some major work is needed to bring these aspects into balance! Each aspect is worked with and healed until a relationship develops where each is nourished by the energy of the other. Then and only then can the client begin to recognize and fulfill his or her purpose in life, drawing on the complementary energies of each aspect, rather than living in a continual battle wherein one aspect demands domination of the other.

Three levels of Male/Female Analysis are conducted in each chakra, and each level may involve a different issue, situation, or circumstance in which one aspect of the personality dominates the other. The types of issues and situations generally correspond to the chakra being worked at that time. For example, in the Solar Plexus Chakra, a woman's female part may believe that oneness can never be felt, so the male aspect takes over and tries to be an overachiever to compensate. The woman may then appear to others as very competitive, aggressive, and dominating. She must be shown how to heal the wounded female aspect within so that it can express equally in her dealings with others. This immediately results in the emergence of her soft, warm, loving nature, thus enabling her to attract this in others.

SUMMARY

If you are happy with your life the way it is, do not try Ro-Hun. Ro-Hun will positively transform the way you think about yourself and about others! However, Ro-Hun is not for everyone; you must be willing and prepared to deal with the unpleasant and dark issues of your psyche. But if you are ready to confront and let go of your fears, phobias, negative thoughts, and belief systems, Ro-Hun will transform your life and give you a more positive and confident, yet compassionate and understanding, view of yourself. This positive "new you" will be projected outward as your newly repatterned energy field interacts with the energy fields of others, and you will attract positive people, experiences, and opportunities to you.

The Ro-Hun process will probably be emotionally intense for most people. The great majority of my Ro-Hun clients react deeply to the scenes and feelings they bring up, and tissues are always kept at hand. However, as each issue is worked through, there is such a feeling of release felt by the client that he or she is always encouraged to continue the process with the next chakra until each is energetically cleaned, balanced, and renewed. Since more than one chakra may be dealt with in a single Table Session, many emotional issues can also be released during that session. In addition to the emotional releases experienced by the client, a significantly broader insight is also provided into his or her energetic, emotional, mental, and spiritual makeup through Ro-Hun than is available through more conventional therapies.

With the release of negative energies, the client is free to attract the positive experiences of life, to learn to open his or her heart and love unconditionally with compassion and understanding for others. In this process, the client also continues to grow and evolve as he or she becomes aware of and incorporates a much broader and higher perspective of his or her own reality into his or her daily activities. And as each of us becomes more aware of what we are as Cosmic, Spiritual Beings, we also become more capable of creating happiness, fulfillment, and joy in our lives and in the lives of those around us.

Ro-Hun is an inspired process of personal growth and transformation that was founded by Patricia Hayes in 1983. Patricia is the cofounder and the chairperson of the board of directors of Delphi University in

McCaysville, Georgia, and is also the director of the Ro-Hun Institute at Delphi. Formal training in all basic and advanced Ro-Hun processes is conducted regularly at the Ro-Hun Institute at the baccalaureate, master's and doctorate levels. In addition, formal training in Ro-Hun processes at the baccalaureate level (Cleanse, Skim, Purification Series, and the Shadow Self Series) is conducted periodically at the Graham Institute of Self-Awareness (GISA) in Yorktown, Virginia, and other locations both in the United States and Europe. For further information, see Appendix C.

Chapter Four

Healing the Spiritual Energy Body

The root or base chakra is the storehouse for a natural, yet powerful, energy called the kundalini. This kundalini energy has the
potential to activate and align all of the major chakras with the
higher centers, bringing illumination and spiritual enlightenment
with the proper sequence of chakra unfoldment.

—Richard Gerber, M.D.
Vibrational Medicine

IN CHAPTERS 2 AND 3, we have dealt with the four densest Energy Bodies in the Human Energy Field (Physical, Etheric, Emotional, and Mental), and have discussed various healing techniques and modalities that repattern the energetic vibrations of these bodies for greater harmony and health on those levels. The outermost energy body of the Human Energy Field is the Spiritual Body. This energy field contains the vibrational patterns having to do with the awareness of our true, spiritual nature. It also holds the patterns of the lessons we have agreed to learn during the current life expression, both in relation to our own personal growth and evolution, and also having to do with our relationship with others—our intentions to be involved in situations that allow us to work out previous karmic debts.

Because of these characteristics, the energetic patterns in our Spiritual Energy Body are those that are appropriate for our greatest growth. However, in most individuals, awareness of our spiritual nature and the Spiritual Body lies dormant and does not consciously affect our daily life to a significant degree. For this to happen, we simply need to consciously "remember" who and what we are, and why we are here doing what we are doing. When this happens, and we become aware of the patterns in our Spiritual Body, we become more enlightened beings and are truly aware of our unique and vital role in the drama of the cosmos.

Thaddeus Golas says in his book, *The Lazy Man's Guide to Enlightenment,* that, "Enlightenment is any experience of expanding our consciousness beyond its present limits. Perfect enlightenment is realizing that we have no limits at all—and that the entire universe is alive."[1] All is energy, not only in this dimension, but also in all higher dimensions and planes of existence. When we choose to attune to this Truth, we have begun to claim our true place as a cosmic citizen in a living universe.

Meditation has been practiced for thousands of years as one method of attaining further spiritual enlightenment, and there is growing evidence that repeated meditation does have a discernable physiological effect on the brain and on the body. Electrical brain wave activity generated by the two hemispheres of the brain are more in step and function with greater coherence in meditators than in nonmeditators.[2] Long-term meditators also frequently gain the ability to consciously control certain physiological body functions such as heart rate, blood pressure, and skin temperature.[3]

During the meditation process, various techniques are used to focus the attention inward to experience the awareness of the present moment. These techniques include listening to your own heartbeat, becoming aware of your breath as it enters and leaves your body, or expanding your awareness to include and recognize all aspects of what it means to be "alive" in your version of reality. Over a period of time, this introspection and meditation begins to develop the nervous system in such a way as to allow deeper levels of consciousness and to encourage the release and flow of energy within one's own internal energy system.

Many books have been written on how to meditate and on the benefits of meditation. But they all come down to the same thing—it is a practice you have to master by yourself, and no one can help you other than on points of technique. Meditation is a personal experience, and as such, each person learns from repeated experience whether or not certain postures, mantras, or music are appropriate to aid him or her in entering into a deep meditative state.

Let's discuss points of technique for a moment. I have attended many workshops and lectures to learn how to meditate, and every teacher teaches what works for him or her and can only offer these favorite techniques to you in hopes that they will also work for you. You can try to learn to meditate by focusing on a flame or a pinpoint of light, on an orange spot on the wall or ceiling, or by humming a mantra that is important to someone else, all with the same goal of "emptying your mind" of all earthly thoughts so that you can become aware of the cosmic.

These simply have not worked for me because I cannot empty my mind of all thoughts and remain conscious. My engineer's left-brain mind excels in bringing in thoughts so that I can analyze them, evaluate them, and determine their truth in relation to the other beliefs and truths I hold about myself and my surroundings. That is the job of my conscious mind, and it does its job so well that there is always something going on in my head for me to consider. I simply cannot ask my very active, creative, analytical, imaginative, logical, dynamic mind to be absolutely quiet and expect to get results. So what should I do? Give up on the hope of ever achieving an inner calm and stillness where I can make a conscious connection with the higher dimensional part of my own being?

Inner Light Consciousness Meditation

While I was agonizing over this situation, the answer was presented to me. At the time, I was attending the Fellowship of the Inner Light Church in Virginia Beach, Virginia, and its minister was holding classes in what he called the Inner Light Consciousness Meditation technique. This particular meditation technique is an adaptation of the Seven Terraces Meditation developed by the late Rev. Paul Solomon, who had founded that church several years before. I sincerely thank Paul's wife, Sharon Solomon, and the Paul Solomon Foundation for giving me their kind permission to use the material and information from Paul's workshops and lectures in the preparation of the guided imagery meditation that is available from Evergreen Healing Arts Center (see Appendix C) on a specially prepared CD. Additional resource information about Rev. Solomon, his teachings, and the books, tapes, and CDs available from the Paul Solomon Foundation can be found on the Paul Solomon Foundation website, www.paulsolomon.com.

The concept that drew me to the Inner Light Consciousness Meditation technique was that it did not ask me to empty my active mind; instead it enlisted the creative energy of my mind to provide an image-rich visual experience (guided imagery) that lead me up my own spiritual mountain and into the Temple at the top where I could remember and connect with my own innate inner abilities. By the time I had climbed to the top of my seven-terraced mountain, I was in an altered state and could develop and draw on healing energies to heal myself and others in my "Healing Room"; I could locate, access, and read my own Akashic Record or, with their permission, the Akashic Record of someone else in my "Hall of Records"; I could ask for and receive guidance and information on any subject that would be in my highest good in my "Learning Room"; and I could enter my own Sanctum Sanctorum within, and open myself to the beauty, grandeur, and unconditional love of the Universe in my "Meditation Room."

ILC MEDITATION GOALS

Instead of simply attempting to still the active mind and wait, the ILC Meditation technique enlists the tremendous capacity for creative imagery within the mind to actively focus on and visualize a very specific sequence of images designed to awaken the inner senses and establish a repeatable and positive experience of our inner nature and true selves. Through the guided visualization found on the ILC Meditation CD that is available from my Healing Center (see Appendix C), the meditator's awareness and consciousness is first gently dissociated from the Physical Body, and then you are led to develop and awaken your inner senses so that you can experience the beauty and harmony of your inner dimensions. Through regular repetition of this guided visualization, you are communicating to your subconscious mind in the language it understands and uses (images and symbols) that it is your intention to become more enlightened. The subconscious mind then has the green light to begin reprogramming the neural pathways in your brain and in your body to enhance and accelerate this process.

The process used in the ILC Meditation sequence does not involve simply attuning ourselves to the infinite and waiting for something to happen. Instead, the ILC Meditation is an active process that provides a structured framework to awaken the inner senses and develop our innate, natural intuitive abilities. It also teaches how to use these natural abilities to actively connect with our higher spiritual Self, to bring physical and emotional healing to ourselves and others, to gain access to our soul records for guidance and insight, to receive useful and practical information for use in our daily lives, and to expand and liberate our consciousness so that we may experience the grandeur of the universe, the infinite love of our Creative Source, and all the abundance the spiritual dimensions freely make available to each of us.

Awaken the Inner Senses. As you continue your meditation practice, you will find that you become more and more aware of your developing natural intuitive abilities. And as your inner senses begin to develop, your meditation practice will become more meaningful each time. This development of your intuitive abilities is sometimes called psychic development, inner sense development, or inner awakening. By whatever name it may be called, it is merely developing your own natural ability to use the inner counterparts to your own five outer physical senses.

The ILC Meditation is a guided visualization through a specific sequence of steps that are designed to increase your ability to see with your inner eyes, hear with your inner ears, feel with your inner kinesthetic sense, and smell and taste with your higher sense organs. As you continue your meditation practice each day, your inner vision will become sharpened and your natural abilities for clairvoyance, "clear seeing," will become more developed. I look forward to receiving an occasional short "video clip" or picture during healing sessions. Invariably, these images provide practical information that is directly relevant to the situation at hand.

As your clairaudient, "clear hearing," ability to hear words and messages develops, you will be better able to receive positive guidance from both your Higher Self and your spiritual guides; this may sound just like someone speaking normally to you. This guidance will invariably be in your highest and best good and will be just the words that you need to hear at that time.

Similarly, the objects you come across in various areas during your meditation are designed specifically to heighten your ability to feel (both textures and temperatures), taste, and smell this exciting dimension of your mind.

Knowing your environment with your five inner senses is perhaps the most important experience of the entire meditation, since this really determines the overall effectiveness of your meditation experience. If you took a walk down a path in a real forest and could not see the trees, hear the birds, smell the earthy undergrowth, etc., your experience would not be nearly as exciting and vibrant as if your senses were all wide open. Similarly, the guided trip through your meditation will fully come to life for you only when you use your inner senses to their full abilities.

Bridge the Duality of Mind. We normally tend to perceive the reality around us in terms of pairs or opposites—up and down, right and left, inner and outer, good and bad, right and wrong, darkness and light, etc. Our brains are even divided into two hemispheres with the left hemisphere governing the logical and analytical aspects of our personality, and the right hemisphere governing the creative, intuitive, and feeling aspects. It could even be that this division of functions within our brain forces us to perceive our outward reality in terms of opposites.

But perhaps the most fundamental division of perception that we generally tend to believe is that on one hand there is a physical, three-dimensional world we live in day by day, and on the other hand there is a separate spiritual world we hope to experience "someday." There is a portion of the ILC Meditation that is devoted exclusively toward development of the inner senses that correspond to the outer physical senses, and there is another portion devoted exclusively to development of your inner spiritual awareness.

However, one of the goals of the ILC Meditation process is to bring these two "separate" experiences closer and closer together during your meditation time so that your mind begins to integrate these into a single perceptual outlook that you can bring into your activities as you go through your day.

As you become more and more consciously aware that there really needs to be no division between the physical and spiritual aspects of your life, every activity you undertake is done so with a greater understanding and wisdom than ever before. It will become quite obvious to those around you that you are bringing greater clarity and understanding into those activities, honesty and compassion in your dealings with others, and joy and happiness to yourself and to those you meet. Unconditional love, and acceptance of others (and yourself) just as you are, cannot be misunderstood.

Integrate Your Energy System. The purpose of the human chakra system, as stated before, is to receive and assimilate vibrational energies of different frequencies from the Universal Energy Field for the purpose of supporting and maintaining the energies in both our Physical Body and our individual Human Energy Field. For maximum health and well-being, it is essential that the chakra system be periodically balanced and systematically cleansed of vibrational patterns that interfere with the normal healthy flow of chakra energies.

The Inner Light Consciousness Meditation technique includes powerful processes to bring down from the spiritual dimensions the highest vibrations possible into each of the seven chakra centers. This has the further reinforcing action of bringing into your daily physical life those patterns and feelings of harmony, balance, compassion, and unconditional love.

Heal Yourself and Others. In the heightened state of conscious awareness known as meditation, many activities are possible which are not normally available during your everyday life. One of these activities is the ability to heal yourself and others. As you develop your ability to focus and direct the limitless energies that respond to the mind, you may wish to bring specific healing energies to yourself or to others.

Most of us are able to do this to varying degrees with prayer; however, the Inner Light Consciousness Meditation technique provides a powerful guided visualization process that enlists the creative energies of your own mind and also those of the higher spiritual dimensions. This process can bring healing to whatever part of your entire being requires it: Physical, Etheric, Emotional, Mental, and Spiritual.

The only requirements that must be met for these healings to be effective are that you (or the person to whom you wish to bring healing energies) consciously give permission to receive these healing energies, and that your Higher Self (or the other person's Higher Self) is willing to accept the healing energies on a subconscious or soul level. The spiritual doctors and healers from the higher dimensions will never provide what is not requested, nor will they ever provide healing if your Higher Self has not given its permission. To do otherwise would violate your own freedom of choice, and that simply does not happen.

Access Your Akashic Record.　Another activity that is available while in the meditative state of heightened awareness is to access your own individual Akashic Record, or if you have their permission, the individual Akashic Record of another person. An Akashic Record, as Edgar Cayce called it, is the complete record of every experience, every thought, every word, and every deed of an individual being while incarnated on this earth during all of its lifetimes, and constitutes that spiritual being's individual soul record.

For those who believe in reincarnation of the spirit and the Universal Law of Cause and Effect (Karma) from a spiritual point of view, all previous lifetime experiences can be recalled consciously for the purpose of your own information, education, and spiritual growth. By repeatedly accessing your own Akashic Record, you can become aware of repeated situational patterns that determine how you feel about yourself and how you interact with others in your present life. By becoming aware of how negative patterns were generated, it is much easier to begin a process (e.g., Ro-Hun, Regression Therapy, etc.) of forgiving and releasing all the players in those experiences, including yourself.

Receive Guidance and Instruction.　One of the several reasons people meditate is that they may be looking for spiritual advice or guidance on a particular issue they are dealing with at that time. This advice is often sought from their Higher Self as the spiritual source of all wisdom and knowledge about their entire being. But each person's individual Higher Self is also the focus through which all knowledge and wisdom available in the entire universe can flow.

Your request for specific information from the higher dimensions will be honored as long as possession of that information or knowledge is in your highest interests. In order to be granted, what you ask for must serve to further your own spiritual growth. You can ask for frivolous information, such as next week's winning lottery numbers, but you probably won't receive it because that usually would not further your psychic or spiritual growth. How many psychics do you know who have won the lottery?

Nevertheless, if the request for information on any subject whatever is valid, you will receive the answer. "Ask and ye shall receive," it has been promised. It may be provided immediately by your Higher Self; however, if your Higher Self does not have the information, you will be informed that you will receive it after consultation with those who do have the information. Usually the answers are provided within minutes or hours, but always within three days. In this case, learn also to look for answers in your dreams, or be aware of unusual messages you may receive.

Spiritual Enlightenment. The Inner Light Consciousness Meditation technique provides a guided visualization or "journey" that is used to occupy and focus the creative, active mind. As this journey proceeds through both the physical and spiritual realms, the mind tends to become less analytical and responds more and more with feelings. The active mind begins to relax more and more each time the journey is undertaken, because it knows what to expect and also knows that each step becomes safer and more comfortable.

As our inner senses become more sensitive and aware of the spiritual energies in the higher dimensions, we begin to realize that our consciousness does not have to go "higher" or "up somewhere" or "out there" in an attempt to experience the sense of connection and oneness with our Source—we merely have to become more aware that this Source energy is all around us and within us, everywhere in the universe. We just need to expand our own awareness to include the reality of these higher vibrations in our individual lives.

A very special, sacred space is provided within this meditation so that each person can completely let go of all the busy mental images in his or her mind, and let the feelings of inner peace and awareness expand without limit until he or she connects in love and compassion with the universal consciousness that many call God. It is here in this sacred space that, if you are properly prepared for the experience, you can allow the kundalini energy within you to rise for the purpose of increased spiritual enlightenment.

THE KUNDALINI ENERGY

In yogic and Hindu literature, kundalini is the process that activates the energy of the chakras and also assists in awakening the higher centers of consciousness. In many ancient texts, the kundalini energy is depicted as a coiled snake that normally lies sleeping in the Root Chakra. But when this energy is unleashed through a deliberate process such as meditation, it rises up the central energy column just in front of the spine, activating each chakra along the way. When this kundalini energy reaches the Third Eye and Crown Chakra, the individual may experience a sensation of bright light flooding the brain, followed by expansion of the consciousness and a feeling of intense bliss.

This can be a beautiful, overwhelming experience of pure ecstasy that, if repeated regularly, can lead to spiritual enlightenment. But if the subject is not fully prepared, it can also be an extremely painful and damaging experience that can result in severe physical, emotional, and mental scars. The kundalini energy is very strong, and if it encounters any blocks in the chakras as it rises toward the crown, negative side effects are quite possible.

Richard Gerber says that, "The chakras are the energy repositories of karma."[4] If complete chakra cleansing is not accomplished before attempting to raise the kundalini, these patterns constrict and distort the free rising flow of kundalini energy as it reaches that chakra. The kundalini energy will hammer away at these energy blocks until they are burned through. As we have seen in previous chapters, there are several techniques and processes to repattern the Physical and Etheric Energy Bodies, and the Ro-Hun technique has been expressly developed to remove negative or nonharmonious energy patterns from the Emotional and Mental levels of each chakra.

Kundalini energy has been compared to an electrical current that passes through the thin filament of a light bulb. As the current passes through, light and burning heat may be produced. The more resistance to the current, the more heat and light are produced. Blockages in the chakras to the flow of kundalini energy must be removed before the flow of energy will be smooth.

All this is said not with the intent to discourage the kundalini experience; instead it is intended to encourage proper preparation before attempting to raise your kundalini energy yourself. The key is the preparation of all chakras by clearing the negative energies from each, and balancing the energies between and among the chakras. When this has been done, the kundalini has a clear and free energetic pathway to travel.

As a matter of course, I encourage my own clients and students to satisfactorily complete at least the basic Ro-Hun Purification and Shadow Self series prior to attempting kundalini release during their own meditations. This allows me to monitor the energetic clearing progress in each of their chakras and also provides the client with enough information to decide when he or she is ready to allow his or her own kundalini energy to be released.

Using the ILC Meditation CD

The guided imagery of the Inner Light Consciousness Meditation CD has been carefully crafted to provide the meditator with a meaningful and consistent set of visualization and imagery cues that define a journey from your day-to-day physical consciousness into your spiritual awareness and back again. It is important to note that your experiences and new insights of your spiritual journey are always brought back into your conscious world so you can integrate this new knowledge into your conscious daily activities.

The ILC Meditation CD that is separately available (see Appendix C) contains two meditations: an initial preparatory meditation that must be done for forty consecutive days, and a shorter version of the same meditation that may be used whenever desired after the forty-consecutive-day period.

The initial meditation journey, labeled "Inner Light Consciousness Meditation (Forty-Day Journey)," guides you through the initial preparation phase. You will be asked to do the Forty-Day Journey at least once a day for forty consecutive days to install and reinforce the imagery cues that make up this meditation sequence. The number forty is very symbolic to the subconscious mind, and represents a new beginning, a starting over with a completely fresh slate. In the Bible, when something happened for "forty days and forty nights," there was a significant new pattern established for the beginning of something new and fresh. The story of Noah's flood and Jesus' challenges in the desert just before he began his ministry are but two biblical examples.

Forty consecutive days' meditation on your part is also important because it calls for a completely new lifestyle pattern to be brought into your everyday experience, one of expanded awareness of who and what you really are. A significant amount of determination and perseverance will be required to complete the initial forty-day sequence, and only you can know if you have the patience and are willing to invest the time that is required.

There are four files on the "Inner Light Consciousness Meditation Forty-Day Journey" CD: two meditation files mentioned above and two data files. The two data files are instructions on how to properly use the CD in a long-term meditation program. The audio files should play on any CD player but may not play on your computer. The data files are saved in the Rich Text Format (.rtf), so they should be able to be loaded into most word processors such as Microsoft Word or WordPerfect on your PC computer. The files are:

- A **data** file called **"ILC Instructions.rtf."** DO NOT PRINT THIS OUT UNTIL AFTER YOU HAVE COMPLETED THE ILC FORTY-DAY JOURNEY FOR FORTY CONSECUTIVE DAYS. It is important to lay a solid foundation first with your Forty-Day Journey before you start working in each of the four rooms of your Temple.

- An **audio** file called **"ILC Forty-Day Journey."** This is the guided visualization for your Forty-Day Journey, and lasts about thirty-three minutes.

- An **audio** file called **"ILC Meditation."** This is a guided visualization you may play during your meditation period each day AFTER you have completed the Forty-Day Journey. This guided visualization is a condensed form of the Forty-Day Journey and lasts about fifteen-and-one-half minutes.

- A **data** file called **"readme.rtf"** consisting of these instructions on how to use the CD. NOTE: THIS FILE SHOULD BE PRINTED OUT BEFORE YOU BEGIN YOUR INITIAL FORTY-DAY JOURNEY. To print out this file, load the CD into your computer. If the meditation starts playing automatically, stop the playback of your audio player (RealAudio, WinAmp, etc.). Start your word processor and open the file "D:readme.rtf" where D is the CD drive letter. Print out the one-page file from your word processor.

THE FORTY-DAY JOURNEY

Select a time and place that you can comfortably set aside for meditating each day, either in the morning or in the evening as you prefer. Prepare yourself by breathing deeply and slowly several times, and let your body and mind become comfortable and relaxed as you prepare for your meditation session. When you are ready to begin your meditation, select track #2 (ILC Forty-Day Journey) on your CD player, press the "play" button and close your eyes. If your CD player has an autorun feature, insert the CD, and it will skip over the first data file and automatically start playing the ILC Forty-Day Journey after several seconds. Follow the words and images given to you and really get into the feeling of each image as you journey through your meadow and up your spiritual mountain to your own Sanctum Sanctorum, your Temple Within.

Use the ILC Forty-Day Journey track #2 on your CD for at least one meditation per day for forty consecutive days to fully "program" your subconscious mind for the life-enhancing changes and transformations that will soon become apparent in your daily life. If you miss a day or drift off to sleep while listening to the CD, you must start all over from day number one and complete your forty consecutive days while awake. Meditation is a conscious activity; sleep is not!

The Forty-Day Journey begins with the relaxation of the Physical Body into a very safe place. It is important for the conscious mind to relax, and it cannot relax if it must continue to be concerned in any way for the physical well-being or safety of your body. You want to take your consciousness or awareness into a state wherein the Physical Body can be safely left behind without worry or concern. This releases and frees the mind from its analytical (conscious) role and lets it expand and travel to the higher dimensions where all things are possible.

The Point of Perfect Balance. The Point of Perfect Balance is that safe place that you feel within yourself when you know that all is well physically. Your body is resting comfortably in a chair, and there are no disturbing sounds, sights, smells, or feelings anywhere in this relaxing space. The lights are subdued, and it just feels good to take this time for yourself and relax very deeply in the knowledge that everything is right with the Big Picture of this moment. As you take several long, slow deep breaths, allow yourself to feel the air coming into your lungs and its life-giving energy spreading out to every cell and molecule in your body, relaxing it even further.

When everything feels good and you know it is right, look up and just observe that your meadow is beginning to form right there in front of you. When you are ready, just step from your Point of Perfect Balance in your Physical Body to the Point of Perfect Balance in your meadow. See yourself standing in your meadow now, still, safe, and secure in the knowledge that all is still right with your world.

The Meadow. The ILC Meditation always begins and ends in your own personal, private meadow. You can make the details in your meadow look and feel however you want. But on a subconscious level, the meadow is always a powerful symbol as a place of peace and tranquility. Forests can be dark and unknown; deserts are arid and barren, and seas can be unpredictable and unforgiving. But a meadow is always a place where the sublime beauty and harmony of nature can be enjoyed in all its peaceful fullness and glory.

The meadow is also the most important place in your entire meditation journey. It is in the meadow where you learn to heighten and expand your inner senses. It is here that you develop your natural inner abilities so you can see with your inner eyes, hear with your inner ears, and sense with your inner knowing all the vibrations and patterns in the higher dimensions of your true spiritual being. This ability to use your inner senses just as if they were your normal physical senses forms the foundation upon which the entire ILC Meditation sequence is based.

Each time you meditate with the intention of opening your inner senses to the world you are visualizing, your experience becomes more tangible, more personal, more real. As you step from your Point of Perfect Balance into your meadow, you will begin to feel the reality of your meadow—feel it, see it, taste it, hear it, smell it, and breathe it all in. You will smile pleasantly at the blue sky and the white clouds, and actually feel the warmth of the sun shining on your skin as you move through your meadow. Feel the grass as it tingles beneath your bare feet, be very aware of all the brilliant colors of the wild flowers, smell the sweet fragrance of the flowers, and reach down to touch the silky petal of a flower.

The meadow experience is so basic and important to the ILC Meditation process that you should not leave the meadow until you are able to sense, see, hear, taste, smell, and touch all the objects in your guided meditation. If you have difficulty visualizing and sensing, for example, the meadow grasses brushing against your ankles and legs, you should take off your shoes and socks and actually go for a walk through a grassy meadow with your eyes closed. Focus all your awareness on the feeling of the meadow grasses under your feet and against your bare ankles and legs. Pay very close attention to the feeling, and remember that feeling so you can instantly recall how the grasses feel when you step into your meadow in your meditation.

Similarly, you may want to sit down in a real meadow, close your eyes, and just listen very intently for twenty minutes or more. Listen to the birds; hear the wind rustle the leaves on the trees and the grasses around you. Remember all the sounds of nature that you hear in your meadow and discard or ignore any man-made sounds. Sit back and lean against the rough bark of a real tree and feel its ridges in your back. Learn to recall the feeling of these ridges as you meditate. Visit a florist and enjoy the unlimited variety of the sweet perfume of the flowers. Remember and be able to recall these beautiful smells during your meditation.

While you continue to meditate each day, let your meadow experience become more and more real to you. Bring the memory of the external world feelings into your meadow experience and allow your inner senses to expand and feel the same sensations, the same feelings as those in your outer world. When you can bring life, animation, color, sound, and feeling into your meadow, your inner senses are truly awake and alive, and will bring significantly enhanced meaning to the remainder of your ILC Meditation.

As you stroll through your meadow and heighten your inner senses of vision, hearing, and smell, there are additional specific areas for you to visit. These include a field of corn, a fruit tree, and a swiftly flowing mountain stream. Each also has a very specific subconscious symbolic meaning, and these are discussed below.

Somewhere in your meadow there will be a field of corn. It may be very large or quite small; the size of the field does not matter at all. The corn itself is the important symbol to understand. As you enter the corn field and walk down the rows with ripened ears on each stalk, remember that corn is a universal symbol of abundance and plenty. And since this corn is in your meadow, the corn is all yours, and you are free to pick as much abundance as you wish and take it with you. The abundance you receive will be that type of abundance that you need at that time, whether it be abundance of prosperity, joy, happiness, love, health, or friendship.

Do not be bashful in reaching out and taking the abundance that you require. Remember, this has all been placed in your garden for you to use however you want. You could refuse to claim your rightful share of God's promised abundance, but why would you want to do that? The truth is that you really do deserve everything good that you can receive from life so long as receiving it does not harm yourself or anyone else in thought, word, or deed.

So forget about whether you deserve it, whether you have a right to ask for it, or whether you really need it. You have a right to ask for anything! All of life's abundance is right here in your own cornfield, available for the taking any time you wish. And as we learn how to accept these gifts without embarrassment, we begin to appreciate our own worth as individuals more and more each day.

As you exit the cornfield, you will come across a fruit tree that is full and ripe with your favorite fruit. It doesn't matter whether it is a pear tree, an apple tree, a peach tree, or whatever—it is your favorite fruit, and you know it will taste juicy and delicious. The fruit tree is there in your meadow to help you awaken additional inner senses and to reinforce the senses you have already exercised. You not only see the fruit and its inviting color, but you touch and feel the rough tree bark and the weight and size of the fruit itself. And as you bite into the fruit, you savor its succulent juices and taste its delicious sweetness in your mouth.

With the fruit tree experience, all of your inner senses that have outer counterparts have now been stimulated in your meadow—sight, sound, smell, touch, and taste. Each day, as you repeat the meditation and experience your meadow, you will reinforce and strengthen your inner abilities and senses. Soon the inner experience of your meadow will become as vibrant to you as a walk through a real meadow on a bright sunny afternoon, and you will know that you are becoming more and more prepared for your inner spiritual experiences with each meditation session.

As you finish eating your fruit, soon you will hear the bubbling and gurgling of a clear mountain stream in the distance. As you walk toward it and kneel down by its banks to wash the sticky fruit juice from your hands, gaze into the running waters and let your consciousness extend into the waters so you can feel the energies and the strength there.

The river with its bubbling waters is a reflection of your spiritual energy, your own life force energies, at that time. Become very familiar with the way they feel to you. Do not analyze whether they are more or less than at any other time, but just observe how the river surface looks at that time. Is it flowing smoothly and strongly, or is it choppy and turbulent? Is the river wide or narrow? Is it moving rapidly or sluggishly? Just mentally note all its characteristics at that time so you can record them later in your meditation journal.

Many factors can influence how the river appears on any given day, and the river may look very different from time to time. The pressures of a busy schedule, the emotional impact of words said or not said, the desire to appreciate the beauty of everything you look at, these all affect your moods and attitudes. As you learn to detect the differences in the way the river appears and correlate that with what is going on in your external life at that time, you will become even more aware of the importance of opening your inner self to the flow of life force energies to bring additional balance and harmony into your daily routine.

The Bridge. As you look up from the river, you will notice a bridge that crosses over the river. Each person will probably see the bridge differently. Just take a moment to see what it looks like to you: what it is made of, how long it is, how high it is, and how it is constructed. You should record these mental notes in your journal when you finish the meditation. You may find that it begins to appear differently or has different construction characteristics as you proceed through your Forty-Day Journey.

The bridge begins on the meadow side of your stream and goes over to the mountain side of the stream. As you pause on the meadow end of your bridge, expand your senses to feel how the energies on this side of the bridge feel to you—all the energies of life here in your meadow. Then you will slowly cross the bridge to the mountain side of the stream and again let your expanded senses feel how the energies seem to you there. Is there a difference in how each end of the bridge "feels"? Again, journal the feelings you sense on each end each day you meditate.

The bridge is, of course, the subconscious symbol that represents the separation between the physical and spiritual portions of your Forty-Day Journey. It also represents the degree of separation between the physical and spiritual realms of your own consciousness.

If you are just beginning your spiritual journey, you may begin with a very long and shaky bridge. But as you continue each day, you may find that the bridge becomes shorter and stronger. If you do see this, you can be sure that your own spiritual nature is becoming more and more closely integrated with your own physical nature, and vice versa. You will become aware of your own spiritual component and bringing it more and more into expression in your everyday life.

The Mountain Terraces. As you leave the bridge over the mountain stream, you will see your spiritual mountain in the distance and a pathway that leads from the bridge toward your mountain. The journey up the mountain represents, of course, the ascension of your consciousness up toward your Higher Self, the mountaintop, the spiritual part of yourself that is eternal.

As you proceed along your pathway, you will notice that it takes you through several terraces or gardens, each of which has a different color. The first terrace is the Red Garden, the second is the Orange Garden, the third is the Yellow Garden, and so on. Each of these gardens has a different vibration, a higher vibration than the previous one. This journey through the gardens is also an energetic journey up through your own chakra system, and you will feel the energy of the lesson or the purpose of each chakra as you climb toward the mountaintop.

The Red Garden is the Garden of Expectancy. Here you want to create a sense of anticipation and expectancy without expecting anything specific to happen, except that you will be changed as a result of this experience. Here you can end the way you saw yourself before and can begin a new way of living, a new way of communicating with others, and a new way of seeing yourself. As you walk into your Red Garden, you will notice that everything in the garden is colored red—the trees, the rocks, the earth, everything is red. Learn to feel what the Red Garden feels like, and really get into the energy of expectancy for a moment. And only when you feel the excitement, the anticipation, and the expectancy of the energies here—only then do you notice that the path continues on upward toward your mountaintop.

The Orange Garden is the Garden of Transformation, where we realize that what we could not do yesterday is now within our reach today. Today, you can reach higher and believe more in your own abilities. Here, you learn to leave all your perceived limitations behind and grow into your full capabilities. When you have felt the orange energies and the feelings of deep transformation, then you will notice that the pathway continues onward up the mountain.

The Yellow Garden is the Garden of New Birth, Expansiveness, and Joy. It is here that you can experience the expansiveness and joy of living a full, creative, joyous, and productive life. Here you will feel the excitement of anticipation, of finding out what your new life will bring—a life without limitations, life filled with exploration, wonder, learning, growing, and creativity. Again, when you feel the yellow energies of expansiveness and joy here, you will see your pathway continuing on up the mountain toward the next terrace.

As you begin walking along the pathway, you will notice that it now becomes much steeper. This is symbolic of leaving behind the three lower terraces (chakras) that relate to the physical body; you are now approaching the Green Garden, the doorway or gateway to the upper three terraces (chakras) that relate to the spiritual aspects of your being. The journey now becomes more difficult, and the pathway becomes steeper.

It is important here to note that the lower three terraces that represent the lower three chakras and the physical aspects of your being are not inferior to or less important than the upper three terraces, representing the spiritual aspects of your being. It is devastating to separate or isolate these chakras into the beast below and the heavens above; they must all be in alignment and functioning equally to bring harmony, balance, and health to your being. In addition, when the upper and lower chakras are balanced, we are best able to bring our spiritual awareness into the everyday reality of our lives.

When you enter the Green Garden, the Garden of the Companion, and bring it to life through your inner senses, you will notice a brilliant being of light approaching you from the deep green forest. This is Living Love—total, unconditional Love, coming to greet you. As you look into this being's eyes, you can feel all the unconditional love the universe holds for you personally. Here your thoughts are, "I don't know exactly who or what you are, and I'm not expecting that you meet any of my own expectations. I simply want to know you better." And you know that this Companion will always be there walking with you; you know that you never have been and never will be alone—your Companion is always there for you.

The Blue Garden is the Garden of Communion, where you reach that point in your life's spiritual journey where you are alone with your Companion, sharing and blending your energies with each other, knowing that there is nothing you want or need to hide. When you feel these energies here in your Blue Garden, you will again see your pathway continuing on up the mountainside to the Violet Garden, the Garden of Responsibility.

The Violet Garden is where you accept the responsibility to use your talents and abilities wisely. With reverence, awe, and gratitude, accept the gifts and the information that is offered to you, and the abilities that will be needed to help you express your essence on the Earth plane in the way you have chosen to meet your own challenges and lessons. Here is where you make the commitment to yourself to always use these abilities when you should, to always use them in a way that will help and aid yourself and others, and to never withhold or misuse them in any way that would bring harm to yourself or others.

Here, you may want to say to your God, "Thy will be done." But God will say back to you, "Oh, no! This is YOUR life! You're missing the meaning of your life if you turn it all over to me! What do YOU want? THY will be done!" The quickest and surest way of expressing that unconditional love you felt in the Blue Garden is not to give your will away to God, but to align your own will with the will of God so that your own "Godness" can be manifested through you in all that you speak and all that you choose to do.

The difference between a person who has awakened in the Violet Garden and one who has not is that the person who has not will send you a Christmas card that says "Good will to all mankind." But a person who has awakened in the Violet Garden will send you a Christmas Card that says, "I will good to all mankind." The first is a nice statement, but there is no responsibility attached to it, and there is no clarity about who is going to do it. But the person who sends the second Christmas card has awakened in the Violet Garden, is expressing his or her will for all to hear, and is taking personal responsibility for that expression.

As you look upward, the mountaintop is still obscured in clouds, and your pathway is not clear. But when you connect with the feeling of gratitude for this experience and accept the responsibility for your words, thoughts, and actions, the clouds part and the loving hands of God lift you up and gently set you down in your White Garden.

The seventh terrace, the White Garden, the Garden of Enlightenment, is symbolic of your own inner sacred space, your Temple within not made with hands, the garden of limitless power, absolute harmony, and eternal duration. These are the energies that you tap into as you breathe in and feel the energies of the White Garden. There in your White Garden is your Temple, your own personal sacred space within where the real power and effectiveness of the Inner Light Consciousness Meditation can be realized.

The Temple Experience. The Temple Experience is the pinnacle of your meditation. When you have prepared yourself to enter your Temple and then consciously choose to enter into your own sacred place within, you are truly standing in your own divine energy, your creative essence through which you can accomplish the goals of your meditation time, whether that be for healing, reading Akashic Records of yourself or another, obtaining wisdom and insight on any subject whatsoever, or to experience your connection with your Source.

As you proceed toward your Temple, you will first come upon a clear, reflecting pool of water. When you look down into it, you can see yourself very clearly in the reflection. Then, as you step down into the reflecting pool and walk along its bottom, you are metaphorically cleansing yourself.

Here, you know all your thoughts, whether good or bad, and you know whether or not there is something you would try to hide or sweep under the rug and just ignore. Here, you cannot ignore any facet of your personality, but must accept everything that you know yourself to be, and then ask silently that anything that is not in service to the Light be washed away from you, leaving you cleansed and purified.

As you climb out of the reflecting pool on the other side, you will see that everything you are, even your clothes, are now washed and made pure—so pure that you radiate a white light outward for all to see. As you approach your Temple and prepare to enter it, you will kneel on the Temple steps and offer a simple prayer for further cleansing and preparation to enter the most sacred part your being. This is simply another reinforcement to your subconscious mind for your intention and desire to completely prepare yourself for the spiritual experiences inside your Temple.

The first thing you will see after entering your Temple is a tall violet flame rising up from a square inscribed in the vestibule floor. This is the eternal flame of purification and transmutation, which burns forever in your own spiritual essence. In the infinitely high vibrations of its perfect light, no lower vibrations can exist. You will step into this flame for a moment, and as you do, any remaining impurities within you (such as lower or base thoughts, feelings, or intentions) are immediately transmuted into a lump of gold, which will appear on the floor beside your feet.

As you step out of the Violet Flame of Transmutation, you will pick up this piece of gold, take it to the altar there in the center of your inner Temple, and offer it both as a sacrifice and letting go of all the impurities within you, and also as a symbol of newly purified material with which to expand this Temple not made with hands. After making your offering, you will rise, look around your Temple, and see that there are four rooms you may visit for various purposes.

The Healing Room. The first room you will visit is your Healing Room. As you enter it, you will be greeted by Archangel Raphael, the

Archangel of healing, harmony, and balance. You will also see a "healing window" on the far wall with the eternal light of God shining through the window, and a healing table will be in the center of the room. Here, you can bring healing on the Physical, Etheric, Emotional, Mental, and Spiritual levels to yourself or, with his or her permission, another person. You will thank Archangel Raphael for being there, and then tell him that you are here just now on your Forty-Day Journey and that you will return to your Healing Room when you are ready to begin your healing work.

The Hall of Records. The next room you will visit is the Hall of Records that contains the Akashic Records of all persons who have ever lived on the earth. You will be greeted by your Recordkeeper, the one to whom you will make your request for a specific record and who will retrieve and deliver the requested record to you. As you also give him or her a big hug, you will tell him or her that you are here on your Forty-Day Journey and that you will return when you are ready to access and read your own personal Akashic Record or, with his or her permission, the Akashic Record of another person.

The Learning Room. The next room to be visited during your Forty-Day Journey is your Learning Room. As you enter it, you will see your Instructor waiting for you. As you look into his or her eyes, you will feel the infinite depths of wisdom and knowledge that he or she has ready to give to you if that knowledge is in your highest and best interests. Any valid question will be answered, usually on the spot and always within three days. If your Instructor does not have immediate access to the answer, he or she will retrieve it and pass it on along later. But you have to learn how to listen so you can hear or know the answer when it is provided. Again, you will let your Instructor know that you will return for specific information after completing your Forty-Day Journey.

The Meditation Room. The last of the four rooms you will visit on your Forty-Day Journey is your Meditation Room. Inside this pleasant, inviting space is only a comfortable chair in the center of the dimly lit room. You will sit down in the chair, relax, and allow your consciousness to expand into the experience, awareness, and knowledge that the universe has to offer you at that time. If you are properly prepared, you may attempt to bring up your kundalini energies here; otherwise, it is your sacred space to just relax and be at peace for a while.

Descending the Mountain. After visiting each of the four rooms in your Temple, you will stop briefly at the altar and offer thanks for this experience. Then you will exit through the Temple doors and prepare to return to your meadow.

As you descend your spiritual mountain, you will bring with you all the memories and energies of your Temple experience in the White Garden into the Violet Garden and merge these energies. Then you will bring these merged energies down into the Blue Garden and merge them once again. In a similar fashion, you will blend and merge all the energies of each chakra garden with all the others, balancing and harmonizing the energies of each chakra as you descend. This is a very important process and brings back into your physical awareness the memories, knowledge, insights, and higher energies of your spiritual meditation.

Returning to Your Meadow. As you cross your bridge and return to your meadow, you will again sense the vitality and energy of all the life in your meadow and, when you are ready, gently step back into your Point of Perfect Balance in your meadow and then into the Point of Perfect Balance within yourself. You will bring with you all the insights and knowledge of your meditation experience, as well as the healing energies of balance, renewal, and regeneration.

A note is appropriate here to alert you to the fact that you may find your mind wandering again after you have been through the Forty-Day Journey several times. You may begin to feel that you know a certain part already because you've been through it many times before and may let your mind begin to wander a bit, and extraneous thoughts may creep in for your conscious mind to consider. Stay focused on the Journey! It has been very carefully and purposefully crafted to engage the conscious mind by providing specific images to focus on. If other thoughts begin to intrude, focus again on the words of the Journey, and let yourself *feel* the feelings associated with the words. Engage your inner senses again and begin to *experience* the Journey instead of just listening to it. And once again, if you suddenly become alert and realize that you drifted off to sleep for a bit and don't remember following the imagery, you must start over from day number one. Meditation is a conscious, directed activity—sleep is not!

AFTER THE FIRST FORTY DAYS

When you have successfully completed at least forty consecutive days' meditation using the ILC Forty-Day Journey track #2 on your CD, you are ready to begin using the tools that you were introduced to during your forty-day preparation. *Now* you may print out track #1 on the CD. It contains the special instructions and background information you will need to use the tools in each of the four Temple rooms.

To print out the instructions for using the four rooms, place the CD in your PC computer and bring up a listing of the files on the CD. You will not see the two audio files but will see only the two data files. Double-click or open the file called "ILC Instructions.rtf" and print it out. This is a fourteen-page document in MS Word format that provides all the information you will need for continuing this very profound meditation. For all subsequent ILC Meditation sessions, you should now use the second audio file, "ILC Meditation," which will be track #3 on your CD player.

After you have successfully made the forty-consecutive-day meditation journey, you are well prepared to delve deeper into the mysteries in each of the rooms in your Temple. You have prepared both your mind and your body for a much more profound meditation experience. Up to now, you have been preparing yourself for the real work that will now be done in your individual Temple rooms. Now you may begin to actually use the tools available in each of your Temple rooms. Now your daily meditation will consist of a special time to take yourself or someone else into your Healing Room for a true spiritual healing on all levels. Or you may wish to read your personal Akashic Records to obtain specific information from previous life experiences that have a direct bearing on your current situation. Or perhaps you want to visit your Learning Room to receive practical guidance and information from your Higher Self that you can use in your everyday life, or perhaps you would like to spend your meditation time in your Meditation Room in quiet solitude and communion with your guides, angels, and higher dimensional spiritual beings.

Because you are going to be doing deeper work each time you visit one of your rooms, you will need to spend more time in that room. This may be perhaps just a few minutes, or it could be up to a half hour or more, depending on what you wish to accomplish during that visit. Therefore, it becomes important to shorten the length of time spent going through your meadow and up your mountain in order to leave sufficient time for your Temple experience without requiring too much time for your overall meditation schedule.

To retain an effective Temple experience, there are certain trigger points and steps that should not be omitted in a shortened version of the ILC Meditation sequence. There is also specific additional information you will need to prepare yourself for the work in each Temple room. The shortened ILC Meditation itself is the audio file "ILC Meditation," and the procedures for using the tools in the four Temple rooms during this shortened meditation are contained in the file "ILC Instructions.rtf." Instructions are provided for using the Healing Window and Healing Table found in your Healing Room, for accessing and reading your own Akashic Records in your Hall of Records, for obtaining reliable and practical information on nearly any subject from your Higher Self in the Learning Room, and for attaining a deep meditative state and connecting with your spiritual self in the Meditation Room.

To summarize:

- Open your word processor and print out the data file "readme.rtf" on the CD.

- Put the cd in your CD player, select track #2 (ILC Forty-Day Journey), and press the play button. Use this meditation for forty consecutive days.

- Open your word processor and print out the data file "ILC Instructions.rtf" on the CD.

- Put the CD in your CD player, select track #3 (ILC Meditation) and press the play button. Use this meditation as often as you like.

The ILC Meditation contains a very powerful and effective set of spiritual tools you can use to change the way you live your life and interact with others. But in order to make a difference, they must be used regularly and purposefully. At this point, you must walk your own walk. Paul Solomon and I have given you these tools to let you explore your own consciousness and abilities, but we cannot do the exploration for you. May the adventures into the conscious awareness of your own spiritual nature be more exciting and enlightening than you have ever dreamed possible!

Spiritual Regression

Spiritual Regression is an advanced hypnotherapeutic approach that lets us experience our true spiritual nature by allowing us to recall the memories, words, deeds, thoughts, actions, and indeed even the form or appearance of our spiritual essence, or spirit, during that interval of time between physical incarnations. (*Note:* See the Glossary for the distinction between "soul" and "spirit" as I am using them here in this book.)

As mentioned previously, the Spiritual Energy Body holds the vibrational energy patterns of our higher intentions, our sense of what is right and wrong (conscience), and our desires to increase our awareness of our purpose, place, and mission for this lifetime. We just need to become consciously aware of these Spiritual Energy patterns so that we may incorporate and apply them in our daily physical life. But what is the best way to come to understand and experience our true spiritual nature that is reflected in these patterns in our Spiritual Energy Body? Albert Einstein summed it up quite concisely in his statement "Knowledge is experience. All else is just information." Experience is the great teacher, and we are here in the greatest schoolhouse of all—our physical lifetime.

However, the one thing we have been told that we cannot experience as human beings is the great mystery of what happens after the final act of human lifetime: our own death. The uncertainty, the unknown, and the fear of what lies ahead "beyond the veil" have all given rise to many different propositions and theories, several of which have formed the basis of our religions and the quest for reassurance that death is not the end of our awareness.

A small but growing number of people have had near-death experiences (NDEs) as a result of accidents, trauma, death on the operating table, etc. and have returned to life to tell their astounding stories. They have seen beyond the veil and experienced reassuring sensations and feelings of love and togetherness after getting a glimpse of the higher dimensions or space to which they were attracted. In fact, according to the mission statement of the International Association for Near-Death Studies, Inc. (IANDS), it has been formed "to respond to people's needs for information and support concerning near-death and similar experiences and to encourage recognition of the experiences as genuine and significant events of rich meaning."

For the great majority of people who have not experienced NDEs, what lies beyond death is still a mystery. But now, this seems to be changing. Three activities have begun to meld together to create a great catalyst for awakening our own ability to answer these questions for ourselves.

First among these activities is a general awakening of the consciousness of individuals to the spiritual truths that lie at the core of many religious orders. We have begun to seriously look for and find the kernels of spiritual truth that form the foundation of religious beliefs and dogmas. And as we observe the resurgence in the activity of searching for God and goodness in the meaning of our lives, we are asking to know the spiritual Truths of not only our own being, but also life and death, and to understand what lies beyond our own physical death.

Second, as we become more awakened spiritually, we are taking back the responsibility for making our own choices and decisions of what to believe and include as a part of our own personal Truth. We are beginning to question institutional thought in general—not only the specific religious dogmas we are asked to believe in church (and what a variation there is between churches!), but also what we are told to believe and subscribe to in the cultural and political organizations to which we belong. No longer are we merely nodding our heads and blindly following the herd, subscribing to thoughts and beliefs that someone else wants us to believe. The alternative healing revolution we are seeing today is another grassroots extension of this phenomenon—we are now asking hard questions and expecting factual answers from those in charge. We want information we can understand and use in our daily lives.

And third, in this era of exponentially increasing spiritual awareness, the tools to obtain, assimilate, and process new information on many levels are becoming available at an astounding pace. New hypnotherapeutic processes to gain access to spiritual information are being developed and refined by a growing number of serious hypnotherapeutic and past life regression researchers, and the ability to quickly disseminate this new information has also increased dramatically. Not only are new titles on these subjects being printed daily, many researchers are rapidly sharing their findings and information with others via e-mail and the worldwide web (Internet).

Certainly these new investigative processes will continue to evolve and be refined as many more hypnotherapists begin to include the ability for their clients to become consciously aware of their own true spiritual nature and the activities they participate in between physical incarnations.

THE PROCESS

The form of Spiritual Regression I practice is patterned after the groundbreaking techniques of Dr. Michael Newton, *Journey of Souls* and *Destiny of Souls*; Dr. Shakuntala Modi, *Memories of God and Creation*; and Shepherd Hoodwin, *The Journey of Your Soul*. The procedure involves taking the client into a very deep hypnotic state of relaxation, and then simply knowing to ask the right questions. It has never been so obvious to practicing hypnotherapists that "ask and ye shall receive" is in fact a fulfilled promise. Once the conscious analytical mind is gently put into an observing mode for a while, all information associated with that client's soul record (his or her personal Akashic Record) and spiritual essence is available for recall and review, with only one apparent constraint: conscious recognition of the memories, experiences, and information recalled must serve the client's highest and best good at that time.

Spiritual Regression departs from the more well-known Past Life Regression Therapy in two significant ways: the depth of hypnosis required is greater, and the focus of investigation and the type of information received is much broader.

In Past Life Regression, the client and therapist are working primarily with the memories and experiences available to the subconscious mind. These memories and experiences can be accessed when the client is in a light to moderate Alpha state. The traditional focus of Past Life Regression is to observe and participate in previous experiences in order to understand the mental and emotional patterns formed by those experiences and how those patterns are negatively affecting the client's current lifetime. The information available to the client from his subconscious mind includes all the experiences from his or her current and all previous lifetimes—each action taken, word spoken, and thought formed while incarnated.

However, in order to witness and understand the experiences of the client's spiritual essence while still in the spiritual realms or dimensions between incarnations, a deeper level of hypnosis is required. It is not enough to merely be able to enter light to moderate the Alpha state of hypnosis; the therapist must be able to take the client well into the lower Alpha/upper Theta state for access to your true spiritual consciousness, the superconscious mind. In this state, the client has access to all the beautiful memories and knowledge of his or her spiritual essence from a much broader and more enlightened perspective. This broader perspective includes all the experiences not only of the soul record while incarnated, but also of the true spirit essence while still in the spiritual world between incarnations.

The Information

Information available to the spirit, or superconscious mind, includes all the information available to the subconscious mind, as well as an understanding of the purpose for each incarnation, the agreements made by specific spiritual beings for helping one another to learn certain lessons, and an understanding of interpersonal dynamics from a spiritual perspective. The amount and type of information available to each client depends on, among other things, the level of advancement of the client's soul and the degree to which receiving such information would be in his or her best interests at that time.

Additional information available to the superconscious mind, but not to the subconscious mind, includes your spiritual name and appearance, the name and appearance of your spiritual guide, the beings in the particular group of spirits with whom you frequently incarnate as close relatives or friends, the energy characteristics and forms of beings in the spiritual world, and the activities that spirit beings participate in while in the spiritual world. In addition to understanding the information available in the spiritual realm, the deeply hypnotized client is also able to experience the activities and feel the deep emotional feelings of love, mutual respect, and compassion that pervade the entire spiritual dimension.

Each Spiritual Regression session will last about three hours. If you come to me, I will want to know what information you are seeking and what experiences have led you to Spiritual Regression. After the interview, you will be asked to rest in a comfortable chair, or remove your shoes and lie down on a comfortable healing table. You will then be given several suggestions that will allow you to quickly and safely relax into a comfortable and very deep state of hypnosis. When you are deeply relaxed, I can then begin conversing directly with your subconscious mind and will begin bringing you into an even deeper state wherein your awareness or consciousness becomes a part of your superconscious mind. Even though deeply hypnotized, you will still be able to hear and understand everything I say quite clearly, and you will respond to any questions I may ask.

While in this extremely heightened state of awareness, assuming that it is in your highest interests at that time to receive the information you are seeking, you will be able to experience your most recent past life, safely and painlessly move through your transition (death) at the end of that lifetime, move back into the spiritual world from which you incarnated, recall the activities you participated in while in the spiritual world between lifetimes, and become aware of the spiritual decisions, choices, and agreements you made for your current lifetime before incarnating.

When the examination of this most recent part of your spiritual record is completed, I will gently bring you back to full conscious awareness. Following a Spiritual Regression session, you will be able to consciously remember your entire journey into the spiritual world, including the information and memories recalled and the sensations and feelings you experienced there. We can then discuss the details of your new information, as well as their implications for your life. This information is usually so profound that you will want to expand your concept of reality in a way that you can accept these new experiences as an integral part of your new Truth. To aid in fully remembering and processing all your spiritual experiences and information, a cassette tape of each Spiritual Regression session is normally provided.

It should be noted here that the process of Spiritual Regression can be initiated from any one of several different therapies. The client may come specifically for a Spiritual Regression session; in this case, the client is regressed to their most recent past life experience, progressed to the end of that lifetime, and taken through physical death and into the spiritual realm, which may then be explored and experienced. Alternatively, the Spiritual Regression process may be initiated at the end of a Past Life Regression session, or at the end of any of the several past life regressions normally experienced during any of the RoHun Transformational Therapy sessions.

CASE STUDY #1

To illustrate the entire process of Spiritual Regression, Barbara (not her real name) came to me to address, among other things, a fear of driving on freeways where she would have to wind in and out of fast-moving traffic. She had an ominous feeling that if she went fast on the highway, she would surely have a wreck and die. She also wanted to understand her deep sense of dislike for her mother that bordered on hatred. The following transcript is taken from a Ro-Hun Purification Session when we were working in the Solar Plexus Chakra area and is edited slightly for continuity of thought.

A normal practice in Ro-Hun is to take the client through the death scene in most past lives and then go to a quiet, peaceful, spiritual place to reflect on the lessons of that lifetime. The process of exploring the spiritual world further, as is done in Spiritual Regression sessions, is often a very logical and natural extension of the RoHun process to access this additional information that is available to the superconscious mind. If the RoHun therapist is prepared for and trained in the Spiritual Regression process, this additional tour through the spiritual world can

add much fascinating and relevant information to the client's understanding of his or her true spiritual nature.

We had worked on Barbara's Solar Plexus Chakra area before, but
when I again scanned it with my hand, I felt some congested energy
remaining in the area, so I began an energetic manipulation technique
to stir up the vibrational patterns there to release any memories that
might still be retained in her field there. When I did this, she reported
that she saw a top wobbling unsteadily, as if something was out of balance there. As I continued to manipulate the energies in the emotional
region of the Solar Plexus Chakra, she saw and smelled an apple blos-
som. When I asked her to look closely at it, she began to see a little boy
climbing in an apple tree. It was her son, Erik, laughing and hiding from
her in the branches. Her husband was nearby, but his name is not pro-
nounceable; they are in either Norway or Sweden.

When I had her look into her husband's eyes and connect with his
inner thoughts and feelings, she knew that he was in love with another
woman, but he wasn't ready to tell her yet. Then they all went home,
and they sent their son over to his grandmother's house to stay while
she (the client) visited her sister over the mountains for several days. But
as soon as she left, her husband got rid of all her clothes and belongings
from the house. He had arranged with the driver of the carriage that she
would die in an accident—the carriage would run away down a hill and
go over the edge of a cliff, killing her.

Then Barbara saw herself in the carriage, bouncing and swaying
along the narrow mountain road, and the horses suddenly began to gal-
lop faster and faster. There was a bend in the road coming up, and the
driver jumped off and watched the carriage with her in it go over the
edge of the cliff. The coach was smashed on the rocks below, three of
the horses died, and the fourth was screaming in pain. She looks down
and sees that she has also died, and that her body is "bent wrong." Then
she missed her son Erik very much, and as soon as she thought of Erik,
she was at his side at his Grandma's house. Erik and Grandma were in
the kitchen talking, but then Erik sensed his mother and asked where
she was. Grandma, who is unaware of the plot, said his mother was at
her sister's house. When the client sent love to Erik, she felt that he
sensed it, so she was satisfied and was now ready to leave. I asked her to

go back out the kitchen door and tell me what she saw there. She reported seeing "a blue hole" above her, and felt she must go up through it. As she rose up through the blue hole, I asked her to report what she was seeing and what she felt.

C (Client): I see my guide waiting for me.

HB (Howard Batie): How does he appear to you?

C: He's light, he's tall.

HB: And how do you call him? What is his name?

C: It's Jare-ub.

HB: Very good. Is there anyone else here? Is there anyone else to greet you?

C: No, not yet.

HB: All right. And where do you want to go now? What do you want to do? Is it important to talk with Jare-ub for a while?

C: I'm concerned about Erik. But Jare-ub says he will always remember me happily and that his new mother will be good to him because she can't have children.

HB: I want you to walk over to that full-length mirror there, right there in front of you, and tell me what are the energies you see? How do you appear? What colors are there?

C: Gold and white. I'm feminine, but not clearly. Just a light energy.

HB: And what is the name you are known as?

C: Eesa.

HB: OK, Eesa, I want you to walk over to Jare-ub and ask him if there's anything you can do now to make sure that Erik remembers you fondly?

C: He says that I did the right thing in going to see him. He says I did touch his energies, and Erik felt it.

HB: Good. And in that last lifetime, what was your lesson to learn, the purpose for that incarnation?

C: Compassion. I learned compassion.

HB: Good. Now what have you decided that your next lesson will be, for your next lifetime?

C: It is not known yet.

HB: Not known yet. OK. Ask Jare-ub when it will be time for you to know what to choose, and how will you know? How will you know what choices you have?

C: I must observe other beings for a while. Right now it is time for me to heal.

HB: How will you be healed?

C: By being in the light. Just by being here and feeling the love.

HB: Good. I want you to look around now, and see if there's a place here, a special place where that love is.

C: It's everywhere. It comes from the Source.

HB: OK. Let's just rest here for a while, rest in this light. . . . And that period of restfulness is so refreshing, so healing. . . . Let me know when you're ready to continue, when you're all rejuvenated and ready to go.

C: I don't want to go—I like it here!

HB: Yes. What are you doing now?

C: I'm waiting for the others in my group.

HB: Good. Well, they're probably waiting for you, too. I want you to get up and move toward them now. Just feel them being drawn to you, and feel yourself being drawn to them. Can you see them approaching?

C: Yes . . . different colored lights.

HB: Good. What colored lights are there?

C: Green, blue, purple.

HB: Beautiful, aren't they?

C: Right. And yellow. We make a rainbow together!

HB: Yes, you do. How is it that you develop and grow as a spirit being?

C: To incarnate into a body to learn the lessons and to teach others. We receive lessons and we teach lessons for our spirit.

HB: What kind of lessons does the spirit need to learn?

C: Compassion, love, trust, giving, endless giving.

HB: And what is the lesson that you have chosen for your next incarnation?

C: Endurance.

HB: And how will you choose a body to learn that lesson?

C: My parents will be killed and I will be alone.

HB: And you'll have to do it all by yourself, won't you?

C: Yes. I'm almost ready to incarnate again.

HB: OK. I want you to move to that place of final instruction, just before you incarnate. And here, where you receive your final instructions and guidance, I want you to look around and see if there's anyone else here.

C: No, they've gone already.

HB: Good. Now I want you to tell me what you feel. How do you feel about this mission that you're coming up to?

C: Confident.

HB: OK. And now it's time to incarnate. I want you to feel yourself floating down, floating down through that blue hole, right down, right down to Earth, and I want your energies to touch that little baby growing inside your mother. Just feel those energies, those brain patterns. Become accustomed to this new little body. And tell me what you feel about this new body.

C: It needs food.

HB: About how old is the baby growing inside your mother? How many months old is it?

C: Maybe six. The baby needs more food, and my mother coughs a lot.

HB: How does she feel about this baby growing inside her?

C: It's just another. I'm the fourth.

HB: I want you to just take your awareness right outside Mommy's womb now, and look at your father. Just feel the energies of your father. You can see him, but he can't see you. And I want you to tell me what feelings he has as he looks over at his wife. What does he feel about his wife?

C: He loves her. He's sorry that she's pregnant again. She is not strong.

HB: But do you have a feeling that she will make it through the pregnancy?

C: Yes. She will not die immediately.

HB: OK. Let's come forward in time. To a time just after you've been born. You're just a newborn baby now. What's your mother doing now?

C: She's trying to feed me, but she doesn't have much milk. Her sister is helping.

HB: Good. I want you to come forward in time again. Where's your mother?

C: She's dead.

HB: How long ago did she die?

C: I was five years old when she died.

HB: And how old are you now?

C: Five.

HB: Is your father there?

C: No. He got sick and died, too.

HB: So you've been left by both your parents, haven't you? Do you remember that this was the plan? This was your agreement, your contract, and their contract with you!

C: Yes.

HB: I want you to thank your mother and father for fulfilling their part of the bargain, so that you can learn your lesson of endurance. And I want you to see yourself getting older and older now, growing up . . . and tell me, what's the next most important event in your life?

C: Chris is going to war.

HB: And who is Chris?

C: Chris is . . . he lives near my house. I grew up with him.

HB: How old are you now?

C: Eighteen.

HB: Good. I want you to go over to the wall and look at the calendar on the wall, and tell me what year it is. What year is it right now?

C: 1914.

HB: And where are you?

C: In England. We're at the station. There's a lot of men are in uniform . . . they're going to war on the train. There's lots of people crying.

HB: How do you feel about Chris leaving?

C: Very sad, very afraid. I don't think I'll see him again. And I love him.

HB: OK. I want you to blow him a final kiss as the train pulls out . . . Now I want you to come forward in time, and I want you to tell me if Chris ever comes home.

C: No. He was killed in France.

HB: So your parents died, and the man you loved died—twice you had to go on alone. I want you to keep coming forward in time until another very, very important event occurs in your life.

C: I'm sick. I'm dying. There's a disease in my chest.

HB: How old are you here?

C: Oh, maybe thirty, thirty-two.

HB: And as it gets worse and worse, you get closer and closer to the point of death. I want you to just gently step out of the body now, step right out of the body and let it go. And tell me what you're experiencing. What are you feeling here?

C: Relief! I'm being pulled up. It's the blue hole again.

HB: OK. Let yourself lift right up through that blue hole. Right back into the light again. And as you turn around and look back on that lifetime, it was a short lifetime, wasn't it? Just thirty years or so. How do you feel about that lifetime? Did you achieve your purpose?

C: It wasn't a strong lesson of endurance. It was just a taste. I'll have to repeat it again sometime.

HB: OK. Very good. Is there anyone here to greet you?

C: Yes, Jare–ub's here.

HB: Good! What does he say?

C: "Welcome back."

HB: I want you to begin moving toward your group now. You've already been greeted and you can just move yourself right over to your own group now. And feel yourself starting to come into their presence. And how do they greet you?

C: With love. They don't say anything, there's no words, but it's just a knowing.

HB: Good. OK, Eesa, we're done for now. So when you're ready, I want you to return to Barbara's body there on the table in the healing room, and (client jerks on the table) I want you to focus again on that Solar Plexus Chakra. . . . OK, tell me how it feels to you.

C: Clean.

HB: OK, let me just scan it, too. . . . Yes, it does!

After the Ro-Hun session was completed, Barbara and I reviewed the information provided to her conscious mind from both her subconscious and superconscious minds. It was clear to her that much of her anger toward her mother was simply her own anger at being repeatedly abandoned, physically and/or emotionally, in this and several other lifetimes as well. As she became aware of this pattern, she began to see that it was all part of a prior agreement between the two of them so she could consciously learn the lesson and experience the feelings of endurance. However, the much more important lesson learned was that, during the several Ro-Hun sessions, she had repeatedly encountered her spirit self and was relating information, observations, and feelings from the spiritual dimensions. As this knowledge was presented repeatedly to her conscious mind, there was now absolutely no doubt that she had released perhaps the biggest fear most individuals have, but are reluctant to talk about: the fear of their own physical death. Just to know—not "believe," but to KNOW from personal experience—that her consciousness will continue eternally lifetime after lifetime has liberated her completely from one of the most damaging and limiting thought boxes we put ourselves in. This is truly bringing our original, spiritual nature directly into our day-to-day physical world and is immensely healing in itself.

CASE STUDY #2

Sandy (again, not her real name) had come to me for quite different reasons. After she had visited my website and learned that I offered Spiritual Regression, she was very strongly drawn to find out why she felt that the weight of the world was on her shoulders and to learn what she could do to unburden herself of this responsibility. She seemed almost driven to discover what deep secrets she had been harboring for so long. She was also interested in learning about her connection with an aquatic world that she had repeatedly seen in her dreams, the meaning of "White Star" as it applied to her, and any information concerning the relationship with her current partner.

After several suggestions to relax her mind, Sandy easily slipped into the Alpha state, which I then deepened even further. I then had her locate her timeline and move backward in time to the most significant experience for her to become consciously aware of at that time. Very soon she nodded her head and we began to explore these past memory patterns. This particular session is noteworthy because of the wide range and detail in the information provided on many topics, including not only several past life scenarios, but also a description of the spiritual appearance and name of herself, her children, and her guide; a tour to an aquatic world much different than Earth; her experience of blending with the vibrations and tones of music as an enjoyable pastime; what function she performs as a service in the spiritual world; how a spirit being prepares for incarnation; and the process of connecting with and developing within the mother's body and energy field.

HB: Where are you now? What are you experiencing?

C: I can't see anything. It's like I'm blind, but I feel that I'm somewhere near an ocean—I can hear the waves sounding against the shore. There are other people somewhere near— I feel their presence, but I can't see them. I'm in a dark cave, and it's hot in here. I'm very, very old, and there are many books in the cave with me, and I have a sword here, too, a kind of talisman, a protection. I'm not a fighter, but it feels very heavy and very important to me. I'm keeping it for myself. It's been placed into my energy field on my left side, and I carry it there with me. It's really used to cut away all old and outmoded thoughts and patterns. I have it with me always because I'm really a Bearer of Right, and the sword is like a Code of Conduct, and I'm the Keeper of the Code. And there's another being here in the cave with me—it feels like a magical beast here in the cave.

HB: What does this magical beast feel like to you? Can you describe it?

C: It's all the memories and knowledge of the Wise Ones from long ago. It's like an energy field that just surrounds me and stays with me. And I'm here with the sword to protect it and keep it safe. It's all the memories and history, and I'm here to see that it's not lost. I'm part of its remembrance and I'm spending time in its remembrance.

HB: And this is the memory and history of what?

C: Of a time when the people in the land were very savage and rough, and they needed to have things remembered, and I volunteered to be one of the rememberers, one of the keepers. I think this magical beast protects me. Yeah, because I don't seem to be able to do very much, I'm not able to see, and yet I don't seem to need anything . . .

HB: How long are you going to have to keep this information, to preserve it? What are you waiting for?

C: (Long pause) OH! (Pause) I feel like I'm going to bust open . . . I think for the people to be able to understand. I need to give it to them somehow.

HB: OK. Now with your sword and the help of the magical beast there, I'm sure you'll be able to preserve that information until they are ready to hear it. What about the people that live in this place, on this world, the beings that live here?

C: I don't feel any people around. I think I've been here a long time, but I don't feel any people. I don't know what will come, but what came before seems like a tunnel, a tunnel of light and energy and I somehow know I was here before. I was in a place that was like a very busy marketplace, you know. Somehow, I had to go to another place, to this cave and do this. And before that, I was like a student, a young man, I was a grown man.

HB: OK. Go back to that time when you were a grown student, become that man again, and look around and see what you're doing there. Are there other people around?

C: It's like a market, an open market, and I'm happy, laughing, and going through the market on my way somewhere. I'm on my way to see a special girl. She has brown hair, pretty, pleasing face, happy to see me.

HB: What do you decide to do together?

C: We're in a garden, walking in the garden. She's very nice. I like her.

HB: Now I want you to come forward in time, just a few years. Is that woman still with you?

C: No. I'm in trouble. I seem to be locked up. I'm not free to go anymore. (Big sigh) I think I told her about things I wasn't supposed to tell her. I think they were supposed to be secrets, kept secret, and I told her.

HB: What kind of secrets were these? Secrets about what?

C: About the knowledge, about the history, about the Keeper, the information, and things. About the stars and the Wise Ones and the things I wasn't supposed to tell.

HB: Where were the Wise Ones from?

C: They're not from here. . . . I don't know where they're from. They're not from here.

HB: What kind of information and knowledge did they bring?

C: We are children of Anon [Uh-Non´], and we barely see the light within our being. And we are supposed to guard that information because not all are ready to hear. The information is about the genetic code, and . . . (sigh) they took away my sight! But I can still see; but just differently. And I don't know where I am, but I seem to spend the rest of my time alone in this cave where I have a beast, and I have a sword, and I have a lot of books that I can't read with my eyes, but that I'm protecting somehow or holding. . . . And I'm weary of being here.

HB: What is it that you want most?

C: I want to get this information out! (Starting to cry) I want to be able to share the information. I don't want to have to hold it secret, or have this weight on me any more.

HB: OK. Now, I want you to see yourself in that lifetime there; describe again your appearance in that lifetime.

C: I feel like I'm an old man. I'm blue and clothed in blue and love. I have a minimal comfort area, a pot for cooking, and books, and a cave. The cave seems to be blue or have a blue light coming from it. And the dragon sleeps. It's not awake any more.

HB: OK. As you look down at yourself and your clothing, are you the kind of a being that has a finite existence? Are you a being of a race that experiences death?

C: I've been alive for a long, long time. No, I think I've always been, but I haven't always been in this form. And I've been on many worlds.

HB: Have you visited these, or were you there for an extended period of time for a certain purpose?

C: I was there to teach all subjects. About the stars and about the Earth, the planets, the Earth itself. I had a good resonance with it, with the Earth and all things. They were a part of one another, of all things.

HB: OK. Now I want you to go back to the cave where the magic beast is there helping to protect all this knowledge. You said before that part of your energy, a part of your self was somewhere else. I want you to get in touch with that, get in touch with that right now and tell me where that other part of you is, what form you're in . . . this other part of your energy.

C: I'm a girl, very happy, about eighteen or nineteen in a garden in a temple.

HB: And what's your purpose there in the temple? What do you do?

C: There are other girls here, but we don't have anything to do.

HB: Let that young girl come forward in time and get older, several years, until there's a very important event in your life. And stop at that point right NOW, and describe what you're seeing. What is happening to her? What is she doing?

C: Everybody's running, and everybody's scared. Everybody's running. I'm looking for my children, and I can't find them. A girl, a boy, and another girl. The Earth is cracking, heaving, caving. There's fire and it's very frightening. My husband is somewhere nearby but not of any help. We had an argument—there was material, scrolls, papers, and work, and crystals, and things that had information contained in them, and we had an argument about where they should be. And I wanted to put them in a device, a protective vault-like thing, and I went back to do it. He was supposed to do it, but he didn't do it. He didn't think it mattered. And I had to get my children, and I can't find them, and everything's cracking, and we're all going down.

HB: What is this land that you're living in?

C: Atlantis. (Very agitated) I didn't get the information. I didn't keep it safe. I couldn't keep my children safe.

HB: Now come forward a bit more in time. And what happens to you? What happens to that woman that's running for her life?

C: She dies. In the Earth, swallowed up. She was very strong-willed, insisted upon her own way, but she was smart and kind and she felt a duty, a responsibility toward the work that she was working with.

HB: After you observe yourself die, I want you to describe to me in detail what you're feeling now and what you're seeing, where you're moving. What's happening here?

c: I seem to be in a very pleasant area. I seem to be no longer that person. I seem to be looking at that life. The children are there, too. They're there, but they're not really my children any more.

HB: I want you to reflect on that lifetime you just left. I want you to reflect on your purpose for that lifetime. Why did you go back to that lifetime? What things were you to learn there?

c: What was I to learn? . . . I think somehow I've been taking care of information over and over and over, and I don't seem to be able to share that information yet. And yet . . . (sigh) I don't understand, I don't know.

HB: Do you feel it's time to share that information?

c: I want to! (Angrily) It always seems to be so hard down there!

HB: I want you to look around and see those beings that were your children there. Look into the eyes of the oldest child there; here in the spiritual world, what is that child's spiritual name?

c: Seems like Flavia [Flah´-vee-uh]. She likes to sing, and she's innocent. An innocent personality.

HB: Look over at your son there in the spiritual world, and go over to him and take him in your arms, and call him by his name. What is his name here in the spiritual world is?

c: Alon [Uh-lon´]. He's a courageous, gentle soul, a gentle man.

HB: Good. And now look over there at your youngest daughter. What's her spiritual name?

C: Sherone [Shur-own´]. She's a warrior! OH (Great surprise) OH! SHE'S THE DRAGON! (Becoming very emotional, panting and sobbing in surprise, ignoring my instructions for calming:) She's the dragon protector! She's the same being somehow! OH!

HB: What are your feelings as you look into her eyes right now and know who she is?

C: Whew! (Laughing) She's a mighty protector! She's amazing! Oh, my!

HB: Now I want you to look around here in the spiritual world as see if you see your guide there. Do you see your guide standing nearby? This one who has agreed to always be there, to be a helper, to help you learn and grow. Do you see your guide there?

C: His name is Michael. He's very regal and dark-skinned, dark hair. Very regal. Michael. There seems to be a green and orange-red color around him. Green on the outside and orange . . . gold, orange, and green.

HB: Good. Now right there by Michael, I want you to see a full-length mirror standing there by him, and I want you to move yourself right in front of that full-length mirror and describe what you see there in the mirror, your true self, your true nature. How do you appear here in the spiritual world?

C: Female. I'm very gold and green. My energy is gold and green. I seem to have a lot of fire energy that I didn't see at first. My hair seems to be red there also. It has gold. Red and gold at the same time. And I seem soft yet strong, and I'm at ease. . . . And there seems to be some pink. I seem to be able to feel for others. I think I work here with those just coming back. Yeah.

HB: As you look at yourself in the mirror, what is the spiritual name you have that others know you by?

C: I am called a star.

HB: (Misunderstanding) Is there any special kind of a star, or is it just a star?

C: No, not a star, Estar [Eh-star´].

HB: Good, Estar. Now when you play, what do you play at, what do you do for recreation?

C: I like to sing, I like to dance, I like to listen to the music in the gardens. I don't know how to describe it, but it's sort of like it moves as waves with emotion. It's like every person has a music about them. Every person's field has a vibration, and you can join with others and allow the music to come forth from your field. And different music is brought forth by the intention of it being brought forth. By joining your energy with different people, you become the music itself, and you create it from your energy.

HB: Are there other things that you like to do when you have time for recreation?

C: I like to be by the water. There's fountains and falls and oceans and . . . oh, there's a place called Narada [Nuh-rah´-duh] Falls and I go there a lot. There's a crescendo of water pouring down over rocks. It's very beautiful.

HB: Where would you like to go now, if you could go to any world that you want to go to? Where would you go, a special world . . . perhaps you've been there before? Just let your consciousness go there now. Go there for a nice, pleasant visit, and see what there is there now, and describe what it is that you're seeing. What are you experiencing here?

C: Seems to be very pastel, lots of soft colors and layers, almost like foggy, but not foggy. Misty. And there seems to be . . . I don't know . . . I hear things in the colors of the mist of the fog. Here I commune with the sounds that are there. This isn't Earth . . . I think it's far away. You can sort of move through it, too, you know. You don't really need to walk, you just kind of float, swim. . . .

HB: Through that mist?

C: Yeah. And we don't look the same here. We have almost transparent bodies here. We just move through the mist. This seems to be a very aquatic place. We're semihumanoid and seem to breathe through gills. We have an almost like amphibian skin, and our limbs have webs. We live in the air, but it's like a fluid, very pastel. And there are others still around here.

HB: Can you describe them?

C: We breathe them. They're all around us. We sense them and are a part of each other. They have different forms. What I like most about them is that they all have good minds—they're thinkers. It's easy to feel and know their energies, and when you do, you know what has been known before. You just experience whatever you want to. They are a very ancient race, and I feel I'm a part of them. We keep to ourselves now. Used to go out more, but not now. It's peaceful here, but it has not always been calm. We are very mental, but can also feel. It's like a living library—a collective. I'm very content to just dwell here.

HB: Very good. Now I want you to go back to the spiritual place where you were first. When you first came back to the spiritual world, what did you feel here?

C: I was very disoriented.

HB: When somebody is disoriented when they first return, how do you help them adjust? What do you do?

C: They get blanketed in a cocoon of light and sleep for a while. And when they wake, I give them nourishment and sustenance—emotional—and then they sleep until they're ready to wake up. And everything is explained to them and they are told how to create what it is that they need the most. The things they are comfortable with, or that were a part of their last life—we assist them to create it because they can create anything they want.

HB: What if they create things that are not good for them?

C: It's not possible. It doesn't work that way. Not to harm. Not to harm. They're able to experience any other pleasant experiences. If they would do harm, they would not have come back to this place. They would have gone to another place.

HB: What kind of place would that be?

C: It's a quick turnaround. This is a place of study and reflection, attunement, and planning for the next phase, next life, or next level of being. Those that wish to do harm to themselves or others are not allowed here. They go into a quick rebirth.

HB: For those beings, what is the purpose of quick rebirth?

C: To again work on their experiences. They do not get to have the opportunity to have the reflection. They don't get to plan. It's almost like a boomerang.

HB: Are they allowed to choose the lifetime that they go to next?

C: It's already in motion. Because if they intend to do harm, they get plugged right back into a scenario that needs to be worked out. There is not nearly as much choice for them. The choice is already predominately made by their own energies.

HB: Now what about those people who are ready to come across and won't have any trouble adjusting. What do you do with them?

C: Well, they're greeted by their friends and family and loved ones. My role is more with those that have some need to get acclimated, helping them to rediscover what it is that they used to do here at home. And to be like an assistant, if you will. And their guide goes with them to the Hall of Records and to the Temple of Love and the places where they spend time taking a look at and getting acquainted with the life they just finished, and just reviewing how well they succeeded in accomplishing their contracts.

HB: When you help take a person into the Hall of Records, what do they see there? What do they experience?

C: Depends whether they are looking at their lives or looking to be in touch with someone else's in an empathic theater if you will. There are machines there that can holographically scan that lifetime and you get to replay the events and emotions and feelings and interactions and get a perspective of being outside of it and having more insight of an experience rather than something that is totally consuming you while you are experiencing it.

HB: And what's the purpose of the looking at this lifetime?

C: To see if you accomplished your mission. To see if you worked through the experience that you came there for.

HB: How do you choose the experiences that you want to work on?

C: You choose all experiences until you've gone through them all. You choose a part, an experience that you haven't done yet. You have a theme. A personality theme, if you will, that determines the type of a personality that you will have. This is what you will experience. Then you have a secondary theme that will try to pull you off that course.

HB: What was the personality theme or type that you chose for yourself? And does it vary from lifetime to lifetime?

C: It varies from lifetime to lifetime. The one that I chose for this lifetime has to do with emotionality and adventure or experiences and security. My primary theme is to feel all parts deeply. To feel it, to be able to be it, and to be able to empathize and to establish and to communicate the things that are felt, and my secondary theme is not wanting to miss any adventure.

HB: And when you've selected the themes for your lifetime, what do you do next when you're preparing to incarnate?

C: Well, I choose a hot spot, so to speak, an issue. I choose an issue like relationships or family or finance or health. Something that will be a medium through which I will be able to be on track and pulled off track. The duality of the two themes will have a tone. Mine appears to be relationships. To be in them, but not lost in them. Be in them, but not of them.

HB: What is it that you want in your current relationship?

C: Freedom. Freedom and trust. Freedom is a right because you can't restrain another person, and you can't own them, you can't make them do anything. You have to love them uncon-ditionally, and let them choose to be or not to be in your life.

HB: As you look down at your current lifetime with (name of partner), what choices are there in front of you?

C: To learn how to just continue to be, and not feel the other person's confusion so much. And to know when to let go, because not everybody's able to be as proud-minded, if you will, or ready for changes.

HB: Good. Now, I want you to go back in time to that time when you're preparing to incarnate. And once again, summarize the issues you want to work on in your current lifetime. You mentioned relationships. What else? Is there anything else you want to work on? Something else you needed to work on for your own evolvement?

C: I think it has to do with patience and being able to be in accord with the timing of things . . . that you can't force things.

HB: Good. Now just continue your preparations for incarnations here in the Tower. Are you alone, or are there others with you?

C: Your guide is with you and you go to meet with your holy persons, whomever you feel connected to . . . Jesus is here, Buddha's here, and many other divine beings are here. They speak with you. I seem to speak with Quan Yin. She says to remember for your heart to be lit with the love that you are. She wishes me goodbye before I leave. You see Quan Yin or your person of eminence as a last step, and then you're put in kind of a sleep.

HB: How does that happen?

C: It's suggested, and you just go to sleep. Your Energy Body is subdued, made smaller, and you are contained, and move into the womb.

HB: At about what point in the pregnancy?

C: It depends. It depends on how comfortable you are there. Many times you come and go several times. Some times it's not comfortable and it's hard to stay there at first, to be contained in such a small space. And you have to go out and come back in and get more comfortable.

HB: As you incarnate into this lifetime, I want you to just sense the energies of your mother and the energies of that baby growing within her. At about what point in time did you first connect with that baby?

C: Well, I connected with my mother before I was conceived. I was very drawn to her. Very drawn to her. I was drawn to her because of her kindness, her innocence, and her love of nature and things.

HB: And then, at the point of conception, what did you sense? What did you feel and experience?

C: Hmmm. My father had no concept of her feelings. He was totally mental, in a mental construct.

HB: Now I'd like you to move more forward in time to about the age of one month. As you're still in your mother's womb, what are your thoughts and feelings? What did you sense here?

C: She's very unhappy because they weren't really in communion.

HB: At this point, did she know she was pregnant?

C: Uh-huh. That's OK. She wanted a baby. That's OK.

HB: When she thought of the baby, what were the feelings that she had?

C: Oh. . . . (sigh) She looked forward to having something to love, but she was tired. She already had three other children. She worked hard . . .

HB: OK. Now come forward in time to when you're about two months old in your mother's womb. How are you feeling now? How are you beginning to adjust?

C: I come and go. I don't stay here all the time. She takes care of everything. He goes to church.

HB: What do you think of him? What are your thoughts, your feelings?

C: Oh, I used to hate him. I did not want to be around him. I think I came in to champion my mother somehow.

HB: Let's move forward to when your mother is three months pregnant. What is your mother thinking and feeling now?

C: She's tired. I'm tired. I'm tired of my dad. They weren't getting along. He's trying to tell me how to . . . trying to tell me God's will, how God talks to man, and man talks to woman, and woman takes care of the child. It's stupid.

HB: Move forward now to five months. How do you feel at five months?

C: I want to be out of here!

HB: Do you feel safe?

C: Yeah. I'm OK, but I just don't like being confined.

HB: Come forward one more month now . . . you're six months old. You're very well formed and developed now. How do you feel?

C: Restless.

HB: OK. How does your mother feel? What are her thoughts? What's she thinking?

C: She's thinking her own thoughts about God and about. . . . She thinks God is love, and not all these rules, and that makes me happy.

HB: Look over at your father. What's he feeling?

C: He's very scared and lonely. But he doesn't know it, so he acts smart. Tries to make sure that he tells everybody what to do.

HB: OK. Now, there in your mother's womb, I want you to come forward even further to when you're seven months old. What are you feeling now?

C: I just want out! I don't like him, and I want out!

HB: And how do you feel about your mother?

C: I want to protect her from him. He doesn't love her. He makes her feel bad.

HB: Come forward even farther. . . . Eight months old now. And what's your father thinking and doing now?

C: He's trying to take care of things. He's around her now. She started to stutter. He was always correcting her. He was always telling her, "You didn't say that right, or didn't spell that right, or didn't do that right."

HB: Is the stuttering because your father is always correcting her or is it because of a condition that she has?

C: She never did it before. I can't stand it! I don't like him!

HB: I want you to come forward even further, to just before you're born. I want you to tell me what are your last thoughts here before you're born?

C: I'm angry, and I want to get out of there! But I'm real nervous, too. It's awfully big out there!

HB: Yeah, it is! What are you going to do out there after you're born? What do you want to do?

C: Fight him!

HB: How are you going to go about that? He's so big, and you're so small. . . .

C: I don't know.

HB: OK. Now, I want you to come right up to that moment of birth. And I want you to take your Wand of Light and circle it all around you for protection and safety. You're just about ready to be born now. How does that feel?

C: Good! Here we come!

HB: Great! And now I want you to feel yourself being placed carefully up on your mother's chest. And look up into her eyes and see the love that she has for you there. Just FEEL that love. And I want you to reach out with your thoughts and tell her, "I love you, too! I love you, and it's good to be here. It's good to be in my own energy again! I'm free! And that feels good!" Let her know that. (Pause) And I want you to look over at your father. . . .

C: He's not there. He's in the hospital. He got thrown off his horse and broke his arm. Mom stayed home to give birth to me.

HB: Just let yourself go out telepathically to him. And I want you to look at him. You can see him, but he can't see you. And I want you to send to him those thoughts and those feelings that you need to tell him. What are those thoughts and feelings?

C: Well, it's OK now. It's OK now. We worked through a bunch of stuff. It's OK now. He really loved her, but just didn't know how to show it. (Sigh) I'm done now.

HB: All right. Now I want you to just let your consciousness lift up, lift up higher and higher and higher, and I want you to step onto your timeline again and come forward in time until you reach right now and you see Sandy's body, your body, resting there safely on the healing table. And let me know when you're back in the present time.

C: Uh-huh.

HB: OK. Just gently move right back into your Physical Body again (client jerked slightly on the table), stretch your arms and shoulders, wiggle your toes, and gently come back to awareness again, fully awake and feeling good. (Pause) Great!

As the amount of detailed information provided in Past Life Regression and Spiritual Regression sessions such as presented above becomes available for review, we are inescapably drawn to conclude that the true nature of what we really are far surpasses what we are normally taught as children to believe about ourselves, or even what we might have imagined as adults. When accumulated and combined into a coherent framework of similar experiences from hundreds and thousands of different clients, we are given a tantalizing glimpse into higher dimensions, other worlds, and cosmic wisdom and knowledge. And as our own vision and perception of our own true nature grows and matures, we are provided with a richly vibrant and intuitively satisfying picture of the world of our spiritual essence and how lifetime experiences in the physical world can be used for its own development and growth on its own path, which inevitably returns to its Creator.

Chapter Five

Growing Home

"Verily, verily, I say unto you, He that believeth on me, the works that I do shall he do also; and greater works than these shall he do. . . ."

—The Master Jesus
(John 14:12)

IN THE PRECEDING CHAPTERS, WE have discussed several healing techniques that can be used on yourself and others to promote the healing of specific energy bodies, including the Physical Body. However, these represent only a fraction of the energy-based healing techniques currently available from which to choose when planning a holistic program for returning to and maintaining a state of complete health. As mentioned in the Preface, these techniques are only those to which I have been drawn. You may also be drawn to these or possibly to others.

It is also important to note that each technique discussed operates primarily on the level discussed, but through the principle of sympathetic vibration, the adjacent energy bodies may also be simultaneously addressed. For example, Reiki works very effectively on the Physical Body. But with our broader perspective of what is really happening and how energy healing works, we have learned that much of the healing work is done on the Etheric Body, the pattern for the Physical. And through resonance of vibrations into the higher octaves, the higher Emotional and Mental Bodies can also be affected in a positive manner.

This broader understanding of how healing works also gives us a much clearer appreciation that the human body is only the densest level of manifestation of our true multilevel energetic nature. Just the mere fact that each of us has an energy field surrounding what we see as our Physical Body should stimulate a curiosity to understand what that field represents, and what happens when my field comes into contact with your field. We need to understand what we truly are and how we interact energetically with others; this understanding will give us the knowledge to begin exploring the real meaning of health and disease on several levels.

As we slowly begin to take baby steps in our search for how best to apply this new knowledge for our own health or the health of others, we are awakening to the first sparks of the real meaning of life itself. However, not all individuals are willing to take that baby step just now; they are still quite content in the valley and yet wonder what the view from the mountaintop would be like. But those who start their journey upward begin to see the real importance of the journey itself. Each time they reach a higher vantage point, they are able to see their entire journey from an even higher perspective.

A reasonable question to ask at this point is, "Now that I have this broader understanding, this greater perspective, this additional knowledge of healing techniques, how can I apply it in my own daily life?" The interesting thing is that it can be applied however you want to use it in your daily life. You could choose to become a healer, but you do not necessarily have to. You could be a waitress, a chief financial officer, a police officer, a teacher, an engineer, or whatever, and still find very practical uses to which you can put this new knowledge in your daily interactions with others. How you view your total self directly influences how you interact with others on all levels.

Each step up the stairs of understanding will surely change how you view yourself, how you view others, how you interact with others, and how you view your own reality and your perception of how you participate in your own reality. Each new belief you take on about yourself, about others, and about your own reality will change the vibrational patterns in your Mental Body—either in a positive or in a negative fashion.

These new beliefs and vibrational patterns in your Mental Body about your "universe" will automatically generate some response that becomes a new pattern in your Emotional Body. You may feel relieved, refreshed, wonderment, awe-struck, and joyous; alternatively, you may feel confused, depressed, worthless, insignificant, or lonely. You have your free will choice and can choose either response. That response, however, will become a new part of your Emotional Body . . . how you "feel" about yourself and others. And this, in turn, will affect the Etheric Body, the pattern for the Physical Body.

Let us return to the question of how to make practical, day-to-day use of this additional knowledge of who and what we are. Perhaps you would like your path to be similar to mine, that of a healer. First, ask yourself if it "feels right." If not, use the new information in your own line of work to recognize that each person you meet, every man, woman, and child that enters your life, is on his or her own chosen path and at the correct place in that path for him or her at that time. Use this insight with compassion, and accept that person without judgment just as he or she is, for the person has chosen to be what and where he or she is on this path, just as you have also chosen to be what and where you are on your own path. Send them unconditional love and support if they are challenged in any way. Even a seemingly insignificant but graciously offered deed such as a friendly smile or a kind word may be just what that person needs most at that time.

But if your deep desires lead you toward the path of healing as a means of helping others, you may wonder if anyone at all can become a healer, or if that is a specially bestowed talent bestowed upon a chosen few. If you believe that healing is something that only a few specially chosen people can do, ask yourself "Who is doing the choosing?"

This question has three possible answers: God, yourself, or "someone else" who has control over your desires and capabilities. In a universe where free will is one of the fundamental principles, the first and last possible answers just do not make sense. You yourself will make the choice to become a healer. But how good a healer you become will depend upon your sincerity, your commitment, and your previous experience and healing knowledge.

If you have absolutely no knowledge of healing and also have never been a healer before, the vibrational patterns in your higher energy bodies that would subconsciously draw you toward healing may be absent altogether. But very few of us have never had an experience of bringing healing to someone else on some level, or have never experienced a healing act from someone else. Even the gentle reassurance to a child that her skinned knee will soon be better is healing on many levels.

Each time we participate in a healing experience, either as healer or the one healed, our beliefs and feelings are affected one way or another. Repeated positive experiences create permanent vibrational patterns in our higher energy bodies, and these vibrational energy patterns are carried forward from one life experience to the next. Those who are strongly drawn to become healers are probably simply remembering their previously gained knowledge and abilities.

Anyone can learn to become a healer if he or she chooses to and feels strongly enough that healing is his or her path, just as anyone can learn to play the piano or paint a fine picture if that is how he or she wants to express his or her own individuality. If the healing path is chosen and you set out to assist others in their own return to health, the knowledge you gain about healing along the way will automatically give you new vistas of what and who you are as a person.

Your identity as an individual, that of a separate being which interacts with others, is defined not by your name or your height or the color of your eyes, but by what you do with the abilities you have right now, and by the motives involved in your actions and deeds. "It's what you DO with what you have that counts." As you learn how to assist in the healing of others, you will soon realize that you are healing yourself as well. Just the knowledge (as opposed to the belief) that you can actually assist others to accelerate their own healing is a quantum step forward in the perception of who you are as a person and as a spiritual being, and of what you are truly capable. The actual experience of bringing healing to others allows us to grow beyond what we previously believed were our limitations. In fact, we begin to awaken to the fact that our only limitations are the ones we create for ourselves individually by faulty or short-sighted belief systems or thought patterns.

Awakening to a New Reality

As each of us goes through our daily routine, we interact with our environment and with others in accordance with our beliefs and perceptions, our likes and dislikes, our biases and prejudices, and our emotions and feelings. Whatever vibrational patterns we have stored in our energy field are radiated out to and are felt by others, even if on a subconscious level. And our interpretation of how others react to us becomes a part of our field also.

If others do not feel comfortable with you and your actions, they will shy away; if this pattern continues, you may come to question your own worth or value as a person. "Why don't people like me?" might turn into "Why am I always rejected?" and this might eventually become "I am unworthy to have friends." But if you are radiating warmth, friendliness, compassion, and tolerance from your energy field, people will subconsciously respond with a similar reaction and be drawn to you.

In this way, we actually create our own reality—our own perception of the world in which we live. But when we consciously recognize the fact that we have the ability to create what is desirable in our lives, we empower ourselves to such a degree that our lives are truly changed forever. All we have to do is choose to live with unconditional love and compassion for others and set aside forever the anger, fear, jealousy, hate, greed, and any other negative reactions we may have had in our energy fields.

The new reality each of us can create for ourselves is limited only by what we can imagine is possible. And this includes a new reality of how we define and measure our own health. When the definition of health is expanded to include the vibrational patterns of each of our energy bodies and the interrelationship of each energy body with the others, we begin to see how we can start taking charge of our own health. We can begin to assume this responsibility ourselves with the understanding and knowledge of how and why disease occurs and health is restored.

It is time to take a good, hard, and very critical look at both allopathic and alternative medical techniques. The best of both approaches should be incorporated into an integrated healing program tailored to meet the specific needs of the client/patient on all levels of his or her total being. It is not enough any more to merely take three pills a day for ten days and assume you will be cured. While drugs can be very effective in combating certain kinds of infections, the potential interactions with other drugs are not fully understood in all cases. Drugs can also have a very powerful long-term effect on the body, even when only prescribed for a short while. Both these effects need to be studied in greater detail to obtain a better understanding of how and when they should be used.

Similarly, the application and effects of alternative medical therapies, and energy-based healing techniques in particular, need to be studied with just as critical an eye. The same healthy skepticism should be applied to allopathic and alternative techniques alike when attempting to determine the potential benefit of either approach to the patient/client. And should an energy-based healing technique be found in properly documented clinical trials to be effective in accelerating the client's healing, it should ideally receive the same amount of marketing hype and advertisement coverage as a new drug that has a similar effect. But we are not there . . . yet!

Fortunately, the growing grassroots medical reform movement for inclusion of complementary and alternative medical (CAM) therapies into a balanced holistic healing program is now being felt. There is a growing demand for alternative medical therapies, including energy-based healing techniques. And as traditional physicians become aware of alternative therapies and their beneficial effects, many are becoming more receptive to integrating a wide variety of alternative therapies and their normal allopathic approaches into a combined program for restoring total health. Health is coming to mean much more that just physical health.

As new drugs are subjected to scientifically conducted clinical trials and analysis and new surgical techniques are refined and improved, traditional medical information continues to grow rapidly. Similarly, as more becomes known about the human energy field and energy-based healing techniques, this information also needs to be seriously investigated and analyzed. However, the traditional scientific method of analysis cannot always be applied to someone's energy field to determine his or her state of health.

Very few can see energy fields, and scientific instruments that can provide demonstrable, repeatable, and reliable methods of measuring or describing the human energy field are not yet widespread. Instead, we have anecdotal reports, verbal descriptions, and in many cases only intuitively derived information that describes what is going on when an energy healer repatterns someone else's energy bodies. Yet this anecdotal and verbal information appears to be so consistent, so repeatable, and from so many different sources that the beneficial results or effects of a healing treatment should also be rigorously addressed.

Just because we may not understand how healing is accelerated does not invalidate the fact that it can indeed be sped up. And the acceleration can be documented quantitatively in terms of how much less pain medication is required, immune system improvements (e.g., white cell count), by how many days hospital stays are shortened, and so on. This *empirically derived* synthesized information needs to be properly documented along with the *scientifically derived* analyzed information, so the best of both approaches can be incorporated into a person's overall holistic healing program.

This is the bright new direction of the "Integrative Medicine" approach to healing and is the basis for the medical revolution now being felt throughout all sectors of the medical community in America. Our physicians are among the best trained in the world, and that training has prepared them in the best way possible to recognize and deal with allopathic emergencies. But they can use only the tools they have been given. In most cases, this is a knowledge of drugs and/or surgical skills. And these tools are simply not effective in dealing with a large number of chronic patient complaints. However, one should not blame the physician for not being taught helpful energy-based healing techniques.

As we become aware of the significant potential for accelerating the healing process through the use of energy-based healing techniques, we will begin to seek out those health care professionals who are knowledgeable in this area. However, each individual doctor is also at his or her own chosen place on his or her own path. Many medical physicians are now beginning to investigate complementary medical therapies and are willing to collaborate with complementary medical therapists for their patients' overall best good. More and more, the traditional and alternative health practitioners will be drawn together to integrate their respective skills and to synergistically enhance the client's potential for returning to a healthy lifestyle of disease prevention rather than disease elimination.

I would not interfere
With any creed of yours
Or want to appear
That I have all the cures.

There is so much to know . . .
So many things are true.
The way my feet must go
May not be best for you.

And so I give this spark
Of what is Light to me,
To guide you through the dark,
But not tell you what to see.

— *Author unknown*

Glossary

The definitions below are given in the context of the way they are used in this book. They reflect my current level of understanding regarding the way we are constructed energetically, and the way we interact with others and with the higher dimensions of our reality.

AHMA: American Holistic Medical Association. An association primarily for holistic medical physicians.

AHNA: American Holistic Nurses' Association. An association primarily for holistic nurses and professional caregivers.

Akashic Records: *See* Collective Unconscious.

Allopathic medicine: Traditional form of medical therapy which concentrates on drugs and/or surgery to treat a patient's symptoms.

Alternative therapies: Nonmedical therapies that are usually chosen by a person instead of traditional medical therapies.

Attunement: In Reiki, an initiation process whereby certain chakras are energetically opened to be better able to receive healing energy. The Palm Chakras are also opened to transmit these energies through the healer to the client. During the attunement process, the energy of certain symbols is also placed into these chakras. An attunement can only be performed by a Reiki Master (Level III).

Aura: The energy field that surrounds the human Physical Body. It is composed of several overlapping and interpenetrating energy bodies: the Etheric Body, the Emotional Body, the Mental Body, and the Spiritual Body.

Awareness: *See* Consciousness.

Base Chakra: *See* Root Chakra.

Block: *See* Energy Block.

Brow Chakra: The sixth chakra, located on the forehead midway between the eyes and just above the eyebrow line. Has to do with clarity and insight, both with the physical eyes and with one's inner vision.

Caged One Series: *See* Shadow Self Series.

Card Session: In Ro-Hun, a process of locating and completely releasing the single most important negative emotional issue the client is facing at that time. Ro-Hun card sessions usually last about an hour, and are conducted with the therapist and the client sitting next to each other.

Chakras (Major): The seven major energy centers located along the front and back of the body; these are most commonly used to describe the human chakra system. They are: (1) Root Chakra, (2) Sacral Chakra (sometimes called the Spleen Chakra), (3) Solar Plexus Chakra, (4) Heart Chakra, (5) Throat Chakra, (6) Brow Chakra (sometimes called the Ajna Chakra or the Third Eye), and (7) Crown Chakra. *See* Figure 1 in chapter 1.

Chakras (Minor): The lesser energy centers associated with each joint, palms of the hands, fingertips, soles of the feet, and ends of the toes. These minor chakras are characterized by "beams" of energy extending several inches from the body, as opposed to the spinning vortexes which are characteristic of the major chakras.

Chi: Chinese word for Life Force Energy that animates all living things— human, animal, and plant.

Clairaudience: The ability to receive guidance and information with one's inner hearing. Information received clairaudiently sounds as if someone has spoken the information to you.

Clairsentience: The ability to receive guidance and information in such a way that you simply know it is *true*. Information received clairsentiently feels like it has the good feeling of Truth and is usually felt in the solar plexus area.

Clairvoyance: The ability to receive guidance and information with one's inner vision. Information received clairvoyantly is usually perceived as something seen, such as a picture, symbol, video clip, or colors/shapes with a particular meaning to you.

Cleanse Session: In Ro-Hun, a single table session (two to two-and-one-half hours) designed to identify and release emotional issues related to the client's parents; also releases client's feelings of unworthiness, fearfulness, helplessness, and of being too critical or judgmental of self or others. *See* chapter 3.

Client: A person who comes to an alternative or complementary therapy practitioner (who is not a medical doctor) for purposes of returning to health on all levels. Doctors have patients; healers have clients.

Collective Unconscious: A term coined by renowned psychiatrist Carl G. Jung to describe the universal storehouse of memories, "the unwritten history of mankind for time unrecorded," also known as Edgar Cayce's "Akashic Records." The vibrational patterns of the Collective Unconscious contain the record of every thought, word, and deed of every soul who has ever inhabited the Earth plane. This information is available to us under the right circumstances.

Color and Sound Therapy: The process of consciously directing vibrational frequencies from several different sources (e.g., the human voice, tuning forks, musical mantras, Tibetan singing bowls, etc.) into each major chakra for the purpose of restoring the proper rate of vibration for that chakra.

Complementary Therapies: Alternative or nonmedical therapies that are chosen by a person who also uses traditional medical therapies.

Conscious Mind: The personality, ego, and intellect associated with an individual person.

Consciousness: The quality of knowing one's own Self as separate from other individual Selves, yet also knowing that on a higher level, all the individually created Selves are but a part of the whole (the Creator or Source) wherein there is no separation.

Crown Chakra: The seventh major chakra, located at the top of the head. Has to do with the upper brain and higher consciousness.

Disease: A condition wherein one or more of a person's energy bodies has a disturbance that prevents smooth, harmonious energy vibrations and patterns within those bodies or between adjacent energy bodies. When this nonharmonious vibration pattern is transmitted down into the Physical Body, it may manifest as pain, improper functioning of organs, or other physical symptoms.

Dowsing: The procedure of placing a pendulum into the spinning vortex of one of the major chakras for the purpose of determining the energy state of that chakra. *See* chapter 1.

Emotional Body: The second subtle energy body surrounding and interpenetrating the Physical Body. This body contains the vibrational energy patterns of both our positive and negative emotional reactions to the thought patterns and belief systems contained in the Mental Body.

Energy: The fundamental component of creation that can be expressed as light energy, kinetic (movement) energy, chemical energy, nuclear energy, etc. Energy and matter are interchangeable ($E = mc^2$); therefore, all we see as matter, including ourselves, is a specific form of vibrating energy.

Energy Block: An area on the Physical Body or in one of the body's energy fields where the vibrational pattern of energy has been disrupted or distorted from its original, natural pattern of perfect health.

Energy Bodies: The subtle energetic layers of our aura which overlap each other and interpenetrate the Physical Body. Barbara Brennan (See her book, *Hands of Light*) has identified seven energy bodies associated with the Physical Body—the Etheric, Emotional, Mental, Astral, Etheric Template, Celestial, and Ketheric Template. For this book, I have combined her four higher layers into what I call the Spiritual Body.

Energy Manipulation: Conscious hand movements and intentions to "stir up" suppressed memory patterns in a client's energy field so that these memories can be confronted, dealt with, and released (*See* chapter 3, "Ro-Hun"). Also a specific set of hand movements to repattern a client's energy field for better functioning on all levels (*See* chapter 2, "Healing Touch").

Energy Meridians: Pathways within the human body that energetically interconnect chakras, organs, and specific areas of the Physical Body. Used primarily for acupuncture, acupressure, and other oriental forms of bodywork to move the life force energy within us.

Energy Modulation: *See* Energy Manipulation.

Etheric Body: The first subtle energy body surrounding and interpenetrating the Physical Body. This body consists of an energy gridwork that forms the template and building instructions for the Physical Body. The blueprint for every cell and tissue of the Physical Body is first formed on this energy gridwork.

Faulty Thought: A thought or belief system which, if subscribed to, limits an individual's full, uplifting expression as a confident, secure, and loving human being. Faulty belief systems include "If you don't believe in my form of religion, you can't go to heaven" and "Human beings just aren't capable of unconditional love." Faulty thoughts include "I am unworthy of abundance" and "I must control others to protect myself."

Foundation Series: In Reiki, the basic series of hand positions which begin each traditional Reiki session.

Golden Rule: "Do unto others as you would have them do unto you." *See* Law of Cause and Effect.

Ground (the client): Return the client to full conscious awareness.

Health: A state of original, natural, and harmonious vibration on and among each energetic level of our being. This is very different from merely "a lack of symptoms or disease."

Healer: One who facilitates the healing processes of another person. It is important to know that no one can heal another person, but a "healer" can greatly accelerate another person's own internal, self-healing processes. The degree to which healing occurs is determined by the intentions and willingness of both the healer and the client to work together for the client's highest and best good. *See* chapter 1, "Taking Responsibility for Healing."

Healing Touch: A holistic energy-based program to align and balance the human energy system through many separate healing techniques that include both physical touch and energy field manipulation. *See* chapter 2, "Healing Touch."

Healing Touch for Animals (HTA): A subprogram within Healing Touch that uses specially developed physical and energetic body manipulation techniques to restore the health of large and small animals. *See* chapter 2, "Healing Touch for Animals."

Healing Touch for Babies (HTB): A subprogram within Healing Touch that teaches the use of Healing Touch techniques and processes that are appropriate for premature and critically ill infants within the Neonatal Intensive Care Units of specific hospitals.

Healing Touch for Caregivers (HTC): A subprogram within Healing Touch that teaches all levels of caregivers the use of specific Healing Touch techniques and processes that address pain management, release of stress and anxiety, acceleration of the healing process, and gentle preparation for a peaceful transition.

Healing Touch Spiritual Ministry: A subprogram within Healing Touch for ministers, nurses, and lay practitioners to provide energy-based healing and laying-on of hands training and education from the perspective of Judeo-Christian teachings. *See* chapter 2, "HT Spiritual Ministry (HTSM)."

Heart Chakra: The fourth chakra, located in the center of the chest on a line between the nipples. Has to do with universal love, balance in all things, and healing.

High Heart: In Healing Touch, the energy center in the middle of the breastbone directly above the thymus gland, approximately midway between the Heart and Throat Chakras.

Higher Self: That part of your being which tells only the Truth, which has only your highest and best interests at heart, and which always loves you unconditionally.

Higher Sense Perception: A term coined by Barbara Brennan (In *Hands of Light*) to mean "a way of perceiving things beyond the normal ranges of human senses." HSP includes clairaudience, clairvoyance, and clairsentience.

Holistic: Addressing all levels of a person's being: physical, emotional, mental, and spiritual. Holistic healing techniques are also concerned with a person's diet, medical treatments, exercise programs, habits such as smoking and overeating, and stress-reduction techniques such as meditation or Tai Chi.

Human Energy Field: The part of the Universal Energy Field that is associated with a particular human being (per Brennan). It consists of the several subtle energy bodies surrounding the Physical Body, as well as the chakra and meridian systems within the body.

Hypnotherapy: A form of psychotherapy that directly or indirectly induces a relaxed hypnotic state in order to gain access to subconscious conflicts and buried traumas, and to alleviate those conditions.

Hypnosis: An artificially induced state of trance, superficially resembling sleep, in which the subconscious mind is open to various kinds of suggestion.

Induction: The process of hypnotically relaxing a person into an altered state for the purpose of gaining access to that person's subconscious mind.

Integrative Medicine: The blending of allopathic and complementary healing techniques into a truly holistic process for the purpose of preventing disease and, when necessary, restoring a person's original, natural state of perfect health on all levels—physically, emotionally, mentally, and spiritually. In Integrative Medicine, a patient may be referred by his or her physician to appropriate complementary therapists.

Intuition: That natural ability, developed to varying degrees within each person, that lets us see, feel, and hear with our inner senses.

Karma: The concept that our every thought, word, and action is eventually returned to us in kind. *See* the Law of Cause and Effect.

Karuna: Sanskrit word for "compassionate action" or "compassion in action." *See* chapter 2.

Karuna Reiki®: A system of additional, specific healing energies that build upon the energies of Usui Reiki. Karuna Reike is taught only to practicing Reiki Masters. *See* chapter 2.

Ki: Japanese word for Life Force Energy that animates all living things— human, animal, and plant. *See* Chi.

Law of Attraction: One of the fundamental principles upon which our universe is based, which states that we attract people, situations, and opportunities that "resonate with" or that are similar to the vibrational energies we project from our own Human Energy Field.

Law of Cause and Effect: One of the fundamental principles upon which our universe is based, which states that we must also experience the effect of the experiences we cause. This is done so that, with the knowledge of both opposites or sides of a particular action, more enlightened choices can then be made at a soul level to influence future actions. "Do unto others what you would have them do unto you." "Whatsoever a man soweth, so that shall he also reap." "What goes around, comes around."

Law of Duality: One of the fundamental principles upon which our universe is based, which states that all of physical creation is expressed in terms of a dual nature: good/bad, black/white, male/female, up/down, light/dark, in/out, here/there, pain/pleasure, etc.

Law of Free Will: One of the fundamental principles upon which our universe is based, which states that the Creator will not interfere with the right of each Spirit to choose for itself what it wants to express. Each Spirit can use this freedom for its own growth or its own limitation. This also implies that there is no judgment by God. Why would He give us Free Will and then judge us for exercising it? This doesn't make sense. Instead, we judge ourselves, learn by experiencing what we create, and evolve ("ascend") in that awareness.

Magnetic Healing: A general term for healing techniques which focus on healing the Etheric Body, which is primarily magnetic in nature, as opposed to the Physical Body which is primarily electrical in nature.

Mental Body: The third subtle energy body surrounding and interpenetrating the Physical Body. This body contains the vibrational patterns of all our belief systems and each individual thought associated with our entire soul record.

Meridians: *See* Energy Meridians.

Mind: The cognitive, analytical, and creative faculties that work through the ego personality to express a person's desires, wishes, and thoughts.

Past Life Experience: A life experience that occurred in the past.

Past Life: A lifetime experience that occurred prior to one's current lifetime.

Patient: A person under the care of, or is being treated by, a licensed medical practitioner or physician.

Pendulum: A small object suspended on a string or thread a few inches long, used for dowsing a person's energy field or chakras. It is used as a visible indicator of the interaction of the healer's and client's energy fields. *See* chapter 1, "Dowsing With a Pendulum."

Physical Body: The vibrational pattern of energy that we recognize by feel, sight, touch, etc. to be our "self." The Physical Body is also the vehicle we use in this three-dimensional world to express our individual essence. The Physical Body is built cell by cell upon the preexisting vibrational matrix of the Etheric Body.

Prana: Indian word for the Life Force Energy that animates all living things — human, animal, and plant. *See* Chi.

Psychiatry: The branch of medicine concerned with psychological illness, especially psychosis, which regards many such abnormalities as organic in origin and that commonly prefers drug treatment to other forms of psychotherapy.

Psychotherapy: A very general term covering many kinds of treatment for psychological disturbances; it may refer to verbal therapies (e.g., psychoanalysis, Jungian analysis), experiential and expressive therapies (e.g., psychodrama), or body-oriented therapies (e.g., Reichian therapy), as well as behavior therapy and psychiatric drug treatment.

Purification Series: In Ro-Hun, a series of three or four Table Sessions designed to locate, deal with, and completely release all the major victim emotional issues that are holding the client back from expressing his or her full potential.

Reflective Healing: An advanced energy-based healing technique for repatterning the Etheric Body to its original, natural, and healthy state of being. *See* chapter 2.

Regression Therapy: A form of hypnotherapy that focuses on the effects of subconscious and previous memories (including past lives) as a means to understanding and releasing emotional blocks.

Reactive Self: In Ro-Hun, the negative emotional energy that is the reaction to a faulty or limiting thought or belief. For example, if you believe the thought, "I am unworthy of abundance," you may react to that thought with a feeling of helplessness. The Reactive Self would then be the Helpless Self, that part of your personality which feels the helplessness.

Reiki: The form of healing that was given to Dr. Usui, a Japanese businessperson, in a transcendental meditation, or satori, about 1920. Reiki healing energy is transmitted through the healer to the client in a form of laying-on of hands. *See* chapter 2, "Reiki."

Reincarnation: The belief that, after death, a person's immortal spirit essence will return in another human Physical Body. The purpose of this process is to enable the spirit to continue learning and growing through the choices it makes during the time it is expressed on the Earth plane. Eventually, when sufficient growth has occurred and the karmic slate is cleared, the spirit can then choose to not reincarnate (return to the Earth plane), but instead to continue its spiritual growth in the higher dimensions. Alternatively, it may choose to again return to Earth to serve in the instruction and enlightenment of others.

Ro-Hun: A very rapid-acting and life-transforming form of psychotherapy that incorporates hypnotherapeutic and energy manipulation techniques to repattern primarily the Mental and Emotional Bodies to a higher level of functioning. *See* chapter 3.

Root Chakra: The first major chakra, located on the front of the body behind the pubic bone. Has to do with survival and security, the "fight-or-flight" syndrome, and the willingness to be fully present in the world.

Sacral Chakra: The second major chakra, located on the front of the body an inch or two below the navel. Has to do with creativity and relationships, and how one feels about him- or herself and others.

Scanning: Movement of the hand or fingers through a client's energy field for the purpose of sensing where areas of energy blockages occur.

Shadow Self Series: In Ro-Hun, a series of four Table Sessions (each two to two-and-one-half hours in length) that release one's abuser/abusive energies. Sometimes called the "Caged One Series."

Skim Session: In Ro-Hun, a single Table Session that allows the client to continue the release of "victim energies," as done in the Purification Series, if necessary. *See* chapter 3.

Solar Plexus Chakra: The third major chakra, located on the front of the body a few inches above the navel. Has to do with expansiveness, personal power and achievement, and control over one's life and the lives of others.

Soul: The "personality of the spirit," as opposed to ego, the personality of the physical being. A soul may be advanced (enlightened) or retarded (not enlightened), depending on its choices and how it expresses itself when incarnated on the Earth plane.

Soul Record: The accumulated record and vibrational patterns of all beliefs, thoughts, words, and deeds of a single spirit throughout the entire history of all its earthly incarnations. As more and more enlightened choices are made while incarnated, limiting beliefs are replaced with positive beliefs in the soul record; harsh and angry thoughts are replaced with kind and loving thoughts. When all negative vibrations have been replaced as a result of deliberate choice, the karmic balance sheet is cleared, and that soul can then choose whether or not to return to the Earth plane. All information in the Soul Record is available to the subconscious mind.

Spirit: An individual essence or spark of life that was created as a spiritual being in the image of the Creator, and that is aware of its own individuality.

Spiritual Body: The fourth subtle energy body surrounding and interpenetrating the Physical Body. This body contains all of a person's vibrational patterns above the Mental octave and reflects our gestalt consciousness of all that has been learned and experienced by the soul.

Spiritual Healing: A general term for healing techniques that focus on healing the Spiritual Energy Body. *See* chapter 4.

Spiritual Regression: An advanced form of hypnotherapy that uses a deep state of hypnosis to allow the client's conscious awareness to merge with his or her superconscious mind. This permits the client to become consciously aware of his or her spirit's experiences in the spiritual dimensions between physical incarnations.

Spleen Chakra: *See* Sacral Chakra.

Subconscious Mind: The subconscious mind is that part of the psyche that is below the threshold of physical awareness. It has direct access to all aspects of the person's soul record, and under the right circumstances, it also has access to the entire Collective Unconscious.

Subtle: Unseen, as in "Subtle Energy Body."

Superconscious Mind: The spiritual consciousness or awareness of a person. The superconscious mind has access to all information of previous incarnations available to the subconscious mind, plus all its experiences in the spiritual world between incarnations.

Synthesized: "The combining of often diverse conceptions into a coherent whole." (*Webster's Ninth New Collegiate Dictionary*, 1985)

Therapeutic Touch: A energy-based healing technique developed by Delores Kreiger and Dora Kunz to modulate a person's energy field in such a way that physical healing is significantly accelerated.

Throat Chakra: The sixth major chakra, located on the front of the body in the throat area where the collarbones come together. Has to do with abundance, and how you express your views and feelings to others.

Universal Energy Field (UEF): A universal field consisting of Life Force Energy that animates the process of life. The UEF contains a wide range of vibrational frequencies that are always associated with some form of consciousness, ranging from highly developed to very primitive. The UEF exists in more than three dimensions and is synergistic in nature in that it builds form, rather than contributes to the decay of form (per Brennan in *Hands of Light*).

Universal Laws: The basic truths and principles that govern the expression of all life in this universe. These include the Laws of Attraction, Cause and Effect, Duality, and Free Will.

Womb Experience: The set of experiences, feelings and beliefs taken on by a fetus from the moment of conception through the moment of birth.

Endnotes

Chapter 1

1. Barbara Ann Brennan, *Hands of Light* (New York: Bantam Books, 1987), p. 40.

2. Ibid., p. 41.

3. Zolar, *Dancing Heart to Heart* (McCaysville, Georgia, Editions Soleil, 1991), pp. 47–49.

4. For simplicity, I have aggregated all energy bodies above the Mental Body into what I call the Spiritual Body.

5. Richard Gerber, *Vibrational Medicine* (Santa Fe, Bear & Co., 1988), p. 163.

6. Brennan, *Hands of Light,* p. 49.

7. Michael Talbot, *The Holographic Universe* (New York: HarperPerennial, 1991), p. 187.

8. Gerber, p. 115.

9. Ibid., pp. 148–150.

10. Ibid., p. 148.

11. Ibid., p. 149.

12. James L. Oschman, "What Is Healing Energy?" (*Journal of Bodywork and Movement Therapies* (Jan. 1998), p. 47.

13. Ibid., p. 48 ff.

14.   "The Healing Revolution," *Life* Magazine (Sept. 1966), p. 39.

15.   Louise L. Hay, *You Can Heal Your Life* (Carlsbad, California: Hay House, Inc., 1984), pp. 146–207.

16.   Gerber, p. 168.

17.   Roger J. Woolger, Ph.D., *Other Lives, Other Selves* (New York: Bantam Books, 1993), pp. 167–168.

18.   Barbara Ann Brennan, *Light Emerging* (New York: Bantam Books, 1993), pp. 309–310.

19.   Richard Gordon, *Quantum-Touch: The Power to Heal* (Berkeley, California: North Atlantic Books, Revised Edition, 2002), pp. 44–48.

Chapter 2

1.   Frank A. Petter, *Reiki Fire* (Twin Lakes, Wisconsin: Lotus Light Publications, 1997), pp. 21–30.

2.   Water Lübeck, Frank A. Petter, and William Lee Rand, *The Spirit of Reiki* (Twin Lakes, Wisconsin: Lotus Light Publications, 2001), p. 19.

3.   Mikao Usui and Frank A. Petter, *The Original Handbook of Dr. Mikao Usui* (Twin Lakes, Wisconsin: Lotus Light Publications, 2000).

4.   Gerber, pp. 318–319.

5.   "Alternate Insurance Coverage," *New Age Journal* (Fall 1996), pp. 67–68.

6.   "The Healing Revolution," p. 38.

7.   Healing Touch Level I Notebook, 2002, p. 63.

8.   Rita L. Kluny, "Beyond Technology: Nursing Care and Healing in the NICU" (*Exceptional Human Experience Journal*, Vol. 14, No. 1, June, 1996), p. 37 ff.

Chapter 3

1. Woolger, p. 30.

2. Ibid., p. 29.

3. Ibid., pp. 254–255.

4. Michael Gabriel, *Voices from the Womb* (Lower Lake, California: Aslan Publishing, 1992), p. 17.

5. Woolger, p. 40.

6. Ibid., p. 97.

Chapter 4

1. Thomas Golas, *The Lazy Man's Guide to Enlightenment* (New York: Bantam Books, 1993), p. 12.

2. Gerber, p. 402.

3. Ibid.

4. Gerber, p. 400.

Bibliography

Ansari, Masud, PH.D. *Modern Hypnosis: Theory and Practice.* Washington, D.C.: Mas-Press, 1991.

Bach, Richard. *Jonathan Livingston Seagull.* New York: MacMillan and Co., 1970.

Barratt, Kathleen. *Dance of Breath.* Privately Published, 1993.

Batie, Howard, MH.D., *Awakening the Healer Within: An Introduction to Energy-Based Techniques.* St. Paul, Minnesota: Llewellyn Publications, 2000.

Benor, Daniel J., M.D. *Spiritual Healing: A Scientific Validation of a Healing Revolution.* Southfield, Michigan: Vision Publications, 2001.

Bradford, Michael. *The Healing Energy of Your Hands.* Freedom, California: The Crossing Press, Inc., 1993.

Breiling, Brian J., PSY.D. *Light Years Ahead.* Berkeley, California: Celestial Arts, 1996.

Brennan, Barbara Ann. *Hands of Light: A Guide to Healing Through the Human Energy Field.* New York: Bantam Books, 1987.

———. *Light Emerging: The Journey of Personal Healing.* New York: Bantam Books, 1993.

Bush, Carol A. *Healing Imagery & Music: Pathways to the Inner Self.* Portland, Oregon: Rudra Press, 1995.

Chopra, Deepak. M.D. *Quantum Healing: Exploring the Frontiers of Mind/Body Medicine.* New York: Bantam Books, 1989.

———. *The Seven Spiritual Laws of Success.* San Rafael, California: Amber-Allen Publishing, 1994.

Custo, Hans. *The Cosmic Octave: Origin of Harmony.* [Translated from German] Mendocino, California: Life Rhythm, 1987.

Dacher, Elliott S., M.D., *PsychoNeuroImmunology: The New Mind/Body Healing Program.* New York: Paragon House, 1993.

Doi, Hiroshi. *Modern Reiki Method for Healing.* Coquitlam, British Columbia: Fraser Journal Publishing, 2000.

Dossey, Larry, M.D. *Healing Words: The Power of Prayer and the Practice of Medicine.* New York: Harper Paperbacks, 1993.

———. *Recovering the Soul: A Scientific and Spiritual Search.* New York: Bantam Books, 1989.

Elman, Dave. *Hypnotherapy.* Glendale, California: Westwood Publishing Co., 1964.

Essene, Virginia. *Secret Truths.* Santa Clara, California: S.E.E. Publishing, 1989.

Fellowship of the Inner Light (authors unknown). *A Healing Consciousness.* New Market, Virginia: The Master's Press, 1979.

Gabriel, Michael, M.A. *Remembering Your Life Before Birth: How Your Womb Memories Have Shaped Your Life and How to Heal Them.* Santa Rosa, California: Aslan Publishing, 1995.

———. *Voices From the Womb.* (Lower Lake, California: Aslan Publishing, 1992.

Gaia, Shanti. *The Book on Karuna Reiki: Advanced Healing Energy for Our Evolving World.* Hartsell, Colorado: Infinite Light Healing Studies Center, Inc., 2001.

Gallo, Fred P., PH.D. *Energy Diagnostic and Treatment Methods.* New York: W. W. Norton and Co., 2000.

Gaynor, Mitchell L., M.D. *Sounds of Healing.* New York: Broadway Books, 1999.

Gerber, Richard, M.D. *Vibrational Medicine: New Choices for Healing Ourselves.* Santa Fe, New Mexico: Bear & Co., 1988.

Gindes, Bernard C., M.D. *New Concepts of Hypnosis: Theories, Techniques, and Practical Applications.* No. Hollywood, California: Wilshire Book Co., 1951.

Golas, Thomas. *The Lazy Man's Guide to Enlightenment.* New York: Bantam Books, 1993.

Goldberg, Dr. Bruce. *Soul Healing.* St. Paul, Minnesota: Llewellyn Publications, 1998.

Gordon, Richard. *Your Healing Hands: The Polarity Experience.* Santa Cruz, California: Unity Press, 1978.

———. *Quantum-Touch: The Power to Heal.* Berkeley, California: North Atlantic Books, Revised Edition, 2002.

Graves, Tom. *The Elements of Pendulum Dowsing.* Rockport, Massachusetts: Element Books, 1997.

Haberly, Helen J. *Reiki: Hawayo Takata's Story.* Olney, Maryland: Archedigm Publications, 1990.

Haraldsson, Erlendur, PH.D. *Modern Miracles.* Mamoroneck, New York: Hastings House, 1987.

Hay, Louise L. *You Can Heal Your Life.* Carlsbad, California: Hay House, Inc., 1984.

Hoodwin, Shepherd. *The Journey of Your Soul.* New York: The Summerjoy Press, 1995.

Hover-Kramer, Dorothea, ED.D., R.N. *Healing Touch: A Guidebook for Practitioners.* Albany, New York: Delmar Publishers, 2nd ed., 2002.

Hurtak, J. J. *The Keys of Knowledge.* Los Gatos, California: The Academy for Future Science, 1977.

Joy, W. Brugh, M.D. *Joy's Way: A Map for the Transformational Journey.* New York: G. P. Putnam's Sons, 1979.

Karagulla, Shafica, M.D. *Breakthrough to Creativity: Your Higher Sense Perception.* Los Angeles, California: DeVorss and Co., 1969.

Karagulla, Shafica, M.D., and Dora van Gelder Kunz. *The Chakras and the Human Energy Fields.* Wheaton, Ilinois: Quest Books, 1989.

Kelly, Maureen J. *Reiki and the Healing Buddha*. Twin Lakes, Wisconsin: Lotus Press, 2000.

Kenyon, Tom, M.A. *Brain States*. Captain Cook, Hawaii: United States Publishing, 1994.

Kluny, Rita L. "Beyond Technology: Nursing Care and Healing in the NICU." *Exceptional Human Experience Journal: Studies in the Psychic/Spontaneous and Imaginal,* Vol. 14, No. 1, June 1996.

Krasner, A. M., PH.D. *The Wizard Within: The Krasner Method of Clinical Hypnotherapy*. Irvine, California: American Board of Hypnotherapy Press, 1990.

Kreiger, Dolores, PH.D. *The Therapeutic Touch: How to Use Your Hands to Help or to Heal*. New York: Simon & Schuster, 1979.

Lübeck, Walter, Frank Arjava Petter, and William Lee Rand. *The Spirit of Reiki: The Complete Handbook of the Reiki System*. Twin Lakes, Wisconsin: Lotus Press, 2001.

MacLaine, Shirley. *Going Within: A Guide for Inner Transformation*. New York: Bantam Books, 1989.

McVoy, Cullen. *Finding Ro-Hun: Awakening Through Spiritual Therapy*. Montclair, New Jersey: Pooka Publications, 1996.

Mentgen, Janet, and Cheryl Hardy. "Energetic Patterns." *Healing Touch Case Studies, Vol I*. Lakewood, Colorado: Colorado Center for Healing Touch, 1999.

Modi, Shakuntala, M.D. *Memories of God and Creation*. Charlottesville, Virginia, Hampton Roads Publishing, 2000.

Moen, Bruce. *Voyages into the Unknown: Exploring the Afterlife Series*. Charlottesville, Virginia: Hampton Roads Publishing, 1997.

Moen, Larry. *Meditations for Healing*. Litia Springs, Georgia: New Leaf Distributing, 1994.

Montgomery, Ruth. *Born to Heal*. New York: Fawcett Books Group, 1985.

Myss, Caroline, PH.D. *Anatomy of the Spirit*. New York: Harmony Books, 1966.

Newton, Dr. Michael. *Journey of Souls.* St. Paul, Minnesota: Llewellyn Publications, 5th Edition, 2001.

———. *Destiny of Souls.* St. Paul, Minnesota: Llewellyn Publications, 1st Edition, 2000.

Nielsen, Greg, and Joseph Polansky. *Pendulum Power.* Rochester, Vermont: Destiny Books, 1987.

Oschman, James L., PH.D. *Energy Medicine: The Scientific Basis.* New York: Churchill Livingstone, 2000.

———. "What Is Healing Energy?" *Journal of Bodywork and Movement Therapies,* January 1998.

Paulson, Genevieve Lewis. *Kundalini and the Chakras: A Practical Manual.* St. Paul, Minnesota: Llewellyn Publications, 1997.

Pert, Candace, PH.D. *Molecules of Emotion: The Science Behind Mind-Body Medicine.* New York: Touchstone Books, 1997.

Petter, Frank A. *Reiki Fire.* Twin Lakes, Wisconsin: Lotus Light Publications, 1997.

———. *Reiki: The Legacy of Dr. Usui.* Twin Lakes, Wisconsin: Lotus Light Publications, 1998.

———. *The Original Reiki Handbook of Dr. Mikao Usui.* Twin Lakes, Wisconsin: Lotus Light Publications, 2000.

Ritchie, George G., Jr., M.D. *Ordered to Return: My Life After Dying.* Charlottesville, Virginia: Hampton Roads Publishing, 1998.

Rothschild, Joel. *Signals: An Inspiring Story of Life After Life.* Novato, California: New World Library, 2000

Selby, John. *Kundalini Awakening: A Gentle Guide to Chakra Activation and Spiritual Growth.* New York: Bantam Books, 1992.

Smith, Linda. *Called Into Healing: Reclaiming Our Judeo-Christian Legacy of Healing Touch.* Arvada, Colorado: HTSM Press, 2000.

Smith, Malcolm. *Healer!* Swavesey, Great Britain: MGOC Limited, 1988.

Shorter, Edward. *From the Mind into the Body.* New York: The Free Press, 1994.

Sutphen, Dick. *With Your Spirit Guide's Help.* Malibu, California: Valley of the Sun Publishing, 1999.

Talbot, Michael. *The Holographic Universe.* New York: HarperPerennial, 1991.

Thomas, Zach. *Healing Touch: The Church's Forgotten Language.* Louisville, Kentucky, Westminster/John Knox Press, 1994.

Wheeler, W. Alexander. *The Prophetic Revelations of Paul Solomon.* York Beach, Maine: Samuel Weiser, 1994.

Wolinsky, Stephen, PH.D. *Quantum Consciousness: The Guide to Experiencing Quantum Psychology.* Las Vegas, Nevada: Bramble Books, 1993.

Woolger, Roger J., PH.D. *Other Lives, Other Selves: A Jungian Psychotherapist Discovers Past Lives.* New York: Bantam Books, 1988.

Zolar. *Dancing Heart to Heart: The Story of RoHun.* McCaysville, Georgia: Editions Soliel, 1991.

Appendix A
Initial Client Interview Form

<table>
<tr><td colspan="6" align="center">**CONFIDENTIAL**
INITIAL CLIENT INTERVIEW</td></tr>
<tr><td colspan="2">NAME:</td><td>ID:</td><td colspan="2">AGE / DOB:</td><td>DATE:</td></tr>
<tr><td colspan="2">HOME PHONE:</td><td>WORK PHONE:</td><td colspan="3">OCCUPATION:</td></tr>
<tr><td colspan="3">ADDRESS:</td><td colspan="3">REFERRED BY:</td></tr>
<tr><td colspan="3" rowspan="2">E-MAIL:</td><td colspan="2">CHILDHOOD RELIGION:</td><td>CURRENT AFFILIATION:</td></tr>
<tr><td colspan="3"></td></tr>
<tr><td colspan="3">PERSONAL STRESS:</td><td colspan="3">WORK STRESS:</td></tr>
<tr><td colspan="3">STRESS REDUCTION / RELAXATION / EXERCISE:

Meditate: Daily ___ X per Week ___ None ___ ILC ___</td><td colspan="3">Knows Chakra System ___   Knows Energy Bodies ___

Believes in PL ___   CM ___   CU ___   Angels ___</td></tr>
<tr><td colspan="3">KEYS:</td><td colspan="3">Suggestibility: Good ___   Fair ___   Poor ___
Visual ___   Audient ___   Kinesthetic ___</td></tr>
<tr><td colspan="6">PHOBIAS:

Water ___   Boats ___   Trains ___   Elevators ___   Claustrophobia ___   Heights ___   Other:</td></tr>
<tr><td colspan="6">CURRENT HEALTH CARE PROVIDERS:

Blood Type:</td></tr>
<tr><td colspan="6">CURRENT MEDICATIONS / DRUGS (including RECREATIONAL):

</td></tr>
<tr><td colspan="6">SIGNIFICANT PAST MEDICAL HISTORY (including SLEEP HISTORY):

Do You Smoke: Never ___   Yes ___   No ___   Packs / Day ___   How Long? ___   When Quit? ___</td></tr>
<tr><td colspan="6">CLIENT'S REASON FOR APPOINTMENT:

</td></tr>
<tr><td colspan="6">WHY ALTERNATIVE HEALING INSTEAD OF TRADITIONAL MEDICAL TREATMENT?

</td></tr>
<tr><td colspan="6">WHAT IS YOUR EXPERIENCE WITH TRADITIONAL MEDICAL TREATMENT?

</td></tr>
<tr><td colspan="6">WOULD YOU CONSIDER AN INTEGRATED APPROACH TO HEALING? WHY / WHY NOT?</td></tr>
<tr><td colspan="6">DESCRIBE YOUR CURRENT LIFESTYLE (Relationships, Home, Children, Job, Hobbies, etc. Use Back of Form)</td></tr>
</table>

Appendix B
Notification to Physician

(Date)

Dr. _____
(Address)

Dear Dr. _____,

   I am a certified hypnotherapist and practitioner of energy-based alternative medical therapies, including Healing Touch and Reiki. One of your patients, Ms. Jane C., has asked me to prepare a holistic healing program for her that includes weight release and which also addresses her Type I diabetes. She is now using an insulin pump, as you have prescribed.

   I have advised Ms. C. that I would be willing to provide hypnotherapy sessions for weight release and energy-based healing sessions to her only on the condition that you, as her physician, are aware that she intends to incorporate these alternative healing therapies into her total healing program. Since I am not a licensed physician, I do not diagnose conditions or prescribe medications. However, I need you to be aware of her requests for hypnotherapy for weight release and to address her diabetes using energy-based healing techniques.

   Upon your acknowledgement of the fact that Ms. C. intends to embark on this integrated approach blending both traditional allopathic and alternative medical techniques, I will begin the hypnotherapy and energy-based healing sessions with her.

   I would greatly appreciate it if you would acknowledge the above information by signing the statement below, and then returning this letter to me in the self-addressed stamped envelope provided, along with any considerations of which you feel I should be aware.

Thank you.

Howard F. Batie, Mh.D.

Director, Evergreen Healing Arts Center

- -

I acknowledge having received the above information.

_____   _____   _____
       (Signature)   (Printed Name)   (Date)

Appendix C
Internet Resources for Healing Techniques

Color and Sound Therapy

Delphi University
(Attn: Charles Curcio)
P.O. Box 70
McCaysville, GA 30555
e-mail: registrar@delphi-center.com
www.delphi-center.com

Healing Touch

Healing Touch General Information:
Colorado Center for Healing Touch, Inc.
(Attn: Cheryl Hardy)
12477 West Cedar Dr., Suite 202
Lakewood, CO 80228
e-mail: ccheal@aol.com

Healing Touch Spiritual Ministry
(Attn: Linda Smith)
P.O. Box 741239
Arvada, CO 80006
e-mail: staff@htspiritualministry.com
www.htspiritualministry.com

Healing Touch for Animals
Komitor Healing Method, Inc.
P.O. Box 262171
Highlands Ranch, CO 80163-2171
e-mail: office@healingtouchforanimals.com
www.healingtouchforanimals.com

Healing Touch for Babies
(Attn: Rita Kluny)
P.O. Box 161372
Austin, TX 78716–1372
e-mail: Rita@healingtouchforbabies.com   or: healingbabies@yahoo.com
www.healingtouchforbabies.com

Healing Touch for Caregivers
www.localaccess.com/healinghands
then click on "Healing Touch for Caregivers"

Healing Touch Website

www.healingtouch.net
(Includes links to HTSM, HTA, HTB, and HTC)

Inner Light Consciousness Meditation

The Paul Solomon Foundation
P.O. Box 2785
Purcellville, VA 20134–2785
www.PaulSolomon.com
The ILC Meditation CD is available for U.S. $15.00
Payment may be made by personal check drawn on a U.S. bank
or by U.S./Canadian postal order made out in U.S. funds or by
International Money Order. Send to:
ILC Meditation CD
c/o Howard Batie
147 Penrose Lane
Chehalis, WA 98532 USA

Reflective Healing

Delphi University
Attn: Marshall Smith
P.O. Box 70
McCaysville, GA 30555
e-mail: registrar@delphi-center.com
www.delphi-center.com

Reiki

www.localaccess.com/HealingHands
then click on "Reiki Healing"
www.reiki.org (International Center for Reiki Training)
www.ReikiDharma.com (Frank A. Petter)

Ro-Hun

The Ro-Hun Institute
Delphi University
Attn: Patricia Hayes
P.O. Box 70
McCaysville, GA 30555
e-mail: registrar@delphi-center.com
www.delphi-center.com

Graham Institute of Self-Awareness (GISA)
Attn: Dottie Graham
148 Breezy Point Drive
Yorktown, VA 23692
e-mail: GISAofVA@aol.com

Spiritual Regression

www.localaccess.com/HealingHands
then click on "Spiritual Regression"
www.spiritualregression.com

Index

acupressure, xxv, 15, 82, 237
acupuncture, xviii, 15, 32, 82, 237
AHMA, 80, 233
AHNA, 80–81, 233
alternative medicine, 81–82
  therapies, xviii–xxiii, 32, 36, 110, 230, 233, 235
aura, 5, 8, 12, 14, 18–19, 21–22, 25, 89, 99, 117, 128, 141, 233, 236

brain centers, 6
brow chakra, 5–6, 103–104, 133–134, 151, 153–154, 234

CAM, 81, 230
Cayce, Edgar, 168, 235
chakra system, xxvii, 5–8, 15, 17–22, 43, 49, 59–64, 68, 73, 77–78, 85, 94, 96–101, 103–108, 112, 126–127, 130–134, 139–141, 143–145, 147, 150–151, 153–156, 159, 167, 169–171, 178–180, 184, 192–193, 201, 233–239, 241, 243–245
Collective Unconscious, 29–30, 124, 137, 233, 235, 245
Color and Sound Therapy, *see*
  Healing with Color and Sound
complementary medicine, 81, 239
  therapies, 230–231, 235
counseling, 82, 118–119
crown chakra, 5–7, 61, 73, 103–104, 140, 153, 170, 234, 236
Delphi University, ix, 98, 110, 156–157

EEG, 16
Einstein, Albert, 4, 187
EKG, 16
Emotional Energy Bodies, 13, 105, 117–120, 125–126, 129–130, 135, 140, 152, 242
Energy Fields, *see also* Energy Fields, Human, 1, 4–5, 7–8, 10–14, 21–23, 25, 28, 37–38, 43–45, 52, 59, 61–62, 64, 73, 77, 79–80, 83, 86, 89, 92, 97–101, 106, 112–113, 120, 122, 125–127, 129–131, 134–135, 143, 147, 153, 156, 161, 167, 203, 225, 228–230, 233, 237–241, 243, 245
Human, xix, xx, xxvi, 1, 5, 8–10, 12, 14, 28, 37–38, 43,

261

☽ ORDER LLEWELLYN BOOKS TODAY!

Llewellyn publishes hundreds of books on your favorite subjects! To get these exciting books, including the ones on the following pages, check your local bookstore or order them directly from Llewellyn.

Order Online:
Visit our website at www.llewellyn.com, select your books, and order them on our secure server.

Order by Phone:
- Call toll-free within the U.S. at 1-877-NEW-WRLD (1-877-639-9753)
  Call toll-free within Canada at 1-866-NEW-WRLD (1-866-639-9753)
- We accept VISA, MasterCard, and American Express

Order by Mail:
Send the full price of your order (MN residents add 7% sales tax) in U.S. funds, plus postage & handling to:

Llewellyn Worldwide
P.O. Box 64383, Dept. 0-7387-0398-2
St. Paul, MN 55164-0383, U.S.A.

Postage & Handling:
Standard (U.S., Mexico, & Canada). If your order is:
Up to $25.00, add $3.50
$25.01 - $48.99, add $4.00
$49.00 and over, FREE STANDARD SHIPPING
(Continental U.S. orders ship UPS. AK, HI, PR, & P.O. Boxes ship USPS 1st class. Mex. & Can. ship PMB.)

International Orders:
Surface Mail: For orders of $20.00 or less, add $5 plus $1 per item ordered. For orders of $20.01 and over, add $6 plus $1 per item ordered.

Air Mail:
Books: Postage & Handling is equal to the total retail price of all books in the order.
Non-book items: Add $5 for each item.

Orders are processed within 2 business days. Please allow for normal shipping time.
Postage and handling rates subject to change.

Reiki for Beginners

Mastering Natural Healing Techniques

David F. Vennells

Reiki is a simple yet profound system of hands-on healing developed in Japan during the 1800s. Millions of people worldwide have already benefited from its peaceful healing intelligence that transcends cultural and religious boundaries. It can have a profound effect on health and well-being by re-balancing, cleansing, and renewing your internal energy system.

Reiki for Beginners gives you the very basic and practical principles of using Reiki as a simple healing technique, as well as its more deeply spiritual aspects as a tool for personal growth and self-awareness. Unravel your inner mysteries, heal your wounds, and discover your potential for great happiness. Follow the history of Reiki, from founder Dr. Mikao Usui's search for a universal healing technique, to the current development of a global Reiki community. Also included are many new ideas, techniques, advice, philosophies, contemplations, and meditations that you can use to deepen and enhance your practice.

1-56718-767-6, 264 pp., 5³⁄₁₆ x 8, illus.   **$12.95**

Also available in Spanish:
Reiki para principiantes
1-56718-768-4   **$9.95**

To order by phone call 1-877 NEW WRLD
Prices subject to change without notice

Chakras for Beginners

A Guide to Balancing Your Chakra Energies

David Pond

The chakras are spinning vortexes of energy located just in front of your spine and positioned from the tailbone to the crown of the head. They are a map of your inner world—your relationship to yourself and how you experience energy. They are also the batteries for the various levels of your life energy. The freedom with which energy can flow back and forth between you and the universe correlates directly to your total health and well-being.

Blocks or restrictions in this energy flow expresses itself as disease, discomfort, lack of energy, fear, or an emotional imbalance. By acquainting yourself with the chakra system, how they work and how they should operate optimally, you can perceive your own blocks and restrictions and develop guidelines for relieving entanglements.

The chakras stand out as the most useful model for you to identify how your energy is expressing itself. With *Chakras for Beginners* you will discover what is causing any imbalances, how to bring your energies back into alignment, and how to achieve higher levels of consciousness.

1-56718-537-1, 216 pp., 5³⁄₁₆ x 8, illus. $9.95

Also available in Spanish:
Chakras para principiantes
1-56718-536-3 $9.95

To order by phone call 1-877 NEW WRLD
Prices subject to change without notice

How to Heal with Color
Ted Andrews

Now, for perhaps the first time, color therapy is placed within the grasp of the average individual. Anyone can learn to facilitate and accelerate the healing process on all levels with the simple color therapies in *How to Heal with Color*.

Color serves as a vibrational remedy that interacts with the human energy system to stabilize physical, emotional, mental, and spiritual conditions. When there is balance, we can more effectively rid ourselves of toxins, negativity, and patterns that hinder our life processes.

This book provides color application guidelines that are beneficial for over fifty physical conditions and a wide variety of emotional and mental conditions. Receive simple and tangible instructions for performing "muscle testing" on yourself and others to find the most beneficial colors. Learn how to apply color therapy through touch, projection, breathing, cloth, water, and candles. Learn how to use the little known but powerful color-healing system of the mystical Qabala to balance and open the psychic centers. Plus, discover simple techniques for performing long distance healings on others.

0-87542-005-2, 240 pp., illus.   **$5.99**

Reflexology for Beginners

Healing Through Foot Massage of Pressure Points

David F. Vennells

Puts reflexology back into the hands of laypersons who want to help themselves and others

Reflexology is one of the most well known and well respected complementary therapies. It is even practiced in many hospitals, hospices, and healing centers. The principles of practical reflexology are quite simple. This book puts reflexology back into the hands of those who have a heartfelt wish to help themselves and others.

Reflexology can have a profound effect on our health and well-being by re-balancing, cleansing, and renewing our internal energy system. As you learn the techniques step-by-step, you will gradually increase your knowledge of anatomy and physiology, while developing a more accurate awareness of the foot reflexes and how to treat them.

0-7387-0098-3 $9.95
5 3/16 x 8, 288 pp., 43 illus., bibliog., index

To order by phone call 1-877 NEW WRLD
Prices subject to change without notice

The Healer's Manual

A Beginner's Guide to Energy Therapies

Ted Andrews

Did you know that a certain Mozart symphony can ease digestion problems . . . that swelling often indicates being stuck in outworn patterns . . . that breathing pink is good for skin conditions and loneliness? Most disease stems from a metaphysical base. While we are constantly being exposed to viruses and bacteria, it is our unbalanced or blocked emotions, attitudes, and thoughts that deplete our natural physical energies and make us more susceptible to "catching a cold" or manifesting some other physical problem.

Healing, as approached in *The Healer's Manual,* involves locating and removing energy blockages wherever they occur—physical or otherwise. This book is an easy guide to simple vibrational healing therapies that anyone can learn to apply to restore homeostasis to their body's energy system. By employing sound, color, fragrance, etheric touch, and flower/gem elixers, you can participate actively within the healing of your body and the opening of higher perceptions. You will discover that you can heal more aspects of your life than you ever thought possible.

0-87542-007-9, 256 pp., 6 x 9, illus.   **$12.95**

To order by phone call 1-877 NEW WRLD

Prices subject to change without notice

Aura Energy for Health, Healing & Balance

Joe H. Slate, Ph.D.

Imagine an advanced energy/information system that contains the chronicle of your life—past, present, and future. By referring to it, you could discover exciting new dimensions to your existence. You could uncover important resources for new insights, growth, and power.

You possess such a system right now. It is your personal aura. In his latest book, Dr. Joe H. Slate illustrates how each one of us has the power to see the aura, interpret it, and fine-tune it to promote mental, physical, and spiritual well-being. College students have used his techniques to raise their grade-point averages, gain admission to graduate programs, and eventually get the jobs they want. Now you can use his aura empowerment program to initiate an exciting new spiral of growth in all areas of your life.

1-56718-637-8, 288 pp., 6 x 9   **$12.95**

New Chakra Healing

The Revolutionary
32-Center Energy System

Cyndi Dale

Break through the barriers that keep you from your true purpose with *New Chakra Healing*. This manual presents never-before-published information that makes a quantum leap in the current knowledge of the human energy centers, fields, and principles that govern the connection between the physical and spiritual realms.

By working with your full energy body, you can heal all resistance to living a successful life. The traditional seven-chakra system was just the beginning of our understanding of the holistic human. Now Cyndi Dale's research uncovers a total of 32 energy centers: 12 physically oriented chakras, and 20 energy points that exist in the spiritual plane. She also discusses auras, rays, kundalini, mana energy, karma, dharma, and cords (energetic connections between people that serve as relationship contracts). In addition, she extends chakra work to include the back of the body as well as the front, with detailed explanations on how these energy systems tie into the spine. Each chapter takes the reader on a journey through the various systems, incorporating personal experiences, practical exercises, and guided meditation.

1-56718-200-3, 304 pp., 7 x 10, illus.   **$17.95**

Chakra Therapy

**For Personal
Growth & Healing**

Keith Sherwood

Your thoughts, feelings, and actions are energy events—to know who you are and why you think, feel, and act the way you do, you must know yourself energetically.

The seven chakras of the human body process and distribute energy, and they transform the frequencies into different sensations comprehensible to us, namely thought, emotion, and physical sensation. Human problems—spiritual, mental, emotional, and physical—are caused by the inability to radiate energy freely due to blockages in our energy systems.

Chakra Therapy is a practical and easy-to-use guide that will teach you how to work with your chakras to release energy blockages. You will learn techniques for increasing your level of energy, and for transmuting unhealthy energies into healthy ones, to bring you back into balance and harmony with your self, your loved ones, and the world you live in.

0-87542-721-9, 256 pp., 5 ¼ x 8, illus., index   **$9.95**

The Healer's Wisdom

**Fundamentals of
Whole Body Healing**

Jennifer Fraser

For those who are new to the theories and practices of holistic medicine, *The Healer's Wisdom* offers safe and effective techniques that can facilitate the energies of health and wellness.

Safely administer home treatments and channel healing energy using basic nutrition, bodywork, herbal remedies, aromatherapy, and energy healings. The text helps to develop your healing instincts and skills, enabling you to empower yourself and others with healing wisdom.

- A down-to-earth guide for laypersons who want to practice holistic healing methods on themselves, friends, and family
- Provides an overview of massage, herbs, aromatherapy, and energy work (chakra treatments, crystal healing, and color therapy)
- Explains how to provide aid in emergencies while waiting for help to arrive
- Provides a quick reference of specific ailments and their treatments

0-7387-0182-3, 312 pp., 7½ x 9⅛   **$16.95**

To order by phone call 1-877 NEW WRLD
Prices subject to change without notice

The Art of
Spiritual Healing
Keith Sherwood

Each of you has the potential to be a healer; to heal yourself and to become a channel for healing others. Healing energy is always flowing through you. Learn how to recognize and tap this incredible energy source. You do not need to be a victim of disease or poor health. Rid yourself of negativity and become a channel for positive healing.

Become acquainted with your three auras and learn how to recognize problems and heal them on a higher level before they become manifested in the physical body as disease.

Special techniques make this book a "breakthrough" to healing power, but you are also given a concise, easy-to-follow regimen of good health to follow in order to maintain a superior state of being. This is a practical guide to healing.

0-87542-720-0, 224 pp., 5¼ x 8, illus.   **$9.95**

Also available in Spanish:
Curación espiritual
1-56718-627-0   **$9.95**

Guide to Natural Health

Using the Horoscope as a Key to Ancient Healing Practices

Jonathan Keyes

The ancient art of medical astrology is only beginning to re-emerge as a powerful system for understanding health and how to heal illness. *Guide to Natural Health* describes a world in which human beings, the natural world, and the stars are part of the same fabric. Through the study of astrology and by working with herbs, diet, and the spiritual properties of stones, birds, and animals, you will learn to harmonize your own health and nourish body, mind, and spirit.

- A unique and valuable application of medical astrology well suited for pagans, astrology enthusiasts, and spiritual eclectics
- Focuses on the "four element medicine tradition," a holistic healing system rooted in the cycles of the planets and natural world
- The only book to work with animal and bird totems as tools for healing
- The only book to focus on ritual as the core of healing work

0-7387-0224-2, 336 pp., 7½ x 9⅛   **$16.95**

Chinese Health Care Secrets

A Natural Lifestyle Approach

Henry B. Lin

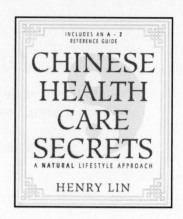

At a time when the medical costs in this country are skyrocketing and chronic disease runs rampant in every walk of life, *Chinese Health Care Secrets* offers a readily applicable, completely natural, and highly effective alternative. It serves as a practical reference on personal health care, as well as a textbook on a health care system from the world's oldest civilization.

It is the Chinese belief that you can achieve optimal health by carrying out your daily activities—including diet, sleep, emotional feeling, physical exercise, and sexual activity—according to the laws of nature. It is especially effective in treating the degenerative diseases that plague millions of Americans. Many of the techniques have never before been published, and are considered secrets even in China. Avoid common ailments brought on by aging and modern society when you take charge of your own health with age-old Chinese wisdom, including:

- An A–Z reference guide of special solutions for seventy-six of the most common health problems
- The secrets of proper diet, sleep and rest, physical hygiene, mental discipline, regular exercise, regulated sex, environmental hygiene
- Appendices full of exercises and acupressure points

1-56718-434-0, 528 pp., 7½ x 9⅛, illus.   **$24.95**

Mastering Reiki

**A Practicing and
Teaching Primer**

John Tompkins, Jr.

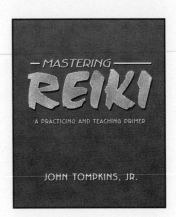

This book is for practitioners of the Reiki healing system who want to expand their understanding of how Reiki works with the energy of the human body. For the instructor, it also provides a complete and accurate teaching program, along with an in-depth look at Reiki's past, present, and possible paths to the future.

Mastering Reiki also includes unique discussions of Reiki history, the Reiki principles, the use of symbols within Reiki, and the advancement through Reiki degrees. Plus it promotes greater personal understanding of the energy system by taking readers on a meditative journey within their own chakra systems.

- Offers students, practitioners, and instructors a more accurate and complete understanding of the Reiki tradition of healing
- Presents a complete format for teaching Reiki
- Explains how to create a Reiki box for sending energy to several people at once
- Includes nineteen Reiki hand positions and their variations

0-7387-0206-4, 168 pp., 7½ x 9⅛, illus. $14.95

The Soul as Healer

Lessons in Affirmation, Visualization, and Color

L. Joseph Nichols

Having self-healed a damaged disc in his neck, a problem that various other treatments couldn't cure, author L. Joseph Nichols introduces new, progressive healing techniques rarely found in any texts to date. The major ingredient missing in most healing practices is the element of spirituality: the soul, or higher self. This book provides a roadmap for those who want to heal themselves and reevaluate just where they spend their energy. It also provides the techniques and philosophies of healing others. You will learn to repair imbalances at the etheric or energetic levels, which is eventually reflected as health at the physical levels.

You will also receive an introductory lesson in "Chironic Healing" (named after Chiron, the great healer of the spiritual realms), the relatively new, yet extremely powerful form of hands-on healing that reestablishes the perfect pattern in the human aura, allowing the body to heal itself.

1-56718-487-1, 240 pp., 6 x 9, illus.   **$12.95**